My father said that Paola Harris would be there the day the *truth* is revealed. Most UFO reporters have their own selfish agenda. Paola is truthful, nonbiased and a loving reporter. The way we met was *no* coincidence. Only *God* knows why.

— Phil Corso, Jr.

Paola Harris has a natural instinct for journalism. She senses the very heart of the story and focuses on the very essence of what the subject is trying to say. From the very beginning of her work, she intuitively understood the deep meaning of the ET presence on Earth and within our solar system. And she has a warm and understanding way of conducting her interviews. Her enthusiasm and insight into the subject plumbs the spiritual depths of the phenomena and inspires the interviewees. This book is a valuable tool that casts light on the greatest story of our time.

— Robert O. Dean,
Retired Command Sergeant Major

Paola's positive approach to the UFO phenomena, which developed in the U.S. in the light of J. Allen Hynek's serious activity, and in Italy with CUN's disclosure effort, has turned into a sincere mission to inform the general public about the real facts about the possible alien presence.

— Dr. Roberto Pinotti (Italy's J. Allen Hynek)
Director, Centro Ufologico National (CUN)

Paola Harris is a lady with all the enthusiasm and energy sufficient for the daunting task she has taken on, namely, to collect and effectively present insightful interviews with some prominent participants in the field of UFO and other anomalies.

—Richard Haines,
research scientist, retired

It is with great pleasure that I endorse Paola Harris's new book, *Connecting the Dots*, as a "must-have" book for any serious UFO buff. Paola is an internationally respected journalist and educator who has boldly researched the truth about Star Visitor contact with Earth. She has literally risked her life, her fortune, and her sacred honor to interview the truly important governmental and elite civilian witnesses to UFO reality. As a dear friend and fellow confidant of high "insiders," I have dubbed her the "Cosmic Lois Lane," courageous sidekick and reporter of the UFO phenomenon from up close and personal. I commend this important volume to every serious inquirer into UFO truth.

—Dr. Richard Boylan

Connecting the Dots...

Connecting the Dots...

Making Sense of the
UFO Phenomenon

Paola Leopizzi Harris

Wild Flower Press
P.O. Box 1429
Mill Spring, NC 28722

Library of Congress Cataloging-in-Publication Data

Harris, Paola Leopizzi, 1945-
 Connecting the dots : making sense of the UFO phenomenon /
    Paola Leopizzi Harris.-- 1st ed.
    p. cm.
    Includes bibliographical references.
    ISBN 0-926524-57-7 (alk. paper)
1. Unidentified flying objects--Sightings and encounters--Research.
2. Human-alien encounters--Research. 3. Interviews. I. Title.
TL789.3.H367 2003
001.942'07'2--dc21

                            2003011832

Cover Artwork: Alberto Forgione
Photographs ©2003 by Paola Harris, unless otherwise specified.
Manuscript editor: Brian L. Crissey

Printed in the United States of America.

Address all inquiries to:
Wild Flower Press
an imprint of Granite Publishing
P.O. Box 1429
Columbus, NC 28722

Granite Publishing, LLC, uses
environmentally responsible paper.

Dedication

To my beautiful mother Elaine Leopizzi,
who always encouraged me to write and
who supported me financially and spiritually,
which made this research possible.

To my close friends, Dr. J. Allen Hynek, Mimi Hynek,
Colonel Philip Corso, Dr. Michael Wolf,
Virginia Morrow (Bridey Murphey) and
my mentor, psychic George O'Steen.

May you always stay by me as I realize now that
I was taught by the "best" of the best.

Acknowledgments

I sincerely thank my children, Lisa and Todd, for putting up with their weird mother, to my brother, Alberto, for doing my graphics and standing by me. Special thanks and recognition go to Russ Croop, who accompanied me on these adventures during the Hynek days, to Patricia Rose Upzak, who unrelentingly pushed me into publishing this book, to Carol Koch and Polly Palmer for helping to edit a portion of this research, to Jim Currant, whose video of Michael Wolf changed my life, to journalist and editor of *Hera* magazine, Adriano Forgione, for sharing my adventures in doing the Michael Wolf story, to Alberto Forgione, my friend and graphic artist, for designing the cover of this book, and to Pam and Brian, my publishers, for bringing this work into print.

Thank you all, for believing in me!

Table of Contents

Table of Contents, continued

Lift Off

Foreword

by R. Leo Sprinkle, Ph.D.
(Author of *Soul Samples*)

Welcome, reader, to the world of Paola Leopizzi Harris. Ms. Harris, who lives in Rome, Italy, has served well as a photo-journalist, futurist, and secondary school teacher in Italian and USA schools. But the position in which she does her best work is not an official position: She brings together high energies, deep issues, and powerful personalities.

My wife Marilyn and I first met Paola in 1981, when she invited several persons to a meeting in Boulder, Colorado. Paola's special guest, J. Allen Hynek, Ph.D., shared with new/old friends his on-going investigations of UFO experiences.

Twenty years later, Marilyn and I were talking with Paola about our occasional visits, the UFO research community, and the personal fate of UFO investigators who seem to share a common destiny. We were driving by car, July 2001, to Albuquerque, N.M., so that Paola could interview Richard Hoagland. During that special journey, I reflected on Paola's activities and her uncanny ability to be in the right place at the right time.

On the surface, Paola is an intelligent, energetic, international traveler who quickly becomes aware of those around her. She conducts herself professionally, but she is able to obtain personal information from others in what seems to be a casual, almost effortless, manner. With a charming smile, and sometimes a hearty laugh, Paola surrounds her interviewee with a comforting trust. She is both a nurse and a healer who eases the stresses that burden the body, mind, and soul of any UFO researcher.

Paola learns about the investigator's activities and invites information about the hopes and fears of solving the UFO mystery. She allows the interviewee to speculate, not only about the phenomena, but also about the social and spiritual implications of the ET presence.

And yet, beneath the surface, Paola is somewhat of an enigma, even to herself. She sometimes puzzles: How was this interview arranged? Why did the theme of this interview shift? What is the underlying purpose of these interviews? When will we know the answers to these questions?

Paola does not view herself as a UFO experiencer, yet she recognizes the pattern of coincidences, or synchronicities that characterize her intuitive decisions. With a busy schedule and limited budget, she travels great distances, under improbable conditions, to arrange interviews with credible persons who report incredible experiences.

Like most UFO investigators, Paola began with a curiosity about the physical conditions that might identify an unidentified flying object. Now, like most seasoned investigators, she is fascinated by the psychical connection of humanity and extraterrestrial communications.

Although Paola is puzzled by the "particle/wave" reality (á la Hynek) of flying saucers, and the "aliens among us" (á la Ruth Montgomery), she is dedicated to her personal mission: To locate and learn from persons who are exploring the intersection of humankind and cosmic cultures, persons who, perhaps, are building a bridge between Heaven and Earth.

Enjoy, dear reader, your opportunity to view the world of Paola Leopizzi Harris.

Introduction

At times, I try to remember back to how all this research began. I personally have never had a UFO sighting, nor do I remember any strange occurrences in my childhood. It all seems like a logical progression of an intellectual curiosity I have. I think in general humankind has a subliminal wish to seek the truth to some fundamental questions about who we are, where we come from and so on. But one thing did trigger an emotional reaction—the 1978 release of *Close Encounters of the Third Kind* by Steven Spielberg. Something in that movie rang true because I empathized with the role of Francoise Truffaut, his utter commitment to understanding that contact, and transforming the meeting with nonhuman intelligence into a truly mystical event, in which we the viewers could participate. His words to the scientists in the film about the roles of contactee Richard Dreyfuss and the other contactees who were desperately trying to make sense of their traumatic experience, were to the effect that "these people were given a special invitation" to participate in an event that would transform humanity, that would change our world as we know it, and that would hurl us into a new paradigm.

I remember sobbing at the end of the film after viewing the exchange of a hand signal greeting of Truffaut with the alien and then I remember Truffaut's famous smile. Ah! What a moment! Something ripped to the core of my soul, some hidden truth, something that would stimulate my intellectual curiosity.

In 1978, I had not yet met J. Allen Hynek (see page 27), but I had begun an education career teaching science fiction in high school in Broomfield, Colo. I graduated from Rhode Island College in 1967 with a degree in English and a minor in French. I had minor jobs in advertising, but I was enjoying raising my two kids, Lisa Marie and Todd, too much to return to work. In 1977, I decided to pursue a teaching degree at the University of Colorado, and my first job was at Broomfield High School in Broomfield, Colorado. I was given a class that no one wanted to teach while the original male teacher was on leave. It was called science fiction, and it was a new English elective. There was a small enrollment of perhaps 40 students, which rose to 186 by the time I finished teaching. It is ironic that the male teacher informed me that no female could teach this class successfully, and, when it was proven otherwise, he wanted the class back.

As part of the classical approach, we read H.G. Wells's *Time Machine*, Herbert's *Dune*, Huxley's *Brave New World*, Bradbury's *The Martian Chronicles* and so many others. The difference was that I began to bring in science articles to support the then sci-fi subject matter. By 1978, I quickly became a futurist, became interested in computers, and I was one of the first to experiment with interactive laser disc technology in the classroom. I even attended the World Future Conference in Vancouver, B.C., in the 1980s, where I was to read Marilyn Fergusen's work about shaping the future, and later I would hear Frijhof Capra speak about spirituality and quantum mechanics. I was hooked on the fact that there needed to be an open approach to this major philosophical shift in thinking, which later was coined as the New Age! I was fascinated!

On the down side, my class was so popular that people were wondering what was going on in the classroom and what secret teaching was making their kids so enthusiastic as to write major research papers, read, when they had never picked up a book before, and increase the enrollment of an English elective, science fiction. In this rural Colorado community where many kids were mainly interested in riding, rodeos, and driving their trucks through Main Street. Something strange was happening and the teacher was weird. I found that the local minister was very disturbed when his parishioners told him that their kids were reading these weird books so he asked for a meeting with my principal who promptly informed him that he believed that the object of education was to teach kids to think and explore. But the minister said this metaphysical material was Satan's work and insisted that I open each and every class cautioning the students that this could be the "work of the Devil"! I told him that I did not want to give the Devil so much publicity and air time and that religion had nothing to do with the study of the future, which I considered to be a scientific pursuit. We discussed cloning, artificial intelligence, life on Mars, telepathic communication, and many other subjects that today have become mainstream subjects and that later would become some of my top interviews.

In the 1970s, the topic was taboo, and the minister took a copy of all the above classics to search for passages that might be inappropriate for high school students. It should be added that my brilliant English department chairwoman came into my office to inform me that "there existed the Devil," and I should be careful what strange material I covered, because it left a doorway open for him. She had no science fiction literary background and could not even begin to comprehend the level of philosophy and science that was reflected in sci-fi classics. It was the science that fascinated me.

Later on, in 2000, this connection between UFOs and religion came back to haunt me when I did a three-hour interview with Mike Siegal on the Art Bell Show along with Phil Corso, Jr. (see page 3). This interview was very informational and objective, but the questions that came in dealt with religious fear that UFOs came from the Devil, and radio callers were reading the Bible to me.

I failed to see the relevance when I was talking about "back-engineering alien technology" from the Roswell crash, unless the Devil is developing microchips and warp drives. I am always respectful of adverse opinions, and I just said, "Thanks for sharing." Mike Siegel was grateful that I handled it well and asked me where had I been hiding, since I had so much first-hand research and was not known yet in the mainstream UFO research, a field where there are so few women researchers.

I was learning. What I didn't know was that, as in *Close Encounters of the Third Kind,* I was being *invited* to participate.

Enter Dr. J Allen Hynek

When I began teaching the science-fiction class, I began buying sci-fi magazines that discussed Kenneth Arnold, the first sightings, Project Blue Book, the Condon Report, J. Allen Hynek, and the latest UFO investigations, such as the Pascagoula, Miss., case. Little did I dream that Dr. Hynek and I would work together some day and become good friends. I quickly made a list of ten people whom I wanted to meet in my lifetime, and Dr. J. Allen Hynek, Richard Sigismond (see page 29), Dr. Carl Sagan and Dr. R. Leo Sprinkle (see page 20) were on that list. The only one I'm still trying to meet is Ray Bradbury. On that list was the name of Bridey Murphy, and perhaps that is highly signifi-

XVIII CONNECTING THE DOTS...

cant, because I noticed that serendipitous things began to happen, events which still amaze me to this day. That will teach me to make a wish list!

While teaching the sci-fi class, a young local girl raised her hand and told me her aunt wanted to meet me because she had been listening to accounts of our conversations in class. I asked this girl who her aunt was, and she said "Bridey Murphy," whose real name was Virginia Morrow. She lived in Denver, and I soon became close friends with her until her death in 1994. She and her husband Dick treated me like a member of the family, and we had numerous conversations about reincarnation, hypnosis and the unknown. Bridey once told me that she already knew me from a past life, a statement that some of my later interviewees also made, an assertion that baffles me to this day. Ginny Morrow believed firmly in an alien presence, and, ironically, she had met Dr. Hynek on the way to a talk show. In the 1980s I refused to link the paranormal or reincarnation to anything having to do with science or the UFO phenomena, which I viewed as only a physical reality. In my ignorance, they were spaceships made of a weird metal! I did not even address the alien presence.

Sometime in late 1979, I was invited to a wedding in Evanston, Ill., and since I knew that CUFOS (The Center for UFO Studies) was there, I made plans to drop into their offices unannounced. I did not expect Dr. Hynek to be around, but I wanted to view the organization and the files. But as it turned out, he was around. As I walked into their organizational offices in Evanston, Illinois, from around the corner, he appeared—a distinguished white-haired man in a gray suit, smoking his classic pipe. I told him that I had a foreign-language background, and he asked me if I could do the Italian translations to sighting reports he was receiving. Later on he would send me a box of files to examine and would call me to put pins in a map of the United States in order to coordinate "same-day sightings." I met Estelle Postelle, his personal secretary and assistant and it was mainly through her that I was trained. I received a CUFOS ID card with my head photographed against the backdrop of what seemed like the Milky Way galaxy. I guess I knew then that my function did not tend toward investigations, but as fate would have it, I did very much what I do now—document events and bring people together, what we now call "networking."

One significant event took place in Boulder, Colo. Expert researcher and social psychologist Richard Sigismond, an old friend of Allen's, lives in Boulder. He is quite well known both for his incredible, almost "unearthly," flower garden and for researching the UFO phenomena, especially abductions. He had not seen Dr. Hynek in a long time. Recently divorced, I asked my then new companion Russ Croop to host J. Allen Hynek in his apartment while I planned a surprise dinner for Allen and Richard. I thought it inappropriate at the time for Allen to lodge at my apartment, although when Russ and I later bought a house, Allen and his wife Mimi were frequent guests. Dr. Hynek agreed to come to Boulder for extended stays.

Richard was adequately surprised, and Allen and he talked over old times and old adventures. I might as well not have been present, as they were drinking wine and happily reminiscing. I look back at those days and I knew nothing of the cases they were discussing. I did not fully understand the impact of the UFO phenomena nor the importance of our relationship. Russ Croop and I always considered Allen a family friend, a kind of eccentric gentleman who would listen to opera and talk with us until the wee hours of the morning about astronomy and UFOs, but I loved the man, as I loved Col. Philip Corso, Dr. Michael Wolf (see page 91), and Ginny Morrow (Bridey Murphy) all of whom are no longer with us, and to whom I have dedicated this work. It is so hard to be so close to, and then lose, these fine people. It is quite difficult for me to go back in time and relive these precious moments.

Allen and Mimi invited Russ and me to Evanston in 1980, just days before we left for Europe. Astonishingly, Allen formally introduced me to his CUFOS board and made me feel that I had an important role to play. CUFOS even bought me a typewriter to use there to answer letters. Allen wanted to network with people, so he asked me to bring Dr. Roberto Pinotti, director of the Centro Ufologico Nationale (CUN) to the U.S. to a CUFOS conference in Chicago because Dr. Pinotti was the only researcher at the time who had many actual slides of UFOs, some given to him by the Italian Air Force. So, while I was in Florence, Italy, I knocked on Dr. Pinotti's door, and my current Italian collaboration began when Dr. Pinotti agreed to come.

For me, that 1981 UFO conference was historic. I heard Budd Hopkins speak for the first time, and I heard John Schussler's analysis of the Betty Cash case. But as we were having lunch with Allen, a nervous man approached us with a courier leather briefcase attached to his wrist. He spoke to Allen about the Roswell photos in his case. I knew nothing about Roswell, just as I knew nothing about Leonard Stringfield, who was carrying information and research. I remember thinking that this man, now departed, had put himself in a precarious situation.

XX CONNECTING THE DOTS…

I realize that I was a neophyte to this field in the 1980s, having done virtually no research and having read only a few books, but my later life not only would provide me with the needed background and data base, but would also introduce me to most of the top players, who would confide in me by giving me information to *connect the dots* in this cosmic mystery.

It is painful for me to talk about J. Allen Hynek, because I really miss his steady guidance. We were both Tauruses with Sagittarius rising. He hated to drive, so at home Mimi drove, and when he came to Colorado, I drove him to his media appearances. I would just sit in the studio and watch him. He was a gentle soul, with white, tousled hair and twinkly eyes, and he always had his pipe in hand, although he did not always smoke it, but just kind of chewed on it. He might forget his hat or his overcoat, and I'd rush back to get it. He seemed to be your typical absent-minded professor, but his mind was clearly on other things.

I was told that Dr. Hynek meditated an hour each morning, facing east, and he was not to be disturbed. Once, while we were listening to the opera "Tosca," he turned to me and said, "I wish I could have some definitive answers before I die." Russ and he would jokingly call the "cattle mutilation" cases "cows in space" and they would laugh together. Later as fate would have it, in 1983, I also met Linda Moulton Howe (see page 34) as she moderated a Denver discussion panel with Dr. Hynek, Richard Sigismond and Dr. R. Leo Sprinkle. These people, and Stanton Friedman in particular, are what I refer to as the "Old Guard," pioneers, warriors, people in the ranks who forged the way, and so few are still living. Today Linda and I remain close, and we refer to ourselves as soul-sisters, although we have not researched any cases together. We have kept our relationship more personal than professional, and we respect each other greatly.

When Allen first came to Boulder, I hosted a reception to introduce him to other astronomers such as David Aguilar, director of Fiske planetarium. I invited psychologist Dr. R. Leo Sprinkle and his wife Marilyn to come down from Laramie, Wyoming. Aguilar later worked for Ball Aerospace, but he always remained curious about this cosmic enigma of UFOs. He thought I was a little crazy, no doubt, but he can testify that I was keeping "credible" company. It was Richard Sigismond who became the benchmark of UFOlogy for me, because he also lived in Boulder. Allen used to go over to Richard's cottage to discuss UFO cases, napping on Richard's couch when he tired.

The most singularly personal memory I have of Allen happened when Russ and I met the Hyneks in Santa Fe, N.M., shortly before his death from a tumor. We stayed at the historic La Fonda Hotel, with its colorful Mexican decor. I remember listening together to a musical combo playing in the hotel lobby bar, which had an orange tile dance floor. Allen asked me to dance a tango with him, while Russ danced with Mimi. What a young spirit he had! As he dipped me at the end of the tango, he said we'd better get off the dance floor before people talked. I was flattered, but he was a 70-some-year-old man with a 30-year-old heart.

In Santa Fe, we strolled by the adobe shops one evening and he began to point out the stars as any astronomer would to an ignorant student. I remember him saying "*Never* mistake Venus for a UFO, Paola! It is one of the brightest heavenly bodies and a common mistake everybody makes!" He said it gently, as was his manner when he listened to the wild stories of alien "abduction." He had infinite patience and treated every person with respect, even those I considered "crazy." I learned from him how to question people and how to stay impartial. I also learned from him how to have compassion for others. I watched him draw information out with this method, and people just loved him.

I saw him lose patience and become angry only once, when the TV show "Night Line with Ted Koppel" called Boulder to place Allen on a panel opposite debunker Philip Klass. Angrily, he said, "Paola, tell them, 'No!' There is no civilized discussion with that man!"

Once, Mimi and Allen asked if they could bring a guest to Boulder. She seemed really nice, and she was an English investigator who, years later, I realized was Jenny Randalls. But I do remember that they discussed the Rendlesham Forest case, many details of which shocked me at the time. I did not know where to place this in my mental data base then.

Later, when Allen became ill, I sadly paid for Richard Sigismond's air fare to California so he could sit by Allen's post-surgery bedside, because I could not go. At least Allen had Mimi, Richard and Jacques Vallée there during those sad latter times. Allen had been advised earlier to move to Scottsdale, Ariz., and in 1986 he called me from there while convalescing, proud that he could take a few steps with a walker. He was happy to hear my voice, and he told me he was improving. That was my last conversation with him.

XXII CONNECTING THE DOTS...

A year or so later, my family and I went down to see Mimi and son Paul Hynek for a couple of days. What an empty house with all those ominous filing cabinets in his beautiful study! It was eerie but it was just the beginning of other losses I would suffer.

After Allen died, Mimi Hynek came to visit me in Rome. I loved her. She was such a brilliantly independent lady with a penchant for archeology. She was a little lost without Allen and spoke about him in the San Marino Conference of 1996. She died in 1997 of a stroke, and I was devastated. It was then that I became aware that I had been schooled by a master teacher, and it stayed with me. They were both gone, and I wanted to slam the door on UFOlogy forever!

Enter Colonel Philip Corso

Sometime in 1995, I found out that my dad in Italy was suffering from a lung tumor, so I packed my things and moved to Rome to be with him in his last days and to explore a new love relationship with an Italian gentleman. This is important, because it seems that at this crisis point in my life, my journalistic and research career began quite by accident, without planning or premeditation. My life in Rome was normal. With a multi-disciplinary masters degree from Leslie College, I accepted a principalship at the high school at the American Overseas School of Rome (AOSR), a prestigious institution with international students. I was living with my marvelous new man, whom I considered to be "the love of my life," and we were doing a lot of world traveling.

All at once my dad died of lung cancer and the roof caved in. To make things worse, my boyfriend and I terminated our relationship. I returned to teach at AOSR, where today I teach high-school photojournalism, American literature and ancient history. It is very rewarding, and I love the kids. Although I rarely talk about my stories or UFOs, those kids who find out or see my web site are fascinated by this weird teacher. My job helps fund the numerous investigations and on-site interviews I have done in this book. There is no money in UFOlogy, and I have spent thousands of dollars on research, money which I will probably never see again. It is only through my mom Elaine's occasional financial support and her personal fascination with the subject matter that this wealth of information has come forth. She has met Col. Corso, Dr. Michael Wolf and Mimi Hynek. My kids and family avoid the subject, and I sometime feel alone and unable to share this quest. It is lonely out there, and as my psychic advisor, the late George O'Steen, said to me once, "the higher you climb on the mountain, the fewer friends you see behind you!"

I was depressed and reclusive after my tragedies, but then a most amazing thing happened. 1997 was the 50th anniversary of the Roswell crash, coinciding with Col. Corso's release at the Roswell conference of his blockbuster, *The Day After Roswell*. I was in Italy at that time, with no desire to travel, when I received a FAX from Richard Sigismond inviting me to travel the 600 miles from Boulder to Roswell for this historic occasion. The FAX arrived at the offices of my friend, Maurizio Baiata, editor of magazines *Notiziaio UFO* and *Dossier Alieni*. Maurizio was then partners with Dr. Roberto Pinotti, whom I had brought to Dr. Hynek in Chicago in 1981. Both men were then consulting with me on some UFO stories.

The invitation changed my life forever and hurled me into a greater arena than I could ever imagine. But I did not want to go. I was healing from personal trauma and not interested in doing anything. Richard and his good friend Ron Keith, who would be doing the driving, insistently FAXed again, saying I could sleep on the floor in their motel in Artesia, 40 miles away from the event, because all the rooms in Roswell proper had been booked since February for this momentous event! This detail is important for the synchronistic things that occurred later. I hesitatingly agreed to meet them July 3, 1997. It was a long, hot drive, and I was ill prepared. I was told to look for a man named Phil Corso and another called Robert Dean (see page 16). I was to invite them to Italy to a major "Contact" conference on the Adriatic in the province of Pescara.

I was also to cover the event and take photos for the magazine. I had long done all my own photography, and I was fairly good at it. As we drove toward Roswell in the van, many thunderstorms unexpectedly arose—weird storms and strange lightening. The colonel later wanted to talk to me about these events.

I said to Richard that I had to check in at the press section to get my press pass and see if I could sleep in Roswell, otherwise, I would never get to attend the morning press conference. I would have been late if I had to come all the way from Artesia, and I felt bad making them rise early. They waited for me in the van as I ran to the press area and told the people there that I was a foreign journalist covering this historic event, and I needed a place to stay. They just said "Good luck!" and handed me the infamous yellow pages. So I placed my little finger at random on the first hotel, the Sally Port Inn, and sure enough, they had a room for three nights. It turned out that all the major speakers lodged there, but what was incredible was that my room was right next to Corso's. I had no idea who he was, what he even looked like, or even what he had written, but some of my best interviews have happened this way, as I am open to anything and do not have a preconceived direction.

I said good-bye to Richard and the guys and threw my equipment and suitcase on the bed and looked for a ride to the Roswell Museum where Col. Corso was to have a press conference. I hitched a ride in a red sports car with William Birnes, Corso's co-author. I did not really understand who he was until I saw him later on stage.

There was a huge crowd around the press table and it was impossible to approach the colonel because his press agents from Simon and Schuster did not want him to speak to individual people. Fate would have it that a young man with blonde hair noticed my press badge and asked me about Italy. He said that I should ask the colonel a question in Italian because the colonel had been there in 1944. I hesitated speaking in Italian in front of all the TV cameras present in that incredible confusion. So this man who turned out to be the colonel's son Phil Corso, Jr., smiled, said "Go on!" and gave me a gentle push, which shoved me into the limelight. In Italian, I asked the colonel about the Santilli alien autopsy footage. My magazine in Italy had dedicated pages and pages to examining it and Maurizio Baiata believed that there was some truth to that footage. Surprisingly, the colonel, being also of Sicilian descent, answered in Italian. He said that if it were *not* real, it was a good facsimile, due to a particular detail he noticed. He explained that in the film he saw an eye covering removed that was similar to the black alien eye covering in his Roswell artifact file, from which Army Research and Development had developed today's night screening devices.

It all seemed incredibly programmed. I got close enough to him to talk for several minutes and he said to me "I know you!"

I answered "I don't think so.' He proceeded to say that he had to tell me about his friend Wilbur Smith and the electromagnetic "pillars" that were spinning in the Roswell desert.

Then everybody crowded in, and I did not know how I was ever going to see him again, until I saw him walking into the room next to mine at the Sally Port Inn. He then said he would give me an interview on July 5, knocking on my door at 8:00 A.M. This was too good to be true, so I was preparing a tape recorder when he showed up at 7:00 A.M. I think he was keeping a low profile because he was the biggest attraction at Roswell. I opened the door and saw this fine gentleman with two autographed books in his hand, one for me and the other for his dear friend Enzio Rapanelli in Foligno, Italy, an ex-military friend from WWII. I never dreamed then that later in my life I would be privileged to spend Easter week in 1998 in Foligno with Col. Corso, his daughter-in-law Liz, two grandsons and Signore Enzio Rapanelli.

We sat in the hotel room opposite one another, a table between us and in an informal discussion the colonel gave me an interview recorded on audio tape and reproduced in this book that not only was totally unexpected but also difficult to deal with at the time. It is printed word-for-word in this book and was printed in *Notiziario UFO* only after his death. The colonel often repeated this story in Italy to anyone he trusted. I was the wrong person at the time, because I wanted to talk only about his book and "nuts-and-bolts" UFOlogy, but he wanted to talk about his contact experience. He was passionately taken by the contact he had, in which the alien gave him the phrase "a new world, if you can take it." He kept asking me "What does it mean?" At that time, I not only did not know but I also did not *want* to know. Naïvely, I decided to shelve the interview because I feared it would hurt the colonel's credibility. I had grown fond of the old man and did not want to do anything to hurt him or to make money off him.

I developed a strict code of ethics with Col. Corso. I decided I would not print revolutionary material obtained from him or other military witnesses. I would keep confidences, and I would not get into nasty, dirty battles with the hustlers and money dealers "in the temple." The colonel was horribly burned and disturbed by the court case that stopped him from lecturing or speaking out in this country. He loved people, especially young people, and he gave them hours of his time in Italy, where he was greatly pleased to share his experiences with the Italians, many of whom still talk about him. He touched many hearts. There were always dubious characters around the Corso family, which did not thrill the good colonel. He sincerely believed in disclosure, but he believed in keeping his integrity—the only thing he could take with him.

I was one of the closest journalists to Corso. I knew him very well as a friend, and I kept my word to his son that I would protect him in Italy, which ironically turned out to be the only country in which he spoke openly. I report here first-hand what I think the colonel would want us to know.

In June 2000, I was invited to Florida to stay with Phil, Jr., his wife, and three sons, to collaborate on some of the materials. I respectfully declined. I love the family, but I was not prepared to take the risk or the responsibility to bring forth effectively the legacy the colonel had collected. Phil, Jr., is a bright man, and he could have handled it himself, for he too well understood the "contact" scenario and the life his dad had led. The two were passionately connected. Phil, Jr., is a special soul whose emotions can get the best of him at times. He and I understand how truly important "granddad" was to the total disclosure of the UFO phenomenon and how "granddad" had influenced the course of the earth-shaking events in WWII just by his actions and physical presence during these events, something I touch on in the section "The Paranormal Factor" (see page 157).

The colonel was a good soldier but always questioned his role in world events. He used to say "Why me, Paola?" Then he would tell me he was handing me a "hot potato," and I would ask, "What do I do with it?" and he would say, "You decide." He never perceived danger, although I will say that horrible stress and pressure came to him for signing an affidavit for Citizens Against UFO Secrecy (CAUS) against the U.S. Government. He called me in Rome at 2:00 A.M. in the morning and asked advice. I just said to him "Colonel, you have done enough for disclosure already. Why, as a patriotic man, are they requiring you to sign this?"

He said only that his credibility was being attacked and that he would be slandered all over the Internet if he did not sign it. I suspect that this event was partially responsible for his untimely death. I spoke to him on a Thursday from Boulder, and he was dead the following Monday. I was devastated, and I cried uncontrollably. A year later, I visited his grave and placed individual roses there from Maurizio Baiata (my boss and editor), Adriano Forgione (my co-worker), and Corso's surrogate Italian family. It did not seem fair. He was such an impressive master teacher.

The Colonel in Italy

Few people realize that Col. Corso twice came to Italy for extended stays. He was happy there, and he spoke at two conferences—Pescara and San Marino. Many people asked him questions. An important document requesting serious dialogue and research on the UFO question was signed there by international researchers. The independent Republic of San Marino then submitted it to the United Nations.

Corso also made an important appearance on the Maurizio Costanzo talk show, which is similar to the Jay Leno show. Costanzo pumped the colonel for details about the makeup of the alien body whose autopsy he saw. Never had this talk-show host been so speechless for so long. Perhaps Col. Corso was the only guest in the history of Italian TV that was able to stop Maurizio Constanzo from speaking for a solid 20 minutes! I was sitting in the front row with my then-editor Maurizio Baiata, and I noticed that the movie-star guests were a little shell-shocked at the first-hand testimony of this very credible witness.

Col. Corso was credible, and he said that he and the generals had made a pact that the last one living would talk. Phil told me that his real motivation for speaking was his grandsons, who would often ask him, "Granddad, tell us what you did in the service." He said that he felt that it was a legacy that the young people could handle. He told me and Adriano Forgione that he was old, that he would not be around forever, and that we must carry the baton. But since I did little public speaking at that time, I preferred to stay in the background. It was too huge a responsibility, and I shared this with the colonel.

He just said that at times he would encourage his young soldiers to give briefings, and they always did a great job, so he said, "Remember, Paola, you are like one of my men, and I know you will do it well. There will always be an empty seat in the front row, and I will be there watching." Now as I do more public lectures, I often see that empty seat and am very moved and nostalgic.

Maurizio, Adriano and I used to take the colonel to Rome's great pizzerias, where he would talk all night. I must have heard his war stories dozens of times. His war experiences alone would fill a book. He was at the famous battle of Monte Casino! His intelligence career and his adventures fighting crime, communists and spies would make 007 seem like a kid in comparison. During WWII, he even used to carry a little stiletto knife hidden in his arm, which alarmed both friend and foe. I saw a facsimile of the knife in a glass case in the Corso home in Florida.

Perhaps the most powerful memories I have of him in Italy were his intimate conversations with Desmond Leslie, British ex-fighter pilot of George Adamski fame. Leslie, who is of noble heritage, knew about aliens and UFOs and was close with Adamski. If those two were talking, no one interrupted them. They would go on until the wee hours of the morning. The colonel's daughter-in-law Liz and one or two grandsons were always present.

It was part of the agreement that the colonel would travel with family, and my editor paid their way, because the colonel wanted the boys to see Italy and his heritage. I became really close to these teen-aged boys who adored their "granddad." I felt like a bodyguard at times, always taking his arm. I was afraid he was going to trip and fall, and I remembered my promise to Phil, Jr., to protect him. When we were at Italian dinners, which are often made up of five courses, the colonel would not eat. So I began cutting up his meat and forcing him to eat. He loved the attention so much that at one point, he wanted to change his ticket to remain in Rome. The colonel maintained that food makes you tired and saps your strength, although I noticed that he loved strawberry ice cream. He displayed incredible energy despite eating very little. He was still talking and raring to go at night when the rest of us were tired and exhausted. I observed that he had great intuition, ESP and dimensional awareness, which I will discuss in the Paranormal Section.

Phil was very generous with gifts for his family and his friends. Once he came off the plane at Rome's Leonardo Da Vinci Airport gently carrying a unwrapped porcelain red rose in his hand for me. Another time he handed me a long, black, laser-pointer pen, telling me it was just like the artifact in his Roswell "nut file." He told me that, like a stupid human, he thought it needed batteries.

He said he had taken the original artifact to the Army Labs at Ft. Belvoir, Md., to have long, low waves put on it. It activated, producing a fine laser light. He said that they did not realize the importance of what they had back then, and also that they should have paid more attention to the Extraterrestrial Biological Entity (EBE) body, the most precious cargo of all, because a careful study of its makeup would enable humans to travel in space. He confided to me that quite possibly the Roswell aliens were humans coming back from the future to warn us. After his first heart attack, he mentioned to me that he had had a dream in which he received a warning of future events occurring in 2003. He was very disappointed with humanity and regretted the deaths and carnage of wars, but he knew he had played an important role in unfolding events on the planet by saving thousands of Jews during WWII, negotiating with key historical figures such as the Montini Pope, saving entire villages from disease and starvation, and fatefully being present in 1947 at Ft. Riley, Ks., to view the alien "cargo" as it was stored in the veterinary quarters. Later, when he viewed the autopsy papers, he recalled seeing the alien body floating in blue liquid. He said the Pentagon was more concerned with its creators, because the EBE seemed to be a clone of some kind. The creators could look like us.

Like Dr. Michael Wolf in later years, whatever Col. Corso related he repeated exactly, without changing the details. These were experiences he had lived. Also like Wolf and ex-NASA ground-crew astronaut Clark McClelland, he wrote papers and documents that later were either destroyed or denied to him. He said that in the intelligence network, you could not leave a paper trail. It is incredible to me that so-called debunkers who have never met the people they are debunking use the lack of documents as their chief reason to claim disinformation and fraud. Corso's documented Italian and American careers are impeccable. One need only have spoken with the man to realize who he was. The release of *The Day After Roswell* took the study of the UFO phenomenon to a new and more concrete level, and, for us journalists, it helped *connect the dots*.

As a journalist who observes and knows these people well, I am appalled at how few researchers do their homework. Although I am highlighting some particular people in this book, I have consulted and spoken with so many more. Sgt. Major Robert Dean, Bill Hamilton and his wife Pamela, Wendelle Stevens, Carlos Diaz, Desmond Leslie, Yvonne Smith, Michael Hesseman, Budd Hopkins, Michael Lindemann and Jim Courant were present with Col. Corso in Pescara, Italy, in 1997 and in 1998 at San Marino. These are some remarkable people. In San Marino, Corso met with Sun Shilli (China), Roberto Pinotti (Italy), Boris Shurinov (Russia) and Gildas Bourdais (France), Antonio Huneas and others. When these people sat with him, they all exchanged ideas and, since I was always present, I saw the enormous respect expressed for him. I also saw a synthesis of research and ideas that I rarely see today in this always competitive and sometimes back-stabbing field. There is so much wealth of information in this group of people that one might consider it a "think tank," or a meeting of the minds, with each person having his or her expertise. If one uses Dr. Hynek's method of compassion and good listening skills, there is no way that the truth will not emerge. Since I have now become a frequent speaker at Dr. Roberto Pinotti's San Marino conference, I can truly say that it is the "United Nations" of UFOlogy and a dignified arena for world discussion.

It is important for contactees, scientists and military leaders to come together, and I saw this at the Pescara conference where Col. Corso explained the propulsion systems on the light ships seen by Mexican contactee Carlos Diaz. He said the craft in Roswell was similar. Diaz, who is now a personal friend of mine, told me that Corso helped him enormously to understand the technical aspects. He is forever grateful to the colonel for verifying his photographs.

The colonel loved to speak about electromagnetism. He explained to me that during WWII in Rome, he had met three scientists who had the key—Fleich, Flock and Castellani. They did research at the University of Rome. Castellani had some famous healing creams that changed the electromagnetic composition of the body. Corso insisted that Adriano and I find the archives to do some research. He added that the EBE would nourish itself with electromagnetism, and taking him away from his environment in the craft would cause him to disintegrate and die. The EBE and the craft were one complex thought complex thought construct.

Then finally, as he promised in Roswell, he spoke about the electromagnetic "pillars." He said that in 1947, Roswell had radar blips that indicated that there were unidentified craft flying around. He said that one night two craft smashed into two whirling electromagnetic pillars that held a storm-induced gateway between them, which was caused by the same kind of unusual electrical demonstrations that I had seen on my 1997 trip there. He added that in the past they had lost planes which simply disappeared. He said one UFO crashed, and one showed up ten years later near Red Canyon, N.M. He says he saw it! The account in the next section is what he told me at Roswell in 1997, and he personally FAXed to my home the drawing of the entity pictured there.

My job as a journalist is to put forth the "word-for-word" interviews painstakingly collected for this book and to let the reader form the conclusions. It is not my job to draw conclusions or to convince anyone! Any intelligent being can *connect the dots*. I thank Col. Corso and all these other researchers for trusting me.

The Old Guard

Chapter 1

The Old Guard

Colonel Phil Corso

July 5th 1997, The Sally Port Inn, Roswell, N.M.

A New World if You Can Take It!

Paula Harris (PH): I hear that you were part of the allied forces that put you in Rome in 1944, and you helped put Rome back on its feet in 1945.

Col. Phil Corso (PC): That's right. I was talking to God, and I asked him, "Did you put me here as a joke? This is your Eternal city, not mine.

PAULA HARRIS AND COL. PHIL CORSO

I'm an American. But since you put me here, I'll show You. I'll show everybody." I was talking to God like a crazy man. "I'll show you. I will put this city back on its feet. I'll give it back to you better than it ever was. Then I went to work. I called in the three chiefs of the black markets, commodities, and money changers. I reorganized "The Ombra" and they worked for me.

PH: I've heard some of those fantastic war stories, but the question I have is "How come it's you? Why *you*?"

PC: I used to say, "Why me? How come? What am I doing here?" It's uncanny. My whole life is uncanny. In Rome, I didn't lose a man.

3

None of my CIG (Central Intelligence Group) agents got killed. That's impossible. It shouldn't have happened. I used to look at the orders I'd write about Communist "arms." Nothing ever went wrong. It's not possible. It's not right. I'd walk down Via Sicilia in Rome at two, three in the morning and I'd walk down the street like I was in another world. Nobody around. No noise. Nothing! Uncanny. Chief of Police Luigi Ferrari told me "you've been here before. Yes. You've been here before." So I told General Trudeau "How'd I get these big positions, White House, big commands? I was drafted in the Army. I'm not a career soldier. So the general said "It doesn't matter how you got the job. We won't try to figure that out. What's important is what you do after you get the job." All my life, even now, I've always felt like somebody's been manipulating me. Who is it? I don't know.

PH: Do you honestly know what your book means? All those people—Linda Mouton Howe (see page 34), Robert Dean (see page 16), Stanton Friedman—have been trying and trying to bring forth the truth. This book is the key to unlock the mystery.

PC: My background, my positions, my integrity—they can't touch that. My experiences fit like a glove with the positions I was in. Something's been guiding me. I don't know what. I can't figure that out.

PH: What gave you the courage to write the book, apart from the fact that you said that you owed it to your men? Are you fascinated by extraterrestrial life or did you already know it?

PC: I knew it. I was pretty hardened to the fact.

PH: When? Before 1947?

PC: Oh no. Years ago. My mother told me, poor woman, that every time she saw a thunder and lighting storm, she used to pray, because she had a crazy little son who, when the lightening started, had to run outside in the storm and watch the lightning. She couldn't believe it. She used to say "What's the matter with you? You love lightning...it will kill you." I said, "It won't kill me." My son claimed that one day he saw me hit by lightning, and I kept walking.

PH: So that when you were 20 or 30 years old, you felt there was something...?

PC: In fact, one night I had an experience. I described the inside of a UFO, and I was the only one on it. But anyway, my whole life was uncanny...the positions I held. I stood one day at Sperry Rand [with] General Trudeau and General Douglas MacArthur, the greatest soldier we ever had, who was chairman of the board...and I said, "What am I doing here? How did I get here? I don't belong here. These two great men are asking my advice. I'm just a draftee from an old town in Pennsylvania. Why me? I don't know."

PH: Let's return to the Roswell Crash. What happened with the gates you said were in that area? (I think he was describing dimensional electromagnetic pillars.)

URSULA ANDRESS RELAXES WITH COL. PHIL CORSO.

PC: The night that this crash happened, Mac Brazel said there was a lightning hit. Wilber Smith, the Canadian physicist, told me about the electrically charged electromagnetic pillars. If a plane or ship in the water hits those gates, the nuclear binding comes apart. When these electromagnetic pillars are moving and something hits them, they create wild fires. The gates are invisible, and if the electric magnetic binding comes apart, even a human can disappear. So on that particular night, there were three of them, three crafts, and all these storms happened, and they must have come through the gate and they hit, and one came through a split second behind the other. The time sequence was off, and one ship became two and happened to arrive ten years later. I saw it. I went out to it!

PH: Ten years later?

PC: I saw it right there in the desert, right near the Trinity site. I put my hand on it. It kept disappearing and coming back. My trajectory, my radar kept picking it up.

PH: You saw the ship?. How did you know to go there?

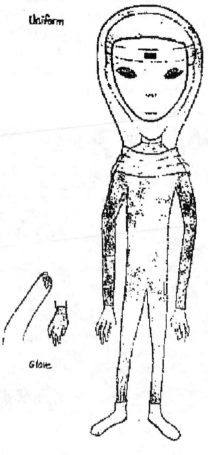

Uniform

Glove

PC: I flew over in a plane first. Then I had them bring me over a big command car. I went across the desert in a command car by myself. I did not go near it. I was a bit scared, but then, I threw some cactus in there and it was crushed. It was solid. It was 110° in the sun and I put my hand on it. It was as cool as ice, right there in the desert near the Trinity site.

PH: Were you alone? Did anyone else see it? Was it by intuition that you knew to go there?

PC: I was alone, but when I told my German scientists...and Wilber Smith, he said "You have experienced one of the truly great events that ever happened in the world." In a gold mine, I met one of those things. You know what message he left me? I had taken my gun out so I put my gun back. He left me a message. I'll write it down for you. "A New World if You Can Take it!" (See insert with Colonel's handwriting) He asked me to come aboard. I said to him, "I know what you have done to my people." Then like a human, I asked him "What can you offer me?" He said "A new world, if you can take it." Then he asked me to shut down my radar for ten minutes. I said to myself, "If I shut my radar down, ten minutes could be an eternity." How did that thing know that I was the only man that could give that order?

PH: Was it a "Grey"?

PC: It had a glass helmet on with a silverfish band and a red jewel or sensor in the middle. (See illustration.) Do you know what that means, "A new world, if you can take it"?

PH: No. But did you write this in your book?

PC: No.

PH: Colonel, you act like this is normal. It doesn't scare you at all?

PC: I was in combat. If you don't act normal, you're in trouble, or you go out of your mind. Do you know what I asked him when I first pulled out the gun. "Friend or foe?" Guess the answer was?

PH: Neither?

PC: That's right, neither. "A New World, if you can take it." I asked Jacques Vallée what that means. Well, I walked back from the cave, I put my gun and knife away, and I walked to the jeep. I picked up my radio and called range headquarters and gave the order, "Captain Williams, this is the Colonel. Shut the radar off for ten minutes. I'm on my way. I repeat, shut the radar down." But as I looked back, the thing was still at the entrance to the gold mine. Whatever the hell it was, was standing at the entrance. There was water there and everything. I looked back, and I saluted him.

PH: And he let you go? Sometimes they try to control you.

PC: Yes. But I can shut my mind off to mental telepathy. I used to do that during the war, or how else do you get through it? When I got back, the sergeant said "Colonel, you'd better pick up the tape at E battery.... There's something going 3,000 or 4,000 miles per hour on the screen. When I was in the air, I saw a green light flashing, and I heard in my mind, "I return your salute." Was I military and just imaging this, or was this thing a soldier too?

:

I have always been very protective of the Colonel, so, although I was given this interview in Roswell in 1997, I decided against publishing it, due to the ridicule factor. However, Col. Corso came to Italy twice to speak at conferences, and on those occasions, he told many others this story. It was important to him that he tell it because of the message stated here. He also wrote it on the dedication of the Italian translation of the *Roswell* book for me. (I wrote its preface in Italian.) I feel that there is timing to this slow-process release of information, and this is the time to consider disclosure. I was lucky to have known the Colonel. I miss his war stories that he used to tell over and over again. I miss his honesty. When I asked him why he had come out with this disclosure, he told me that he thought his men and the world could handle

COL. PHIL CORSO RELAXING WITH FRIENDS.

it. He said he was giving me a "hot potato" and I would know what to do. He said to me "you decide." He encouraged me to continue speaking at conferences and he used as a metaphor, his briefing of his own young soldiers. He called me a soldier although he was aware that I was also a lady. Phil Corso said he knew that he would not be around forever and since his men would always do a good job in his place, he knew I would too. Curiously, he told me personally that he would always be present sitting in the first row so look for an empty seat. Some strange paranormal phenomena has happened to me around the colonel and many psychics who know nothing of my work have told me they see, on an astral level, an older soldier walk in with me when I enter the room and that he is wearing medals.

"I hope I did a good job, Colonel."

Chapter 2

The Old Guard

Zecharia Sitchin

www.sitchin.com

Scholars have traveled the entire world looking at historical artifacts and documents as evidence that possibly humankind could have been seeded by alien races. One of the most powerful proponents of this theory is prolific writer, researcher and historian Zecharia Sitchin, and his evidence is pretty convincing. The following interview took place May 5, 2003, a time when many people had questions about the ransacking of the National Museum in Iraq and the possible return of the planet Nibiru.

In *The Earth Chronicles*, Mr. Sitchin tells, based upon his interpretations of ancient Sumerian clay tablets, the story of humankind, our origins, how we were created, and details of the overall plan. Earth's history originates with the stories of gods who interact with humans, and most divine stories are similar. We know them as mythology. Sitchin researched these concepts for 30 years, traveling the world and examining thousands of artifacts, art works and archaeological locations, to reach the following conclusions.

1. The Sumerians wrote the story of humankind on clay tablets 6,000 years ago in what is now Iraq, where, in the ages past, a sophisticated,

advanced and well organized civilization suddenly bloomed in the Mesopotamian area.
2. They knew the sun was the center of the planetary system and they knew
    of planets that we have just discovered in the last 150 years, including
    Pluto, "discovered" in 1930.
3. The key to the mystery lies in a planet the Sumerians called Tiamat,
    which once orbited between Mars and Jupiter, but which no longer exists.
    In its place lies the asteroid belt. Tiamat was destroyed by an invader—a
    planet the Sumerians called Nibiru, which joined our solar system.

This "12th Planet," Nibiru, is represented in ancient writings and art. It has
a retrograde 3,600-year elliptical orbit around the sun and may soon be returning
our way. Sitchin says that it took him 30 years of research to document this information and that he paused for five years to find an answer to the creation of
humankind itself. This he found in the Mesopotamian epic of creation called
Enuma Elish, which was written on seven clay tablets. Six tablets tell about the
creation of the solar system and planets, and the seventh glorifies the Creator,
much like Genesis in the Bible (the creation of the seven-day week). According
to these ancient texts, humanity was genetically created by the Anunnaki (meaning "Those who from Heaven to Earth came"). Fifty of them splashed down in
the Persian Gulf (432,000 years ago) and genetically engineered a race to mine
gold for them in southeast Africa. They needed gold for a protective shield over
their planet. To create humans, they did some serious genetic manipulation on an
already-existing hominid species. They left behind symbols found in ancient cultures, such as the winged disc, and evidence of nuclear destruction. Mission control for their flying crafts was in what is now Israel, an area that was as
significant then as it is now. (See "The State of the World" chapter, page 211,
which reiterates the key role that Israel still plays in today's world.)

May 5, 2003

Paola Harris (PH): How significant is the destruction of the thousands of arti-
    facts in the National Museum of Baghdad? Does it destroy the legacy left
    by the early people of the fertile crescent, including the Anunnaki?
Zecharia Sitchin (ZS): While the subject of the fate of the archaeological
    objects in the museum should be of concern to everyone interested in the
    preservation of art, culture and history, the matter is, of course, of special
    interest to me and my worldwide readers because my writings, beginning
    with *The 12th Planet*, are profoundly based on the archaeological evi-
    dence from ancient Mesopotamia—beginning with the Sumerian civili-

zation, continuing with the Akkadian, Babylonian and Assyrian, and encompassing the other adjoining civilizations that followed.

The National Museum of Iraq in Baghdad was a major depository of such artifacts, but fortunately not the only one. In the early days of modern archaeology most of the discovered artifacts were carried off to the museums of the archaeologists' countries (London, Paris, Berlin, Milan, etc.) and later divided between them and the local museums. So, first, the loss is not total. Secondly, it is now clear that of the reported 170,000 items in the Baghdad Museum, only 29 (yes, twenty nine) important artifacts were missing (some have been returned since), and these ones have of course been studied, photographed, etc., and are well known to scholars (or even to readers of my book).

Although the loss is not as massive as initially reported, the looting that took place, the smashing of display cases, thus damaging their contents, and the breaking of larger monuments that could not be carried off–this was nothing short of pure barbarism, unforgivable behavior.

So the legacy that these museum collections represent was not and cannot be destroyed; it lives on in the other museums and, of course, in the books on the subject (such as mine), in videos, etc.

PH: Could there be a secret connection between this war and antiquity?

ZS: By advancing from the subject of the artifacts to the issue of the geographic location of the conflict, you are in reality raising two other very significant subjects. The first is that of hallowed or sacred ground; the other is that of prophecy. If you travel in the lands of the Bible, you realize that a mosque is built exactly where a Byzantine church had stood, and that it was built where there had been a synagogue, and that one, too, was built exactly there because the place was revered even in earlier times. Over the thousands of years of Mesopotamian civilization (from the beginning of Sumer circa 4,000 B.C. to the conquest of Alexander and the Seleucid rulers in the last centuries B.C.), royal inscriptions repeatedly state that it was the custom and the duty of kings to rebuild temples exactly where the previous ones stood. Conqueror after conqueror in antiquity adhered to this tradition, but neither the British after World War I nor the Americans this time have such a compulsion to build houses of worship upon ancient sites.

So the issue of interest in one of prophecy. Though Baghdad is a relatively new city and is not a continuation of Babylon, nor built where it was, there are biblical prophecies about the fall of Babylon as part of a

Divine Plan. The question is whether such prophecies were one-time prophecies, i.e., just specific to Babylon (as an example) in the 6th century B.C. only—or whether these are eternal prophecies, applicable again and again when the circumstances and the Wheel of Time apply. I believe in the latter. I have repeatedly stated that "The Past is the Future," because the Anunnaki, the people, and the civilizations they bequeathed to humankind are subject to a grand historical cycle.

PH: In your works you mention that a nuclear explosion destroyed the Sumerians. What kind of arms do you think they employed?

ZS: The use of nuclear weapons in 2024 B.C. is, first of all, of significance because it relates to the more general and bothering question: Why are there wars on Earth? In my book on the subject, *The Wars of Gods and Men*, I raised the question: Is Man born a warrior, or did someone teach us to make war? The answer is the latter: Before the wars of man there were the wars of the gods. It was during the conflict between Horus and Seth, according to unambiguous Egyptian texts, that humans were given arms and enlisted to fight (on the side of Horus that time).

And so it was that in the conflict between the two clans of Anunnaki, nuclear weapons were used to wipe out the spaceport in the Sinai (an event reflected in the biblical tale of Sodom and Gomorrah). Before that there was an international war related to the spaceport (the so-called "War of the Kings" in Genesis, chapter 14). The nuclear cloud from the explosion in the Sinai was carried by the winds eastward to Mesopotamia, and numerous Lamentation Texts describe how the Evil Wind—the nuclear cloud–killed all life in Sumer. Thus, there was no actual explosion in Sumer. The cities, the buildings remained intact; people, animals, plants died.

It is interesting in this regard to recall that as it happened the winds carried the poisonous cloud in such a way that Sumer itself was affected, but not Babylon to the north. So already in antiquity it was pondered: Was this a divine omen, the hand of Destiny? Even the Anunnaki opposed to Marduk, the instigator of the war, considered that to be a manifestation of destiny and accepted Marduk's supremacy. As to what kind of nuclear weapons were used–that the texts do not specify.

PH: What do you think happened to the survivors of the conflict?

ZS: The Sumerian Lamentation Texts indicate that the "gods" realized as soon as the explosion took place that a calamity would engulf Sumer hundreds of miles away. So the texts describe a hurried departure by the gods and their warnings to their followers to escape as well: Not to try to hide, because there was no hiding from the cloud, but to run away, to the north and farther east. The result was the first recorded Diaspora. Remnants—led by their gods–found their way, in time, to what we call Iran and India (thus the same tales of the gods in the Sanskrit texts), to the Far East (thus the Chinese, Korean, Japanese scripts that are based on the Sumerian cuneiform), to eastern Europe (the lands of the god whose symbol was the double-headed eagle), along the Danube (thus the Hungarian legends and language), etc.

PH: If the Anunnaki colonized this entire planet, what other traces are there?

ZS: Everywhere! Besides the lands and people I just mentioned, there were the more distant Americas. In my book *The Lost Realms*, dedicated to the Americas, I show connections—the evidence. You find the same gods, even if called by local tongues (e.g. the Sumerian *Ningishzidda* = the Egyptian *Thoth* = the Mesoamerican *Quetzalcoatl*); the same legends of Creation; the same astronomical recognition of equinoxes and solstices as a guide to temple orientations, etc.

PH: What is your opinion of the return of Nibiru? Many people are becoming fearful of this. What consequences will this return have on the planet?

ZS: Nibiru, which is the home planet of the Anunnaki according to the Sumerians, has a great elliptical orbit that lasts (by definition) one year for its inhabitants but 3,600 Earth years as counted by us Earthlings. I have been asked many times when it will next be in our vicinity (passing between Mars and Jupiter); and if I don't give an answer, the question is changed to "When was it last time," so people just add 3,600 years.

I have done my best in lectures, on my website etc., to stress that 3,600 (a *Shar* in Sumerian) is a mathematical number, not a precise orbital number, because orbits change with each passage. We know it from Halley's comet. We know it from the changing configuration of Earth's orbit. In addition, how Nibiru affects Earth is also not the same each time. Whether other planets stand between it and Earth is also not the same each passage. Is Earth directly exposed to its gravitational, magnetic and other effects? One time, we know, it caused the Deluge, but not after that one (circa 13,000 years ago).

To be specific, I first announced clearly in talks, interviews, and on my website that the claim by others that Nibiru will pass near Earth in 2003 is wrong. Since April 2003, the predicted date, in the meantime came and went, everyone now knows it.

PH: When will Nibiru be visible in your estimation?

ZS: Nibiru is without doubt on its way back from its farthest point out (aph-
elion). The leading searcher for what astronomers call "Planet X," Dr.
Robert Harrington of the U.S. Naval Observatory, agreed with me where it
probably was a few years ago (his sketch or sky-map is given in my book
Genesis Revisited). In that book I also provide the evidence from the discovery by IRAS (Infra-Red Astronomical Station), a satellite launched by
NASA, that twice traced the planet in 1983 by infra-red (i.e. by heat emis-
sion, not by light reflection). So those who need to know, know at least
since 1983. NASA is about to launch a new, more sophisticated infra-red
space telescope. When will Nibiru be visible from Earth with regular tele-
scopes? I cannot say, as I am not in the telescope field of expertise.

Let me make clear, however, what I have stated in my lectures again
and again: The return of the Anunnaki and the return of the planet do not
and cannot coincide, for reasons of space travel and trajectories. I thus
believe that the prophesied *return* or second coming is now, in our time,
applicable to the Anunnaki, even if not to their planet.

PH: Do you see any additional evidence that Mars is an outpost for an alien
race that might also be the Anunnaki?

ZS: As a matter of fact, the evidence from Mars is one reason why I am so
confident of the statement I just made. There is no doubt, from NASA's
own photographs from the '70s, that there were artificial structures on
Mars (other than the "Face")–I include such photos in *Genesis Revisited*.
The experts now admit, contrary to previous claims that Mars is a dead,
airless, waterless uninhabitable planet, that it did have, and still has,
plenty of water, that it even had seas and lakes, that it had an atmosphere,
etc. So the Sumerian assertion that Mars served as a way-station on the
way from Nibiru to Earth, which, when I wrote *The 12th Planet* in 1976,
was deemed by others as impossible, now is admitted as very possible.

The crucial piece of evidence is what I called in *Genesis Revisited*
"The Phobos Incident," when in 1989 a Soviet spacecraft first photographed the shadow of an elliptical object on Mars and then was
destroyed by a missile fired from Phobos, a moonlet (possibly an artificial satellite) of Mars. I wrote then that though it may not be the Anunnaki themselves who are back, it was their "emissaries"–robotic artificial
beings. This was enlarged upon in my TV documentary "Are We
Alone?" in which the Soviet space officials were quite outspoken.

PH: What are the most current discoveries you have made?

ZS: I have made it a point of stressing that the various artifacts, clay tablets, etc. which I use as evidence, were *not* discovered by me. They are the result of archaeological discoveries by others over a century and a half, the work of scholars, translators, epigraphers, biblical scholars, etc. The main "discovery" by me is the belief that while others refer to all that as "mythology," I say: No, these are records and recollections of what actually happened. That is why the overall title for my series of books is *The Earth Chronicles*. If "discovery" is understood that way, my recent discovery has been this: That every year, every month, sometimes every day, as our science advances—in space, in astronomy, in geology, in biology, in genetics, etc.–I "discover" more and more corroboration for what (as I understand it) the ancient people knew. More than ever, the subtitle of *Genesis Revisited*: "Is modern science only catching up with ancient knowledge?" is becoming more and more true.

PH: What is the overall message of *The Earth Chronicles*?

ZS: The message is: *We are not alone.* The DNA on Earth, which is the basis of all life from microbes to humans, is the same as on Nibiru, the same as everywhere else in the universe. Genetically, we are akin to the Anunnaki from Nibiru, for, as the Bible summed it up, we were fashioned by them in their image and in their likeness. Our civilizations are similar to the one they had, because it is they who gave us civilization. Our wars, to consider latest events, are similar to their wars–both wars on Earth and preceding wars on Nibiru. So we, in many respects, are they. And since I believe the Biblical prophecies and think they are universally valid, I have no doubt that we shall one day do what the Anunnaki did: Come to another planet, supposedly for a selfish need or reason, and end up doing there what they did here—cause life to evolve in a manner similar to ours, create civilization there, repeat the cycle, because it is all part of a grand design.

The Sumerians distinguished between Fate (*NAM, TAR*) and Destiny (*NAM*). Destiny was predetermined, fixed, unchanged. That Man is mortal was Destiny; how Man conducted his life between birth and death, how he would die, was Fate—a "destiny" that could be changed or bent by Man's behavior, free will, circumstances, etc. The same applied to planets, which they considered as living entities, and to the whole solar system, and to stars: There is a predetermined destiny, but within it a changeable fate. We are part of it. *We are not alone in our own solar system, and we are not alone in the universe.*

PH: Thank you!

Chapter 3

The Old Guard

Sergeant Robert O. Dean

Pescara UFO Conference, 2001 Pescara, Italy

I caught Sgt. Robert O. Dean in a reflective moment while he was speaking at my conference in Pescara in 2000 on the Adriatic Coast of Italy. He first spoke there in 1997 along with Col. Corso, Carlos Diaz, Desmond Leslie, Wendelle Stevens, and Bill Hamilton, just after I first met him in Roswell, N.M. Robert has been a guest in my home in Rome several times, and he exemplifies the mystical presence of wisdom in the chaos of this world. His delivery of precise disclosure data emotionally changes even the hardened of hearts, because he speaks as an ex-military man who has come to terms with another reality. His talks include slides of art work where UFOs are clearly represented, historically documented and he finalizes a formal presentation with the latest NASA photographs clearly showing UFOs. He presents a convincing historical argument for the extraterrestrial presence.

On a personal level, many people, from my doorman in Rome, who speaks no English, to the waiter at Bar Café Columbia in Piazza Navona who has waited on him several years in a row, all love this white-haired, pony-tailed, distinguished gentleman who walks with a cane but ages so very gracefully. He embodies, love, acceptance and wisdom. He is by far the most charismatic of the top players in the field. I consider him one of my closest "friends of the Hynek kind." His working at U.S. military at SHAPE headquarters in Paris during the '60s changed his military reality enough to compromise his security oath, and, like others, he has paid heavily for it. Italians perennially invite him back to lecture because he surpasses the language barrier enough to project a message of love. He extends an invitation for us all to enter a "a new Cosmic society" teeming with extraterrestrial life. Here he discusses those synchronicities I speak of in this book as he tries to help me understand my role as researcher/journalist over the years.

PH: Paola Harris (PH): I noticed that when you walked in here that you had a lot of memories of 1997.

Sgt. Robert O. Dean (RD): Many memories.

PH: What were you thinking when you walked into this hotel and found Bill Hamilton, Desmond Leslie, Carlos Diaz, Wendell Stevens and Colonel Corso?

RD: Carlito I will see here. I did have a memory of Desmond Leslie who is gone now, and a strong memory of Phil Corso, who is also gone. I loved them both very much, and it immediately hit me that they are not here any longer. I felt a feeling of loss, but I am delighted to be back in Pescara, because there are so many wonderful loving people here.

SGT. ROBERT O. DEAN WITH COL. PHIL CORSO

PH: Do you remember that we sat in the front row here? It was a wonderful time, when we were lucky enough to hear Colonel Corso speak about a very important issue, while in America, they were trying to get him to speak.

RD: It was a great honor to have Phil on the program and on the podium with me. Having Phil and Desmond here meant a great deal to me. Phil is not dead. Desmond is not dead. They are alive and well. They've just crossed over. I will see them again, and I have a feeling that they are with us, here at this conference.

PH: Do you feel that their contribution was significant?

RD: Oh! More significant than people even begin to understand. There is significance to the issue, to the phenomenon, to the truth of the story that will eventually come out in the years yet to come...of how much they contributed, and that will redeem them in the public's eye. I'm looking forward to that.

PH: Do you feel that it is no accident that we were all together at that particular time in 1997 which was the 50th anniversary of the Roswell incident?

RD: Paola, there are no accidents; there are no coincidences. Everything that has occurred was meant to occur. We were meant to meet. I was on the program with Phil in Roswell in 1997. I miss him very much.

PH: 1997 Roswell was a pivotal point.

RD: There are so many pivotal points—these conferences over the years. People show up and express so much interest in this subject. That in itself is important. We will not know the depth of the significance for some years yet, but someday we will...in time!

SGT. ROBERT O. DEAN WITH PAOLA HARRIS

Chapter 4

The Old Guard

R. Leo Sprinkle

Laramie, Wyo., Dec. 28,1998

It was my pleasure to meet and interview Dr. R. Leo Sprinkle, well-known, long-time UFO researcher at the University of Wyoming. Many people with past-life issues and bizarre personal experiences such as alien encounters have been helped by Leo's insightful and innovative approaches over the years. For many years he organized the annual UFO conference at Laramie.

Paola Harris (PH): Can you discuss your personal experience with abduction phenomena?

R. Leo Sprinkle (LS): First, we must acknowledge an ET presence here.

In my memory, the first sighting I had was in 1947 at the University of Colorado in Boulder. I was going to a meeting with Joe Waggoner, a buddy of mine. We were discussing general semantics and how scientists discover what is real. That was exciting philosophically. It was fall, and we were playing a little game of what's up there, when we saw in the western sky what appeared to be an elliptically shaped metal object.

We watched, but we couldn't understand what we were seeing because we knew it wasn't an airplane, helicopter or balloon. It moved faster than any of these. We watched and did not know what it was, but we knew it wasn't a flying saucer. Only kooks saw flying saucers. We didn't want to be kooks. We wanted to be scholars.

Later I thought about it, and it seemed to be the size of a fingernail at arm's length. I didn't talk about it to anybody, and I became somewhat depressed. It upset my notions of science and religion. I lost my scholarship for a quarter. And then, after being in the service in Germany, I returned to Boulder and one time my wife Marilyn and I were looking towards a mountain range here in Boulder called the Flatirons, and we saw a bright red and orange light.

It was beautiful. We thought it was an evening star. We got out of the car to look at it. It went back and forth and had no sound. The light was between the Rocky Mountain foothills and us. As the sky got darker, the object disappeared in the night air. The next day I assumed that I would read something in the newspaper or hear something in the radio regarding what we had seen. Nothing!

I learned two valuable lessons: one, that, after the second sighting, I had to investigate; and two, that it would be a lonely business, because I knew that people were afraid and hesitated to talk about these events. So I started reading books and journals that were available in 1956—books by Frank Edwards and Maj. Don Keyhoe and journals such as the *National Investigations Committee on Aerial Phenomenon.*

When I finished my doctoral studies in 1961 at the University of Missouri, I wrote to Richard Hall, who was secretary of NICAP, and we did a study of some 250 people who were interested in UFO phenomena. We asked their educational background, socioeconomic status, and so forth. We came to the conclusion that these people fell in the normal curve distribution of open-mindedness or close-mindedness. We had taken a psychological inventory.

Some scored high. Some scored low. I tried to do another study of professors of psychology, but it did not go. My colleagues thought it was nonsense. So I said, "OK, I can't do it with them," so I tried again in 1963 and once again in 1964 when I came to the University of Wyoming at Laramie. I continued the study. I decided that if I could get 100 people to complete personality inventories to describe their ESP and UFO experiences, I could do some correlations.

I knew at that time that psychic phenomena were very much a part of the UFO phenomena. Some of my colleagues do not yet understand that.

They think it is unscientific to look at the spiritual or psychic aspects. In my opinion, both physical and spiritual aspects are important.

PH: Did you go through any transformative personal experiences?

LS: I went through hypnosis myself a few years ago. When I was 50 years old in 1980, I finally had courage to go through a hypnosis session with another psychologist to learn about my childhood. He took me back to what seemed to be a 10-year-old experience in 1940 in Rocky Ford, Colorado.

I felt as if I were on board a craft. A tall man next to me put his right hand on my shoulder, and we were looking out at a dark sky with stars shining. He was telling me, or informing me (I don't know whether it was a verbal message or what), "Leo, learn to read and write well, because when you grow up, you can help other people learn more about their purpose in life."

When I was a child I had no understanding what this message meant, but I know as a boy I had bloody noses. I would wake up with nightmares with what I thought were figures in the room and a feeling that I somehow had gone elsewhere. But I did not know where elsewhere was. So as I got older and became a graduate student in psychology, I said, "Oh, I'm just afraid of my father, and these were just nightmares about my relationship with him. He was a harsh and demanding person, while my mother was compassionate and helpful."

So I would have this nightmare about something coming up the stairs and turning toward me. My mother would come in with a broom and chase it away in the hall. A crab? Well, my father was born in July—a cancer—thus a crab?

And so I explained my event to myself psychologically. In 1980, I knew that my body's reaction was such that whatever happened to me at 10 years of age did happen to me. It was a body memory. I finally was able to accept it literally. Just as many people have had experiences as children, but it's not until they get older that they allow themselves to admit it.

PH: Was this being who put his hand on your shoulder human-like?

LS: Human-like, with what I'd call a space suit.

PH: What color?

LS: It seemed like it was gray. When I was a kid, I didn't know what to call it. The only thing that I could relate it to was the comic strips called "Buck Rogers." There were no movies of this kind of thing. And people said,

"Oh, that was just a memory of a movie." Right, it had to be a movie in the future. So their explanation....

PH: Was he a blonde?

LS: I couldn't tell. Just looking up, I could just see the face, but I couldn't tell whether the head was covered with part of his space suit or his hair.

PH: So you knew this was a real physical experience?

LS: That's what I felt. Every time I would hear something beautiful or a sense of truth, I would get that little tingle in my shoulder, which said to me that this was a physical event. So I can't convince others that this really happened, but I do believe it myself. And, as a result of that, I learned that some people feel like they were abducted....

PH: Kidnapped?

LS: Taken away, back to something, but I felt like I was taken *towards* something. *Ad*-ducted. So, when I was 10 years old, I had an experience at Rocky Ford sitting on a chicken-shed roof looking toward the southwest sky. I had the same feeling looking at the sky with my parents, with my family Bob, Jean, my brothers and sisters, and later rationale took over, so I forgot that nonsense.

Yet I had a strong feeling that I had a connection with another family in the sky. And so many people feel that they are here on the planet for a task, for temporary duty. It is rough. It is scary, but it is important. And so we, therefore, continue to discover our purpose.

To me that's why many people go through this fear and doubt, because, not only are they coming into contact with extraterrestrials—which is a shock—but also, they are coming into contact with their own soul's purpose, which is a bear! It is beastly to know that we are here for a high purpose, to help ourselves, and to help humanity to get through this stage in which the Earth is going through some changes.

Humanity, itself, is going through some changes. The outcome, if it's successful, could lead into our being inducted into a confederation of civilizations of other cultures.

PH: An interplanetary federation of some kind? Is this a supposition from your studies or something that you're getting as inspiration?

LS: It is both. If I meditate, that feels right, and if I investigate, that, too, feels right. I've talked to thousands of people who are coming to similar conclusions.

PH: Including the people I've been interviewing, too, because I've gotten the same kind of response.

LS: It is both an intuitive and a sensual kind of exploration, because our senses investigate externally, but our intuition can only be used to investigate internally.

PH: So can you give us a time period for contact? What is the time period? Hundreds of years? A few years?

LS: My own bias is that the ETs are in charge, so that we don't have to worry. Contact will *not* be a formal announcement to the world but, the way things are going, the information will come as a foregone conclusion.

PH: You are saying that we could either become an intergalactic civilization and mix with our cosmic brothers, or we could...

LS: ...blow ourselves up.

PH: What time period are we talking?

LS: Now there are a lot of prophecies about the year 2013 or 2014. Mayan and pyramid. There are a lot of prophecies from individuals for 2001. Nostradamus had his quatrains interpreted about something unusual happening in June or July of 1999. There are some people who talk 2004, 2005. I've heard a wide variety of interpretations.

All we have to do is to continue our work. It's the way I felt when I was in the service. We'd look on the bulletin board when we first got up and throughout the day for a posting of the day's and the week's activities. OK, it said at 1600 hours such and such is going to happen. Now could that mean "right" at 1600 hours, or did it mean at two minutes after or a few minutes after?

What we knew was that we had to get ready for that "all-night march," or whatever it was, and have our gear ready. It might be two hours before the inspecting general comes, before the "thing" begins. So, there are several things we can do. We can scientifically investigate UFOs and the ETs as much as possible, both physically and biologically.

We can psychologically and psychically investigate ourselves. We can learn more about our past lives and what messages we bring to ourselves. We can meditate. We can share information with a wide variety of people and let people—including the ETs—know that we are ready, when we are ready, but, as a society, not as individuals. Then, I believe, we will get signs and symbols that will tell us the next step.

PH: Dr. Sprinkle, why do we have the impressions of government abductions? What are the ETs doing? Many interviews that I have been doing lately suggest that the military has also been doing abductions, probably about

80% of them. I am absolutely in shock that the military would ever use psychotronics, holographics, etc., to tamper with its citizens' minds.

LS: I have a bias about that because some of the people I talk with say that the military helicopters come by and they do this, they do that. I believe that this is happening to some people, and I also believe the ETs do a "double duty." They present us with what "they" are doing, but they also present us with what "we" are doing. For example, many people who describe abduction experiences also describe childhood abuse, so it is easier for psychologists, on the average, to say "Well, you did not really get abducted by ETs—you were just remembering childhood abuse experiences." Then we start looking at childhood abuse as a society, because we are more willing to look at that than at the ET encounters. So what I'm saying is that every institution—education, military, political, economic and religious—is going through this "enfolding" or "imploding"—a collapse or fall from the inside.

PH: How do many people respond to ET encounters?

LS: There are many people who use the term "abduction" and I understand the term, because many people feel as if they've been taken away from home or a car, and into a flying saucer. Some people feel as if it is a very horrifying experience and not only an ET encounter, but others describe what they feel are humans and ETs. So there are a wide variety of descriptions by various people about what's happening to them.

Some people feel like it's a physical phenomenon, and some people feel it's a biological one—nerves, brain waves etc. Some people feel it's a psychological phenomenon, like a sense of a fantasy, a daydream, night dream, or lucid dream, and some people have a psychic experience—an out-of-body experience—so that they are lying in bed and the consciousness or soul goes up into the flying saucer and then comes back. In my opinion, it is physical, biological, psychosocial, and spiritual. All of it. And in my opinion, the ETs provide the scenario for two reasons: one for the individual and one for the society, so that some people have an individual experience that is terrifying, painful, and medical. Some people have an awesome experience that is psychic or spiritual or religious. It's a test—an initiation. The individual is taken out of his circle of friends, the experience happens, then the person has to deal with it. Do I tell my family? Do I tell my friends? Do they accept it? Do they not accept it?

It is just like a person in military service who has an initiation—basic training—and has to learn how to depend upon himself or herself. In my opinion, the UFO experiencer has to learn to depend upon himself or herself and not feel comforted by God, a family, a religion, the military, the government, physicians, councilors, friends, neighbors—nobody!

PH: They are totally alone.

LS: Yes. Totally alone. Then, when they get the feeling like, "I can handle it, I can do it," they start talking to others, and they find out that they can share with others. Then they come together in groups and start sharing this information, so that it becomes a kind of "grass roots" phenomenon. Instead of information coming from the "top down," it's information that comes from "bottom up." So in my opinion, it is both an initiation and a social stimulus. Gradually society becomes aware that there is contact with the ETs.

PH: Thank you!

Chapter 5

The Old Guard

J. Allen Hynek

DR. ROBERTO PINOTTI, DR. J. ALLEN HYNEK, AND PAOLA HARRIS

To Paola Harris
Feb 11, 1981
Dear Paola,

Got home before the storm, which has ended only now. I think our meeting was most productive. I am having sent by UPS the files on the investigations—so that should keep you busy, perhaps sticking pins into a map to familiarize yourself with where the investigations are located—ours and MUFON! Since you have set 2 Associates newsletter, look up Vol. No. 3, July 1980, and look up the details on the Italian Painting—

Palazzo Vecchio in Florence—the Saturn Salon. The Painting: The Madonna and St. Giovanninio. So that painting—and others that might have UFO connections!

I am also sending along with the files some matters that need to be scanned for important items. I thought the luncheon a huge success—the Boulder Connection is off to a great start. And once again, let me say what an excellent dinner you prepared—it was really great. I look forward to another one sometime—except next time it's my turn!

Cheers! Allen

Chapter 6

The Old Guard

Richard Sigismond

April 1998

Paola Harris (PH): Can you tell me about your first involvement with the UFO phenomenon?

Richard Sigismond (RS): Yes. My first involvement was in the late 1940s and early 1950s. I had a surprising event occur at the University of New York, where I was both an undergraduate and graduate student for quite a few years. The event involved the appearance of Air Force and government intelligence agents wanting to know where we had gotten certain information which we had published in a New York state newspaper. The information had to do with the UFO phenomenon and the Air Force's attempts to knock UFOs out of the sky.

The appearance of government agents demanding interviews with us a few days after we had published our material made us think that there was some reality in our subject matter. They wanted to know the name of the informing officer who had given the information to the senior individual who was in our group.

We ridiculed them by saying, "Wait a minute; you know that all this stuff is science fiction. You have been saying for years and years that UFOs don't exist."

But they insisted on speaking to our senior member, who also was a graduate student. We didn't divulge that information, however.

PH: What year was this?

RS: This was the winter of 1953 to 1956 in Buffalo, New York. Today, it is the main campus of the New York City network of colleges.

PH: Have you personally experienced any encounters?

RS: Yes. I have had several encounters, mainly in the course of my work in the field of mineral prospecting. Of course, you know that I have a geology, as well as a psychology, background. I've had some encounters in different places in the West.

Fortunately, in this one, I had one or two people with me who were part of this encounter. I am not personally inclined to go into every detail of certain events of that time.

It was early July, 1967, in Missoula, Montana. We were in an isolated forest area, and it was a very foggy day. The fog was down to the tree-top level. I was doing some prospecting for setting up my own mining company, trying to trace a surface gold when, all at once, there was a humming, buzzing noise that sounded like a thousand bees. It was a sound like I had never encountered before.

Even though I had investigated the UFO phenomenon for many years, I did not say, "Oh, dear. This is the humming, buzzing sound that you get when you are under a big disc." I simply said, "What is this?" I called to my man, George, and I said, "Do you hear this?"

He said, "Yes, I do."

It permeated everything, even our clothes. That was the beginning.

The next day, the fog had lifted, and the ship came out of the sky. It looked like a flying submarine. It came down at the most leisurely pace imaginable. About 150 feet above us, it settled right at tree-top level. We figured it was about 120 feet long and 30 feet thick. We estimated our distances and sizes by looking at a distance between the trees. The object had a metallic sheen of silver or magnesium, a cast-aluminum look. It had no wings, no engines, no seams, no rivets, no welds. It was just one giant cast.

PH: For how long did you see it?

RS: For three to four minutes it was just stationary. We watched it come down very slowly. While it was coming down, it was doing more like 10 miles an hour, 5, 4, 3, 2, 1....

I marveled that at that particular instant it had no sound. It did not disturb the trees that it stood right up against. It was about 30 or 40 feet off the ground.

How it left, by the way, was entirely different. The entire surface shimmered; then it vanished. It did not go away at fast speed. It just simply...vanished.

That was one encounter.

PH: I know you have had several encounters and some contact yourself, but I think we should leave those stories for another interview.

Now, Let's progress to other areas. In what capacity do you investigate the cases that you research?

RS: I am a psychologist and social scientist, and I am highly trained in the field of cultural anthropology and government. I also have a secondary field and interest in geology and minerals.

PH: In the capacity of social psychologist, can you tell me how you collaborated with the famous astronomer and researcher, Dr. J. Allen Hynek, and how and when you worked together?

RS: In the winter of 1967, when I was checking my mail, I noticed a return address on one of my envelopes: Chairman, Department of Astronomy, Northwestern University, Evanston, Illinois. I knew that J. Allen Hynek held that position.

You must realize that those of us who were the early UFO pioneers of the 1950s held him in great disregard, because we thought this man had sold his soul to the Air Force. We believed that he knew that the UFO phenomenon was real and that he had maintained that this was all a bunch of nonsense under pressure from the government. His posture, in essence, had ridiculed pilots and everybody else who had had sightings. He had called the early reports of sightings "cases of mistaken identity of natural and man-made phenomena."

So, with this preconceived notion of Hynek in mind, I looked at that letter and thought about not even reading it. I was disturbed, and I was about to tear up the letter. Fortunately, I opened it, and I read it. The letter contained a sincere request for a private get-together; Hynek also stated that he had heard of my work from people who respected me and what I did in the field.

Hynek's letter said that he maintained private opinions concerning the UFO phenomenon. He also noted that he had private files, implying that he had changed his posture completely. That letter from Hynek led, in a few weeks, to a series of phone calls and private meetings at Northwestern University. That was spring of 1968.

That first meeting was held at the Lindheimer Astronomical Center, because Allen said it would be more private than his office at Northwestern. There, I met two or three of Hynek's closest confidants, who knew of his now-private affirmative position of UFOs. That meeting led to a series of many other meetings over the next 20 years.

PH: You later became very good friends and collaborated on cases with Dr. Hynek, if I remember correctly.

RS: Yes. We became very good friends. We collaborated on his magazine, *CUFOS*. I did a couple of lead articles, including the one on the Carol and Joe case, which came from Hynek. He gave me the lead. It was the 4th of July, 1976. He called and said that he had received a call from a young couple in Colorado. He said, "Can you deal with it, since it is in your field of discipline?"

PH: It is an interesting case because it involved a baby?

RS: Yes. That's right. Carol and Joe, a young couple, were coming back to Colorado from Ohio, where they had recently had a baby. They had come through Western Kansas into Colorado, and they were near the border of the two states at about 1:00 A.M. in the morning. They then observed the typical event where the lights start to flicker and the radio starts to have lots of static. And they wondered what was happening.

They looked out, and they saw a fleet of discs. These very clear disc shapes were coming from four different directions. Then they came together in the sky in a blue flash. One of the discs came down over their car, as the others took off.

Now, what happened after that was that they lost a little bit of time from 1:00 A.M. in the early morning until dawn. And they didn't even realize that they had traveled 100 and some odd miles from the place they had had the encounter. The last thing they remembered was that they previously were sitting on the hood of their car watching this phenomenon.

When they awakened, their car was going about "umpty" miles per hour, as if it were being controlled by someone or something else. They were 100 miles farther down the road and had lost four hours. Joe also noticed that Carol's pant legs were rolled up and that she had shackle marks on her ankles and wrists. And she said to Joe, "You don't look so pretty either. Look at your wrists, too!"

PH: You were able to help them with the missing time?

RS: Yes. I conducted a series of hypnosis sessions, done very scientifically, never at the same time or in the same room, or on the same day. I used deep hypnosis in which the subjects don't remember what they say when they are under.

We must remember that there was a six-month-old baby with them. When Carol looked at the baby on the back seat, she was shocked to see the same marks on his belly similar to those that were on her ankles and wrists. He appeared to have been held down in the same way they had been.

And if we follow the case through childhood, the baby had a heightened awareness, and Carol always felt a presence over the crib. But while in the craft, Carol remembers seeing these entities playing with the baby, passing him back and forth, and making him laugh. It seems he was not frightened, but Carol began screaming "I want my baby back!" while she was being examined separately from Joe on an examining table. Both Carol and Joe had examinations, and Joe had an out-of-the-body experience with one of the alien crew members. They seemed to greet or join in the room.

It is interesting that at first it seemed a frightening experience for them, but later, after all the trauma, they felt enlightened by the contact.

PH: I heard that you are dedicating time to writing a book. Is this one of the cases you are most known for?

RS: It is one of the most interesting cases that I have investigated, Yes, I am currently writing a book, and I will have many more cases. But you must know by now that a lot of people stop by my house to see my beautiful flower garden here in Boulder, Colorado. We discuss flowers and UFOs.

PH: Thanks, Richard. You are one of a kind!

Chapter 7

The Old Guard

Linda Moulton Howe

1999; www.Earthfiles.com

Although this startling interview was done with fellow journalist Linda Moulton Howe on the phone five years ago, it is even more relevant today. I noticed that I often ask people about their early childhood experiences (David Icke (see page 55), Ed Fouche, Pascal Riolo and Linda, for example) in an effort to look for a link as to why people research this strange phenomena.

PAOLA HARRIS, RICHARD SIGISMOND, AND LINDA MOULTON HOWE.

Linda is to be commended for her dedication, courage and professionalism. If they gave out Academy awards for "quality" research, she would truly get one!

Paola Harris (PH): You have always been interested in animal mutilations: how and why did you decide to expand your research into other areas?

Linda Moulton Howe (LH): I started working on animal mutilations in 1979 and my documentary, *A Strange Harvest*, was first broadcast in the USA on May 25, 1980. I spent nine months filming it and during the investigations I found myself touching on everything, from abductions to crop circles, from Bigfoot sightings to the government cover-up, from anomalous technologies to silent helicopters.

PH: Why does your book seem to be organized like an.... encyclopedia of twentieth century mysteries?

LH: *Glimpses of Other Realities* is split into two volumes: *Facts and Eyewitnesses* published in 1994, and *High Strangeness* published in 1998. I began the draft in 1990 and completed the project in the space of eight years, and then decided to publish in two volumes. The first volume talks about crop circles and investigations into animal mutilations between 1989 and 1994, phenomena, which have occurred all over the world. As for abductions, I only included eyewitness reports, where hypnosis was not used, concerning experiences related by people from the '60s to today. In *High Strangeness*, I deal with subjects who are very important to me: there are rumors in military circles of encounters having occurred in broad daylight between civilians and nonhuman beings. It seems that there is an evolution in the spiritual relationship between humans and aliens, a kind of intimacy, which springs up between the two, particularly when someone is dying. If we look back at the dawn of human civilization, this is borne out in historical terms. For example, the connection between the Sumerians, Syrians and Babylonians and alien civilizations, or the Book of Enoch and other key figures of Biblical literature associated with this field. But perhaps it's primarily an introspection of the relationship between humans and alien intelligences. Chapter One of Volume Two reveals episodes involving military personnel, particularly eyewitness reports. Chapter Two, on the other hand, concerns daytime encounters between civilians and non-terrestrial craft, or between civilians and Sasquatch. In Chapter Three, I relate the story of James Sparks and his encounters, during which he was taught a three-dimensional language, made up of symbols. Many alleged abductees say that they have been taught by nonhuman intelligences by means of a symbol-based language. James Sparks[1] came to the conclusion that it's not an alien language, but a language-interface between a real and fully telepathic

---

1. See Jim Sparks: *The Keepers*, Wild Flower Press, 2003.

technological alien civilization and our verbal, linear, three-dimensional system. This subject is expanded in Chapter Four, where I also set out a cross-section of abduction cases dating back to 1990. That was when I realized that all of this was closely connected with the human-alien interaction at the time of death, and the relationship between bodies/containers and the soul, or the spirit.

PH: By moving towards the metaphysical field, aren't you afraid of harming your reputation as a logical and analytical person and, consequently, of losing part of your readership that is used to your traditional approach to the UFO phenomenon?

LH: There are two volumes for a good reason: I knew that the material assigned to Volume Two could not be substantiated and the majority of cases were anonymous testimonies. One of the reasons why it took eight years to write Volume Two is because as a journalist, I was getting into a really tricky area. That's why the two books differ greatly and the material has been split in two. However, as a reporter, I felt that the content of Volume Two had to be regarded by the public in the same way as the strictly scientific material contained in Volume One, so much so that in *High Strangeness*, I quote the astronomer J. Allen Hynek who, by seeking to understand the nature of sightings of lights and flying saucers in the sky, concluded, along with Jacques Vallée and John Kehoe that we are dealing with something that is pushing us to the boundaries of what we believe to be a proven three-dimensional reality. These are phenomena, which appear to go beyond what we call reality. This is the basis for *Glimpses of Other Realities* (Volume Two), whose long, first chapter, "Military Voices," is full of (anonymous) testimonies of individuals who used to be military men or agents, who believe in the absolute authenticity of the material I have presented. A former CIA agent, now retired and living in Washington DC, also confirmed this: he pointed out to me that some of the documents and content of the new book have never seen the light of day before now. And in his opinion, the material has stirred up a real hornet's nest among government insiders in Washington.

PH: Do you think that there is one political faction, which wants all this to come out, and another, which wants to keep it secret?

LH: I think that there has always been strong disagreement among those we call government insiders who use different acronyms and names such as Majestic 12 or Special Studies Groups and so on. There are signs of a great deal of tension between those who want to disclose as much as possible to the public, and those who don't want to leak anything because that could undermine the current religious, political and social status quo. All this has been at issue since the Truman administration, and it's still being discussed today, even though there are people who have been fighting since the '50s to make the information public, and who now approach the film industry, the papers and researchers like myself. This is one of the reasons why I have so much material. I was even sent a copy of SOM1-01 (Special Operation Manual), a document which I published in *Glimpses* and that I consider to be the most important piece of history to come to light in the past fifty years. I received it from an anonymous source in San Francisco, as I explain in my book, and it's a document, dated April 1954, regarding the recovery of extraterrestrial technologies and material. A CIA agent asked me, and not without emotion, how I had come to have these documents, seeing as he owned a similar training manual when he was part of Majestic 12 in the '70s, but which didn't bear the date of 1954.

PH: People are talking about some sort of event which is about to take place...do you feel part of a mechanism to prepare the public for what is going to happen, whatever it may be?

LH: A lot of people think that soon the government is going to reveal everything it knows, but in my opinion it won't, that will never happen. I think that the administrations or government insiders (people who are not elected as representatives or congressmen so that they can maintain their positions), don't want such stories to be divulged, but want to maintain the status quo: I'm absolutely certain of this. I am also certain that our technology was obtained by studying alien craft, and the findings were then applied to our space programs and American industries, just as Colonel Corso said in his book, *The Day After Roswell*. Taxes paid by American taxpayers have always been used for scientific research, and some private industries have earned billions from these technologies, without ever revealing to taxpayers the truth as to how they were obtained. Not to mention the policy of silence surrounding contact with nonhuman intelligences...and this is just a tiny fraction of the things that politicians don't want to leak out.

PH: People, including researchers, who have read Col. Philip Corso's book, *The Day after Roswell* know and accept the situation. At least 40% of the public understand it and are wondering what is going to happen.

LH: The term I would use is 'indifference.' Public indifference to anything which isn't a television program, film or entertainment. What we are discussing doesn't interest in the slightest people who work from 9 to 5. So long as people are only interested in scandals, war, politics, and making money, they won't be interested in extraterrestrials at all. But we know that extraterrestrials will probably land on this planet, and the question will be: are you here to help us or to harm us?

PH: Exactly. Are they benevolent, or do they have hostile intentions?

LH: I have no idea. I am very confused about this.

PH: I think that nowadays it's easier to talk about this, given the amount of information in circulation, but to what extent is it possible to separate science fiction from reality?

LH: The so-called traditional media don't want to have anything more to do with certain subjects, which are relegated to X-Files, a very clever television genre which tackles real issues as if they were science-fiction, entertaining viewers and informing them of the state of affairs at the same time. The most serious issue regarding human-alien interaction, through manipulation of the planet, is therefore restricted, as the twentieth century draws to a close, to old TV drama scripts, and the indifference and cynicism of the media and the general public is clear to see. It won't be photos, documents or videos, which change this apathy. The next level of understanding will result from a landing, from the testimony of alien intelligences communicated to all the nations of the world. However, the most pressing issue at the moment is to establish what the alien intelligences' true plans are, because personally I am certain that there is more than one, and government documents confirm this.

PH: More than one plan or more than one intelligence?

LH: More than one type of intelligence. When we have manifestations of various Extraterrestrial Biological Entities that come from other solar systems or another time or other frequencies (and this all seems probable), how on earth can we know who we are dealing with or what the truth is, when an alien intelligence interacts with the planet? That's why I talk about this, in Volume Two, for a good 512 pages, because at least, during my career, I have had the satisfaction of publishing a trilogy, where I give the best of myself, completely honestly and without any political aims. With the help of investigative journalists, I have made four documentaries, conceived and produced by myself, and have supervised reports of UFO sightings broadcast by a national North American television network. It's been like sending a message in a bottle without any point of reference, and I have no idea what will be coming.

PH: Have you ever had any spiritual experiences?

LH: Yes, in Peru, but in Volume Two I mention what happened to me in the Idaho mountains when I was a girl. It was as if something in the invisible had made contact with my soul, and wanted to explain how I was connected to the forces of the Universe, which, in fact, I had always felt part of, and that I shouldn't let myself be influenced by books and human experiences. Every single human being on this planet has similar experiences, receiving certain information from the invisible. These are events which definitely have a strong impact on people's lives, but which are very rarely discussed. And yet precisely such events may have determined the mythical and religious development of our planet.

Often what we don't talk about can provide us with the most important information. I had gone to the mountains to get in shape. I wanted to take part in the Miss America competition to earn the money I needed for college, as my parents didn't have any. I was with my brother and my cousin, and while I was running up and down the mountain. I saw beautiful golden and orange rays of light in the forest, a light I'd never seen before. I was transfixed, and it was so beautiful. I remember that I went towards the light as if I wanted to touch those rays shining through the trees with a child-like curiosity, and it seemed as if I wasn't living in normal time, as if everything were in slow motion, even though I was fully conscious. I don't know why, but I clearly recall all the details: nature looked like a painting by Van Gogh. It seemed almost as though the mountain was breathing, while the sun was setting and the first stars were rising, constantly twinkling. I felt a kind of light pressure on my arms and hands, like a push to make me raise them and put my hands together in front of me. While I was looking at my joined palms, a voice in my head said: "Now you are one with the light, the light is one with you, and you are in the hands of God." All the pulsing light that surrounded the flowers, the hills and the mountains appeared to ebb away slowly, and in that moment I felt completely changed, transformed, as if in that instant I had been shown the true nature of everything around me.

We come from light, and return to light, that's the truth. I wrote this in the prologue to tell readers that in the end, it doesn't matter what form contact with other intelligences takes, because everything in the Universe comes from the same source and will return to the same source. I tried to go further, sharing everything I have experienced with the rest of my human family, and in the end we will discover that we are not alone in the Cosmos.

Reality is not confined to just what we see. I believe that in ancient cultures there was a much more fluid and variable dynamic between what we call frequencies. The irony of mythology is that we humans, in our industrialized 20th Century world, maintain that angels are just images carved in ancient times, that serve a purpose only on Valentine's Day. Or that the strange creatures of the past, such as centaurs and unicorns, are merely figments of imagination, and that the nine parts of a human that the Egyptians described so clearly are just myth. We are the ones with the more closed and narrow minds of the 20th Century.

PH: I see. It's a real tragic comedy. Linda, where are you going to go from here?

LH: I am working on a lot of projects involving various media such as the Internet, radio, television and books, which will address various subjects. And I will continue my research, particularly the relationship between spirit and matter, the visible and the invisible.

Disclosure Begins

Chapter 8

Disclosure Begins

Monsignor Corrado Balducci

 I have been most fortunate to know Monsignor Corrado Balducci quite well. His openness and kindness to all people, even strangers, is one of his most precious qualities. Our meeting was one of those serendipitous things that happened to me in my career. It is amazing to me how we bonded instantly at the May, 1999, San Marino conference sponsored by the Centro Ufologico Nationale (CUN), where I served as translator for Harvard professor Dr. John Mack.

In my years in Rome, I have many times taken production crews to see Monsignor Balducci to film documentaries, and I have served as translator. None were so important as the director of CSETI, Dr. Steven Greer, who included Padre Balducci in his disclosure project. On September 23, 2000, Balducci invited Greer, his cameraman Peter Sorenson, and me to his home in Rome for what I consider a rather historic event. Monsignor Balducci agreed to be interviewed and filmed as part of Greer's major worldwide disclosure project (see page 61).

Balducci often invited me over to his home for dinner, and he did so again on New Year's Eve, 2002. He is a great host and he likes to leave his Christmas decorations up all year long. His apartment is quite close to where I live next to the Vatican. The following interviews are from three different occasions where I listened intently to this man of the cloth integrate the extraterrestrial reality with mainstream Catholicism. Balducci is perhaps the most empathic person that I have ever encountered when it

PAOLA HARRIS, ANDY ABRAHAMS WILSON, AND MONSIGNOR CORRADO BALDUCCI

comes to listening to people, but he is also very much like J. Allen Hynek in that he has his mind on other things and is a very random abstract thinker. One of the most heartwarming meetings I experienced was when I introduced Balducci to ex-priest Dr. Richard Boylan (see page 48), and they both communicated in Latin. Father Balducci had a captive audience as he cited many of the old church fathers, and although he did not agree with all of Dr. Boylan's ideas, he listened carefully and pensively to what Boylan called his star visitor theology. Monsignor Balducci has an incredible archive of news clippings on UFOs and the paranormal. It fascinates him. Unlike many of us researchers, he excluded nothing in the cosmic mystery and had begun "connecting the dots" long ago. It took me years to catch up to his thinking.

Paola Harris (PH): Is UFOlogy a relatively new study, and is it connected to parapsychology in your opinion?

Monsignor Corrado Balducci (CB): Over the last 150 years this phenomenon has appeared sequentially and with an increasing spreading and frequency rate. Spiritualism and UFOlogy are two types of manifestations and phenomena that are very different from each other, but each is so interesting, controversial and fascinating that public opinion is divided into two different camps: either it is all real, or it is all false. This reaction shouldn't surprise us, because it's related only to the reactions and behavior of the public as they perceive these two phenomena and not to their contents, which are obviously very different!

PH: Monsignor Balducci, why, as a Vatican spokesman do you come forward publicly in favor of the existence of extraterrestrial life?

CB: Because there must be something between us and the angels. If there are other beings, they are surely more evolved than we are. We are at the bottom of the evolutionary ladder because of our ability to "see good, but do evil." Man processes a certain duality and is capable of both good and evil. It is illogical and a bit arrogant to believe that we are the only intelligent beings in God's creation. Perhaps if these other beings do not possess physical bodies, they are not subjected to our same temptations.

PH: Did Jesus also represent these beings?

CB: Yes, of course. Jesus died for all beings in the cosmos. In the sacred scriptures, He is called King of the Universe. Never underestimate the

MONSIGNOR CORRADO BALDUCCI, DR. RICHARD HAINES

great mercy or compassion of God, whose grace and compassion surpasses all, and that means it relates to *all* of creation in *all* the cosmos. That also means that "all is possible." God created us to give praise to Him, as I imagine he created others to do the same. How can God be gloried without a varied creation?

PH: Why is it so important to take UFO sightings seriously?

CB: Because it is based on human testimony, as are our Gospels. Since a great deal of the Catholic faith is based on witness testimony, we must realize how important human testimony is. It would be a tragedy if we began to be suspicious of all people who report that they experienced something unusual like seeing crafts in the sky. From what I understand, there are some very credible witnesses who have seen this phenomenon and have come forward. They are courageous and should not be dismissed. Many church fathers have addressed the extraterrestrial presence in early philosophical works.

In fact, testimony is a form of communication of our faith. Imagine what could happen to individual and social life if the value of human testimony were diminished, an act which would logically cause the decrease and disappearance of our faith, which is essential for daily life!

PH: Do you think that there is a type of theology or philosophy then that can be attributed to extraterrestrial life?

CB: I think that we need to examine it, then formulate "theological and Biblical considerations" on the habitability of other planets. First of all, there is a clarification: We should exclude that angels use spaceships, because they are merely spiritual beings. They are wherever they want to be, and in the rare cases when they show themselves, they have no difficulty in assuming a visible form. We can say the very same thing about dead people. The Holy Virgin, in the very few cases when she seems to contact humans (very exceptional episodes and to be confirmed in their authenticity), continues to choose other very different ways to transmit to us her maternal affection, her urgencies, her maternal claims or her sweet reproaches. We need to separate these realities.

PH: How do you reach these conclusions?

CB: My conclusions come from my research in parapsychology and demonology. There are human testimonies concerning the UFO phenomenon—in particular the abduction phenomenon—which are essential to historical truth and must be considered seriously. These things cannot be attributed to the "Devil." He does not need UFOs. Even keeping their angelic nature, we shouldn't think about the devils at all, because they are connected in their liberty to God in their extraordinary activity, and in that way they are unable to express their terrible and malefic hate for us. Let's remember St. August: "If the Devil by his own initiative could do anything, even a single living being would not stay on Earth."[1] Let's remember also St. Buenaventura: "Is so large the demon's cruelty, that he would swallow us in every moment, if Divine protection doesn't guard us."[2] This has nothing to do with the Devil.

These important UFO sightings by credible people must be taken into account because there are so many witnesses. It is as important as scientific research is! If we live in constant skepticism, we will destroy society and our dignity as human beings. We will believe no one. Catholicism, which is partially based on human testimony—primarily letters of followers of Jesus (Apologists), who explained the religious phenomena of Jesus and the resurrection and presented a certain truth. The church has based many of its doctrines on this human testimony.

Likewise in UFOlogy, we know a phenomenon exists, and although we don't know who these aliens (possibly angels) are, it is possible that they are more evolved than Man is today.

PH: Can you quote some church fathers who suggest the existence of life on other planets"? I heard that Padre Pio said something of this nature.

CB: Yes there are several. Don Andrea Beltrami (1870-1897), the Salesian Father and servant of God, prayed also for the possible inhabitants of other planets. Of the 16 booklets he wrote, one seems to deal with this topic. The second is the recently sanctified Padre Pio, who was beatified by Pope John Paul II on May 2, 1999, and canonized on June 16, 2002. He was asked the following question: "Father, some claim that there are creatures of God on other planets, too."

Padre Pio replied, "What else? Do you think they don't exist, and that God's omnipotence is limited to this small planet Earth? What else? Do you think there are no other beings who love the Lord?"

Another time someone asked him, "Padre Pio, I think the Earth is nothing, compared to other planets and stars."

---

1. ML37, 1246.
2. "*Diaeta salutis,* tit. 7 c. 1, Verona 1748, p. 183.

His answer: "Exactly! Yes, and we Earthlings are nothing, too. The Lord certainly did not limit His glory to this small Earth. On other planets other beings exist who did not sin and fall as we did."

PH: So you are saying that believing that UFOs exist is not contrary to one's faith or Catholic Church doctrine?

CB: The acronym UFO (Unidentified Flying Object), is used here in a wider sense to include the existence of living beings on other planets. The aim of my intervention and speaking out is to underline that something real *must* exist in the phenomena, and that this does not conflict at all with Christian religion, and is considered positive, even among theologians.

First, Something real *must* exist. Secondly, I have made some theological considerations on the habitability of other planets. Thirdly, much witness testimony favors it. Conclusion: Something real must exist.

PH: Is it a grave mistake to think that you are the *official* voice of the Vatican?

CB: These ideas are mine, and I do not represent the Vatican. However, I am told that the Holy Father Pope John Paul II has seen me on Italian TV several times and follows my radio homilies. If there were some objection, I'm sure I would know. I believe there to be no problem here.

PH: Thank you, Monsignor Balducci, for your kindness to me and all your foreign guests.

CB: Compliments and good wishes on your interesting work.

Chapter 9

Disclosure Begins

Richard Boylan, Ph.D.

---

www. drboylan. com

"Contact with the Star Visitors can be gentle and subtle," says Dr. Richard Boylan, who usually begins his lectures by giving a historical perspective referring first to Biblical references, then to the research of Zacharia Sitchin, and most importantly to the oral traditions of the Native American peoples,

PAOLA HARRIS,
MONSIGNOR CORRADO BALDUCCI,
DR. RICHARD BOYLAN

that indeed Star visitors have always been among us and have possibly had a hand in creating us and altering our evolution. He is a gentle warrior with a very strong voice. I often request that Rich keep things mellow in his disclosure attempts. I have even nicknamed him "James, " after James Bond. Why? Because we have had many adventures in our world travels that one might consider dangerous, everything from earthquakes to trips to the hospital. All too often we have had such mishaps at UFO conferences. Once, after giving a great talk at the Denver Global Sciences Conference in 2001, Richard suddenly collapsed in the coffee shop while eating breakfast, and I accompanied him to the emergency room, only to find out that the doctor could not find anything wrong with him, and we were all mystified as to why he had fainted. He suffered three more similar incidents that year. Richard attributes this to psychotronic attacks, and it is possible, considering that there are some very sophisticated psi weapons around. To some, Dr. Boylan is seen as the enemy of the so-called shadow, or covert, government, or "the Cabal" as he calls it. He has done many an exposé and has named names, to the chagrin of many people. He is a chief proponent of Dr. Michael Wolf's disclosure material (see page 91).

Boylan is a very controversial figure, but I greatly admire him, even though we sometimes disagree. People can decide for themselves and I firmly believe that this contact phenomenon is mainly benign. But I, unlike Richard, have never had contact. I support his work, and all the other serious and sincere researchers who are not out simply to "make money." I have too many friends in the field who oppose each other with back-biting and groundless criticism of each other's work. Real "debunking" is expensive, and people do not spend the money. Researchers use "the lack of credentials" or shallow rumors as evidence, and when it comes from the "icons" of UFOlogy, the masses believe them immediately without questioning. I know better, because I do first-hand field research. Dr. Boylan clearly was given classified information in the past, which he shared with his UFO Facts email list—some 1100 members strong—which is filled with wonderful people, often people who have had contact. It is a worldwide network and a great deal of information is shared, in what I consider to be a respectful and courteous manner.

Dr. Boylan has been edging away from conspiracy theory material, since his house and vehicle have been broken into several times and he has had many anomalous computer crashes. I was witness to some of the high strangeness in Richard's life. Once we were driving back to Denver from Standing Elk's Star Knowledge Conference in Rapid City, S.D., and we hit a deer that seemed to come from out of nowhere and almost totaled his rental car. Then the roof of the car mysteriously heated up at 5:00 A.M. before sunrise while we were having a conversation about Col. Corso (see page 3). While we were riding back to Denver together I saw what looked like a rudderless, cigar-shaped helicopter over a desolate lake in Wyoming. The problem was that I was the only one who could see it. I kept screaming at Richard to look, but he saw nothing. It made me feel as if I were going crazy, so now I can empathize with people who have UFO sightings and no one believes them.

Once in Oslo, Norway, Dr. Boylan was very late for his talk, and when he came in, he was very disoriented and had fallen on the ice. I took some Kleenex with iced tea from my cup (the only liquid I had) and washed off his bloody wounds seconds before he began his talk, which turned out to be one of his best, because he described and showed the vast variety of star visitor types! I never know what to expect, and I always tell Rich that I really don't need this kind of excitement in my life, but he insists that I am the "cosmic Lois Lane" for the mild-mannered reporters of the world who do this work. In another instance, he rescued me in San Francisco a day before a 4.7-magnitude earthquake in Napa Valley, and he and his wife Lee hosted me overnight before I took a bus cross-country to cover another story in New Mexico.

People know Boylan as the author of *Close Extraterrestrial Encounters* (Wild Flower Press 1994), *Extraterrestrial Contact and Human Responses* (1994), and *Project Epiphany* (1997), and as a noted hypnotherapist and social psychologist. He has worked with numerous abductees and has done many regressions. It should be noted that most of his clients eventually categorize their "abduction" experiences as spiritual and enlightening.

Recently, Dr. Boylan has been directing his energies toward the acclimation of the special children he calls "Star Seeds," who are being born with an advanced awareness and advanced psi abilities. He has moved away from his former focus on the government cover-up to work with others to set up Star Seed workshops in California and elsewhere in the U.S. to help young "contactees," some born as Star seeds, some known as "Indigo children." These young people possess incredible intelligence and psi capacities, and Rich and his chosen staff help them to cope in a world that does not understand them. This is a revolutionary new venture that is supported in the U.S. by many contact groups.

Dr. Boylan quotes Dr. Wolf as saying that we are at a crossroads of our evolution where we must put down our weapons of war and heal this diseased

planet, or we will destroy both it and ourselves. Echoing the words of Lakota leader Standing Elk (now Golden Eagle, picture at left) and the tribal vision of White Buffalo Calf Woman, Boylan said we are shifting from the decaying Fourth World into an emerging Fifth World for which humanity needs to prepare spiritually. It is a wake-up call to action and a shift in our conventional paradigm.

May 1, 2003

Paola Harris (PH): Dr. Boylan, did your contact experience leave you feeling an obligation towards the Star Visitors?

Dr. Richard Boylan (RB): My contact experience in April, 1992, provided further impetus to my already well-formed commitment to explore the phenomenon of Star Visitor-human contacts wherever it might lead. Three years prior to that first late-night physical contact in the New Mexico desert, experiencers of such contact had begun coming to my office in ever-increasing numbers to pour out their accounts of these extraordinary meetings. I became fascinated, and I vowed to pursue active research, including field investigations. You are aware of my 1992 grand tour of secret bases in the U.S. Southwest, by which I confirmed that Star Visitors and their technology are being studied and back-engineered into American-manufactured devices and weapons, such as the now-numerous fleet of antigravity craft, such as the X-22A manufactured by Lockheed-Martin, the plasmoidal disc made by Northrop, and the Nautilus built by the consortium of Boeing-Airbus Industry. Subsequently the Star Visitors' contacts with me have been less physical and more indirect. For example, I get messages from them through strangers who come up to me at conferences where I speak and somewhat self-consciously say, "You don't know me, but the Star Visitors told me to give you this message," and then they proceed to deliver it. Or I get a short note on my computer from the Visitors. Do I have a sense of obligation to the Star Visitors? I feel a very strong sense of obligation to humanity, to help see it through the tumultuous changes ahead between now and 2012. And I am committed to working in concert with the Star Visitors to awaken humanity to the importance of reforming society to prepare for wholesale public cosmic contact.

PH: What is the single most important disclosure effort yet?

RB: The most significant public disclosure effort paradoxically comes from the very organization that has so assiduously striven to maintain the UFO cover-up. I'm referring to that U.S. Government UFO-policy control group, the Special Studies Group (SSG) of the National Security Council, formerly known by its more popular name of "MJ-12." The SSG is responsible for a graduated program of conditioning the public to the non-traumatic acceptance of Star Visitor presence. Their efforts include facilitating such movies as *ET* and *Close Encounters of the Third Kind*, allowing various Apollo and Mercury Astronauts like Edgar Mitchell and Gordon Cooper to make public statements about UFO reality and even the existence of a government cover-up, and SSG's facilitating a committee of scientists led by a Stanford University professor to make widely published public statements that the evidence for UFO reality and ET life is compelling and deserves attention by serious scientists. This is not to denigrate the next most important effort, led by Dr. Steven Greer of CSETI (see page 61), to gather former military, intelligence and black-project officials to testify to their involvement in UFO and Star Visitor-human projects. His public disclosure press conference at the 1997 National Press Club in Washington, D.C., deserved the worldwide media coverage it was never permitted to receive. Nor does the above excuse SSG's unconscionable delay in proceeding to full disclosure to the public of UFO/Star Visitor reality. The public needs to "storm the gates" if we are to wring admission of the truth from our "rulers."

PH: Do you think the world governments will be the vehicles of disclosure? Do you think that government disclosure will come soon?

RB: As a long as the Cabal of the wealthiest and therefore most politically, powerful persons on Earth control the developed nations' governments, we will not have public disclosure facilitated by established governments. If public revelation of the Star Nations' presence occurs, and I think it will occur "soon," this will happen because of efforts by both private citizens and the Star Visitors themselves. We had a foretaste of this in the skies over Turkey, as reported by Turkey's foremost UFOlogist, Haktan Akdogan. Several months ago, six different airline pilots over Turkey reported seeing a very bright and very large meteorite enter atmosphere and hurl towards Earth. Soon a UFO came up alongside the meteor and sent out a beam which blew the meteorite into smaller pieces, which then could safely burn up in the atmosphere. Had this not occurred, the meteor was large enough to have done substantial damage upon impact. I think that some scenario like this will unfold as we move into severe earth changes over the next six years, which will provide circumstances in which the Star Visitors are likely to intervene, at least by public warnings, to minimize loss of life.

PH: What do you believe the late Dr. Wolf's legacy will be?

RB: Paola, you and I communicated with Dr. Wolf many times, and we grew very fond of this giant of a man. He is, in my estimation, a "Mahatma," Hindi for "a large soul." He spirituality matched his erudition and technological intelligence. His legacy may well be his book, *The Catchers of Heaven,* his attempt to pack as much release of information about the

Star Visitors, and the governments' role in contacts with the Visitors, while maintaining a cover-up to protect powerful special interests. I believe that SSG allowed him to publish the book once they knew he was dying from pancreatic cancer and would not be around long after the book reached the public. Thus, SSG hoped to minimize the chance of his letting out too much information or becoming the backbone of a public campaign to demand UFO truth from the governments.

PH: You were very involved with conspiracy theory. Why have you switched roles to focus on the "star seed phenomena."

RB: Let me start by gently contradicting your question. I have never had "conspiracy theory" as my focus. My focus has always been on the Star Visitors, and the effects of their contacts with humans. Any side research I have done into UFO technology or the government cover-up has been only in the service of further elucidating the circumstances within which the Star Visitors are having to operate as they conduct their outreach to humankind. The more I studied experiencers of Visitor contact, the more I noticed how they became transformed in positive ways as a result of these contacts. These transformations turned out to be generational. I then noticed that the children of experiencers were very advanced, and research revealed that this was due to the Visitors doing some genetic splicing of the experiencers' reproductive material, so that they subsequently had children who were extraordinary. I call them Star Kids, because part of their genetic heritage comes from the stars, and because their generation's destiny is to meet and travel with other cultures who come from other star systems.

PH: How are you currently facilitating the advent of this new breed of child into our "still closed-minded" society?

RB: Following a strong suggestion from the Star Visitors, I have made my central life work at this point in my life the Star Kids, and establishing the Star Kids Project. The first stage of this effort is identifying Star Kids, and inviting them and their parents to Star Kid Workshops There they can meet other Star Kids, feel normal among peers; learn more about their special abilities, and how to use them for the social good. And we help individual Star Kids refine their sense of mission. We also work with those who are over 18 and are designated adult Star Seeds. Eventually we plan to establish a residential Star Kids School, and thereafter a Graduate School. Ultimately we plan to train appropriate Star Kids for becoming ambassadors for Earth to the Star Nations. One of the things we teach the Star Kids is discernment, and caution in being selective about whom to trust with information about who they really are. It is a shame that these innocent children have to be taught to be wary of revealing themselves in a society which may not understand and which is quick to stigmatize. I look forward to the day when the UFO cover-up ends, and these children can come out of the closet and be themselves naturally.

PH: What did you see in the media, especially the film *X-Men II,* that is a significant media contribution to the star seed concept?

RB: The media are finally being permitted to serve up to the public the first strands of visual impressions of the Star Kids. A hint of this occurred in the *The Matrix*, where a scene showed Keanu Reeves interacting with Star Kids who could levitate balls in the air and bend spoons by mental effort. Then there was the unfortunate Spielberg television series "Taken," a dreary repetition of Cabal disinformation about the Star Visitors as cruel, uncaring, hurtful intruders. This series was only redeemed in the last three episodes, where the figure of Ellie, a Star Kid, came to the fore and shone as an attractive example of an advanced, transformed human child. The movie *X-2: the X-Men* portrays young adults with extraordinary powers who have been tutored in a special school to hone their ESP abilities to an advanced edge. While not explaining their powers as due to Star Visitor interaction, the movie does suggest they are a genetic mutation—true, but not a spontaneous one. Being cartoon heroes and entertainment, this movie is not about Star origins, but does serve to soften the public's intellectual beachhead for further revelations about genetically mutated advanced children.

PH: How long do you think it will take for our transition into the Fifth World?

RB: All the indigenous shamans I have talked to agree with the Mayan Calendar date for the transition from current corrupt, materialistic, warfaring, ecocidal Fourth World society into a peaceable, just, communal, cosmic Fifth World society. That date by which the transition will be accomplished is December 21, 2012. That is not far away, nine years. The upheavals attendant on the Earth Changes besetting us and crescendoing will help break the infrastructures upholding the sources of power and wealth for the covert ruling Cabal. That is our prime opportunity to take back control of our society, and refashion it in the better ways that truly reflect the highest and best in the human spirit. If we don't, we face disaster. If we do, then our children will inherit not only a healthy Earth, but will be ready to navigate to the stars.

Chapter 10

Disclosure Begins

David Icke

The bad news is The Cavalry Is Not Coming.
The good news is Humanity Is Meeting It.

No one can be called "Mr. Conspiracy" more than ex-BBC British journalist writer David Icke. Upon my yearly summer visit to New Mexico in 2001, Richard Hoagland tossed some books at me, as was his habit, and he said, "Read these." Among them was *Rule by Secrecy* by Jim Mars, which cited a great deal of Icke's research, such as *The Truth Shall Set You Free,* which is now a classic and read widely in Italy. They were both powerful books, and they made me determined to track down David Icke. Conspiracy theory is my least favorite subject and the most dangerous, but I was curious, as are most people, about people like David Icke, who see deceit everywhere.

I received much negative feedback about Icke from other journalists and people in general. I remember that Hoagland said Icke had the right idea, but he had been "spammed" by the media, which means that disinformation agents had gone to work mixing up fact and fiction about him.

When I first pictured David, I saw reptilians everywhere, since that was the most bizarre aspect of UFOlogy for me, and yet what follows here is a very sensitive interview. I asked David to stay away from the reptilian agenda and told him I was interested in what made him tick. The background of this interview is quite amazing, as it happened on December 8, 2002, in Bellaria, Italy, at the Macroedizioni editorial festival after David Icke finished a three-hour slide show and lecture on his 9/11 conspiracy theory. The audience was properly shocked with his delivery and evidence, and at one point someone shouted, "That's enough! Isn't there anything positive to say!" David let them know that ignorance breeds control, and information is power!

Seeing that he had a six-foot-four, bald bodyguard who looked like Mr. Clean made me instantly paranoid. I was supposed to have one half-hour interview, but it became a two-and-a-half-hour interview. I called it quits because it was after midnight, and I needed to walk back to my hotel. Intent on continuing our conversation, David kindly walked me back. He was a gentleman, very intelligent, extremely articulate and charming, and as I found out, he has a deeply spiritual mission.

As we sat in a small press room before this interview, David was drinking a beer, exhausted and totally dripping with sweat—he had been speaking for three hours. I prepared my digital camera and tape recorder, and I asked him first why he dismissed his bodyguard. His explanation is essentially his code. He told me that humanity's real enemy is fear, and that the Italians gave him the bodyguard, but he did not want to invite trouble, so he told him to go home. Icke was tranquil, and I then asked him why he had chosen this path. Ironically what he told me—*that humanity must take back its own power of decision making and of deciding its own destiny*—was the same message that Richard Hoagland told me was in the Spielberg-Kubrick masterpiece film, *Artificial Intelligence,* newly released that year. After all, folks, it was 2001!

Paola Harris (PH): David, you speak of many things, but you are most known for your conspiracy theories about those who control the planet. What do you feel is happening and why?

David Icke (DI): I would say that these extreme events that are happening are not even to enhance the power of those who rule but to protect what they have. The surveillance explosion, which of course has followed 9/11 in leaps and bounds, is about controlling those who are awakening and communicating to advance the awakening. When you have an all-encompassing word like "terrorist," and you create a situation where you have secret military trials and people charged upon the basis of the authorities saying you are a terrorist, you've basically got a blank check to pick up whomever you want. They are doing it with countries now. All

they have to do is to demonize the country in the eyes of the public....
They could do this to individuals once they got this all-encompassing
war on terrorism. So of course, when do you know this war on terrorism
is won? You never do. This has all to do with the countdown to a window
of time around 2012.

PH: But there is also an economic component here.

DI: Yes. So this is a war that you can fight forever. Lending money that doesn't
exist and charging interest on it has been a card played by these people
since Babylon. Control by debt that doesn't exist. Again it is not so much
that they control finances to give themselves large amounts of money, but
the key thing is that when they draw all the wealth to themselves, the rest
therefore are all dependent on their system. Nothing these people do is just
for gratuitous generation of horror or humor.... It's because everything
they do has an end outcome that advances their agenda.

PH: What can humanity do in the face of this probable reality? What is the
agenda? Are there evil forces controlling us? What about reptilians?

DI: In the book *Children of the Matrix*, I quote from some claimed-to-be-
ancient tablets called "The Emerald Tablets." They are supposed to be
tens of thousands of years old. In them, they talk about serpent people.
These serpent people live in planes unknown to Man.

PH: You mean planes being dimensions?

DI: Planes unknown to Man. So I'm talking to a guy who is on the inside of
this network, who tells me that these reptilians I'm talking about—and
other entities of the same state of being—don't live in this dimension,
and they don't live in the next dimension, but it's as if they live in a crev-
ice between the two frequencies... almost like a false place. I'm reading
Giuliana Conforto's book, *Man's Cosmic Game,* where she is looking at
the paranormal from a scientific point of view. She talks about something
called "inter-space planes" that are little ridges of frequency between the
dimensions, which is exactly what the Emerald Tablets talked about and
exactly what this guy taught me about where the reptilians live. In this
frequency range between dimensions they work to disconnect incarnate
consciousness from multidimensional self, thus isolating incarnate consciousness from this frequency range we call Earth.

So the work to disconnect is there at that level, so we are not getting
the inspirational intuitive knowing from higher dimensions of ourselves.
Therefore, the only way that the people then can get a fix on the world
and themselves is from the information coming by way of eyes and ears.

In essence, what they have done is to disconnect us from our intuitive knowing, while also controlling what of incarnate conscious goes into our eyes and ears. They isolate the droplet from the ocean and then program into the droplet the conditioned reality they want.

Going back to what you said, the consciousness, whatever form it takes, is working to help humanity with this situation. It's a two-way process. *The cavalry is not coming.* We have to connect with the cavalrymen. In other words, if we want to connect with high consciousness, then we have to at least meet it halfway. That is why it is absolutely vital that we work on ourselves to stay connected through this inner-space plane manipulation to our other-dimensional self. This is where we get the tremendous diversity of reality between awakening people and those who are still completely in the illusion, because once you start to awaken and reconnect, you start to view this world not from within it but from without it. You are in this world but not of it. The focus of your consciousness is out there.

PH: I want you to know this, David. This is what I will write about. This is the most important thing you are telling me.

DI: What I think was happening to me in 1991 is that, in some way, I was being plugged in "out there." I remember that I went bloody "*ga ga*" for about three or four weeks because it is like a dam's burst, and these concepts and images were hitting me. What takes years with some people was hitting me in weeks and days. I was looking through the same eyes, but I was seeing things in a completely different world. I could see things happening that I couldn't see before, because the focus of my consciousness was no longer in the manipulation, but it was observing the manipulation through my physical form. This is what's happening to people, and this is why someone who is connected can look at a situation and see what someone who is not connected cannot possibly see, until it's pointed out really simply. They are in the illusion looking at the illusion, while the "connecting" people are outside the illusion looking into it. So it is a completely different point of observation. Therefore, the way we see the world is completely different.

PH: Is "fear" the thing that stops us from doing that?

DI: Exactly. Fear is the prison that holds us in isolation. What is known as paranormal is not paranormal at all. It is just a different condition of reality. That point from where you are observing decides how you see something.

PH: I began by asking you why you are doing this. Now where are you going with this? Do you have a goal? Do you not know what the future is, or do you just go day-by-day or by instinct now?

DI: I do go by instinct, and I will continue to go by instinct. I went by instinct back in the days when I left TV. It's an interesting cycle that is taking place. When I went out after my revelation in Peru in 1991, universities would ask me along. They would sell out the events weeks in advance, with 1,000 people or more, mostly students, coming to laugh. These are the decision makers of tomorrow. I remember standing up in front of about 1,000 people at the University of Nottingham one night and it was about 10 to 15 minutes before I could start to speak because of all the noise and things being thrown on the stage. When things began to calm down, I said "You think I'm mad, don't you? Mentally ill, don't you? Well, what does that say about you, because you actually spent money at the door to be here?" You couldn't hear a sound. They listened to me in silence. However, once they realized that what I said made some kind of sense, the audience just dropped off, the invitations stopped.

I had to try to get there by putting on my own events. I would, on a number of occasions, hire a small church hall in villages, and I would turn up and put the chairs out. I would do the talk to 15 people if I was lucky, and I would drive home poorer than I arrived. But the people had come to listen to what I had to say. The cycle has moved on to hundreds of people from Britain and other countries and America, who just come to listen to what I have to say. It is an incredible cycle where audiences are reaching great levels not to ridicule me but this time to hear me. Back in those desperate days, when money was pouring out of my life and I was looking the street in the face, and I had kids to bring up, although the incarnate me was getting desperate, on another level I knew it was going to be all right.

I published *The Robot Rebellion* when I was first looking at the conspiracy in 1994. That was the outer, outer, outer limit that any publisher could publish, so I faced starting my own publishing company. I was told I would write five books in three years and I did this right to the month. Now when I write, I know what I write will be published. In energy terms, all my books run straight at the people. They are without fear. If the evidence points in a direction, then that's the direction that is published.

PH: I thought all this might make you skeptical and disillusioned with humanity, but you seem to be optimistic and encouraged and at peace with yourself.

DI: I'm extremely optimistic. When you look at something—whatever it is—and see it in as many forms as you can, you have to realize that it is not only humanity that is multidimensional. What you are observing is also multidimensional. When people say "Tell me what's going on," or "What do you think is going on?" I say "What level of what's going on do you want? Do you want the physical level?" I will tell you about the Bilderbergers, the Freemasons and how they connect.

Do you want the next level? OK. Then I will tell you about the entities that aren't actually human but who are orchestrating the whole thing. Do you want the next level or the next level? If you want that level, it's all a freaking game! Let's not get caught in the illusion! I made a decision years ago: There are different people making different contributions to this whole tapestry of knowledge, and mine was going to be that I wasn't going to let the system that I am trying to expose set the agenda for what I said and how I said it. I was going to set the agenda. What I've decided to do is to have a simple philosophy of being led by information, and if the information leads me into really bizarre areas and I feel it is justified, then that is what I communicate! I was talking about the spiritual stuff in the early '90s, because I was seeing the spiritual, and it made me see the suppression of spiritual knowledge, which started me asking, "Why is this suppressed?" and "Who is suppressing it?" Suddenly I'm on the journey that's led to today.

Chapter 11

Disclosure Begins

Dr. Steven Greer

MONSIGNOR CORRADO BALDUCCI, LEFT, AND DR. STEVEN M. GREER.

http://www.cseti.org

In my personal view, the single most impressive disclosure effort was the historic Disclosure Project Press Conference (May 9, 2001) headed up by Dr. Steven Greer and CSETI. I first interviewed Steven by telephone in 1998, after which I invited him to come to Calabria, Italy, for a 1999 spring conference along with Sgt. Major Robert Dean.

I was impressed with his courage because he did a "no-holds-barred" lecture with video backup. We were all impressed, but most of all, we Italians became suddenly informed about the many unknown political implications of the cover-up. We soon became close friends who remained in contact via e-mail. The Italian people love him and appreciate him for his candidness.

Sometime later, Greer then returned to Italy with Peter Sorenson to film our Italian disclosure witnesses for his documentary in the fall of 2000. His video testimony included Monsignor Corrado Balducci, Dr. Roberto Pinotti of the Centro Ufologico Nationale (CUN), Alitalia pilot Max Poggi and physicist Clarbrunno Vetrucchio, who now works for the Italian Space Agency. Since I was present at filming, I know how valid this testimony was. I saw that Steven was very determined, professional in his demeanor, and courageous. At times it was almost scary how aggressively candid he was during the filming. While I tend to "soft pedal" sensitive material or try to screen controversial pronouncements, he is a veritable "steamroller." He has personal reasons for pushing this issue, since so many of his friends have died of mysterious causes. He is your typical angry young man, and rightly so. He is also one of the most animated, dynamic speakers ever.

I admire Steven mainly because he is truly a warrior as much as he is a sentimental family man, with a wife and three daughters. I met them all in Colorado when he was searching for the funding for the disclosure taping, and I saw what it took to actually organize this impressive effort. The synchronicities are incredible. It seemed unbelievable that I could be sitting with him in Colorado, at dinner in Oslo, Norway, and filming near the Rome train station. I saw myself as somehow being led, being invited to help pave the way for something that involved all these key players, while I never consciously understood how I got there. I just knew I was at the right place at the right time for the most important disclosure efforts in our human history, again much like the invitation of Close Encounters.

Telephone, 1999

Paola Harris (PH): How did you feel when you heard that Colonel Corso had died? How do Americans feel about it?

Steven Greer (SG): Corso lived longer than the average male in the U.S., even though some of the circumstances surrounding his death aren't clear. People younger than he die in mysterious circumstances while they are searching for the truth, and that's even stranger.

PH: Are you referring to Arizona Congressman, Steven Schiff?

SG: I am referring to five of my staff. As you know, I've got a metastatic malignant melanoma. My doctor, who treated me for six years, died in January, and a former CIA director was killed when he was about to give us valuable evidence and research materials. There have been other deaths over the past two years, but all we can do is carry on.

PH: Colonel Corso is one example. We need witnesses of this caliber to come forward with hard facts.

SG: In Italy are there any military personnel—witnesses who may be of a lower rank than Corso, but of similar stature—who are prepared to come forward?

PH: I don't think there are any in Italy.

SG: Well I think there are. UFOlogical projects and conferences are being organized in Italy, and I'd like to take advantage of this interview to call on people who know something to speak out. In particular, I'd like to stress—in support of the activities with which Corso was involved—that sometimes they [the projects and conferences] have been badly organized, which reduces their intrinsic effectiveness as a tool for disclosure. There is a direct relationship between the people involved in this cause, its context and its effectiveness. You know that in the past we had people like Colonel Corso, Pavel Popovich in the former Soviet Union, and the astronaut Gordon Cooper in the U.S., who came forward with their sightings and experiences.

PH: And Edgar Mitchell.

SG: Mitchell isn't a first-hand witness. I'm talking about eyewitnesses, military personnel, scientists and aerospace engineers who have had some sort of involvement with aliens and were present at highly ambiguous events of an extraterrestrial (ET) nature—something which never occurred during the 50-year cover-up. When they see Philip Corso or Gordon Cooper, a lot of people say "Ah, they'll finally put a stop to all the secrecy."

But that's not the case, and it never will be, as we need to take a multidisciplinary approach to the issue, which doesn't just gather dozens of top-secret witnesses from all over the world and give them a forum where they can speak out, but which combines their testimony with scientific proof, official evidence, government documents, etc.

In fact, Corso's information wasn't coordinated alongside that of other people of similar moral standing, and even though he had mainly charitable and non-commercial aims, in the end, scientific and political communities and the main channels of communication paid no attention to it at all. It's important to discover the truth all over the world, and to do this we need much more sophisticated measures than people think.

At CSETI, we have concluded, after a thorough investigation lasting several years—starting with Donald Keyhoe who had been involved in the same project since the sixties—that the weight of evidence is essential in a multidisciplinary context. Around 200 top-secret witnesses who have come forward should participate in an information blitz which will stop anyone denying the truth. I think it's really important.

What happens if the uncorroborated story of a person such as Colonel Corso comes out, and then that story moves outside the reception zone of the main political, information, military and scientific circles? This is what we at CSETI asked ourselves in the context of Project Starlight, which we have been working on for five years. The main aim is to find a Philip Corso in Italy, in the U.S., Germany, England and the former Soviet Union, and to combine their knowledge and testimonies in a well-organized global process of disclosure, perhaps through the U.N. or in that small nation in Italy—San Marino—which Michael Hesemann told me about.

The difficult part will be to move all these witnesses...we have identified around 200. Some are people who are very much involved in this area, and others were just there by chance when UFOs landed or appeared on radar performing extraordinary maneuvers. By presenting various people, from different social backgrounds and experiences—with top secret clearance in their official positions at the time—who have been concerned with various aspects of this phenomenon for over 40 or 50 years, their cases become much more compelling than that of one unknown, anonymous individual. It could all be done through a government agency, or by a series of well-made TV documentaries, but we don't have the funds for this....

PH: Why are aliens often referred to as hostile?

SG: The aim of depicting ETs as hostile is to launch the trillion-dollar mechanized operation to deploy military space stations throughout the cosmos. It's an operation which obtains funds from all over the world instead of raising the majority of funds from Europe and the U.S., in order to militarize space and draw aliens into hostile and violent clashes, and to do this, you need to demonize the enemy. No war can be fought, no-one will abandon order and peace, if you haven't first inculcated hate, fear and loathing for the enemy. By orchestrating false abductions and mutilations, someone is laying the psychological foundations for conflict through popular culture and the UFOlogical community. And it's ironic that the UFOlogical community itself is the main culprit in terms of disinformation, furthering a program connected to the funding of a vast military operation. We're playing a very dangerous game, and no good can come of it.

PH: What do you think of abduction researchers who interpret the phenomenon as a negative alien project?

SG: I'd just say that whoever takes abductions at face value hasn't put two and two together, and in some cases intentionally ignores facts which strongly support the hypothesis that the abduction phenomenon is to a large extent—*if not entirely*—carried out by humans.

PH: If the abduction phenomenon is a human activity, where does the alien presence fit in?

SG: At the start, it was obscured by tons of false material. It's a very complicated subject. True alien phenomena are rare, but they exist. They have waited patiently for a long time for us to mature and evolve into a calm species capable of interacting openly with them. They have tried to come forward gradually, waiting for the time when we reach some semblance of maturity, showing ourselves to be a species capable of interacting peacefully. We had an opportunity in the forties and fifties, and we failed. That was when the film *The Day the Earth Stood Still* was released, in a drive for pacifism: People at the State Department were trying to send a message to military personnel, who, in turn, were trying to militarize relations between human and alien life-forms.

PH: Is it true that there is a cosmic federation which hasn't just visited Earth, but has also established relations with certain government leaders, requesting permission to be here?

SG: This is a subject which must be approached with caution. I believe there were meetings similar to what you describe, but we subsequently betrayed the ETs. And that's not all. The so-called Extraterrestrial Federation was, and is, being targeted by bombs and weapons used to track them down and kill them. Basically, if we believe that ETs are collaborating with the military, it's because the military has craft similar to alien craft.

PH: That's like Ed Fouché's theory.

SG: Yes, I know Ed. I help people piece together all the facts. Take cloning for example. Dolly the sheep was not the first cloned animal. Anything that's part of the public domain, even things considered to be at the cutting edge of science, is five or ten generations behind, compared with true advances in technology and biological sciences. People say that a being they have seen is a "Grey," but maybe it isn't an ET...it may be "alien," but not ET. It may be a biological form—a kind of life-form similar to an alien.

I'm almost certain that science has the ability and the resources to simulate alien events in such a way as to control the public's perception of the phenomenon. Because they need to do this to pave the way for a holy war in space, which right-wing groups, religious fanatics and the military crave. These people are desperate for a holy war to break out, and if it doesn't happen spontaneously, then they'll start it. To give you an idea of how serious this is, one of my top-secret witnesses, for example, didn't testify before Congress, during a meeting set up by CSETI in 1997 in Washington, because during the break he was told to leave, and Intelligence agents—the very men with whom he had worked some years previously—spirited him away to the Virginia countryside, where he was held until midnight. This military witness was an intelligence contractor for the Air Force and other departments during the eighties, and participated in meetings where plans were made to use reproduced alien vehicles.

These [vehicles] were made by a consortium of companies in the U.S.: Northrop, Lockheed Martin, SAIC and others, in the context of a terrible project—which could be activated without the slightest warning—whose aim is to simulate an ET attack on the Earth. In other words, human settlements would be attacked with means similar to those made by alien technology, but which in reality, would be rendered operational in a base in Utah. The final point is: We are very vulnerable. Our leadership—the National Security Council, the U.N. Security Council, all the Joint Chiefs of Staff, all these people whom I have met—are very anxious about a surprise attack by an apparently alien force, which in reality is made up of human resources deliberately made to resemble ET resources. This is very important, because, if this is indeed the case, and a large number of people have confirmed the existence of this base and such a project, an *Independence Day* scenario could unfold—human beings trying to start a world war, in a battle against real aliens. This is exactly what happened in the Gulf of Tonkin during the Vietnam War, where we simulated attacks on our own ships to get more funding for the war. This is highly dangerous, as a small group of people has got the power to create events of this magnitude, fooling world leaders.

The energy and propulsion systems which could replace all the sources of pollution in the world already exist, but would put an end to the crude-oil and fuel-gas industries. Government members are extremely interested in UFOs, an interest which goes beyond normal bureaucratic concern. So the crux of the matter is that the "Government," as it is referred to by the public, is really quite outside the loop when it comes to this subject. We have gathered the best evidence and top-secret testimonies (which can be accessed on our web site), and we have questioned these members of the government, encouraging them to take control of the situation and learn about these issues. This will depend on their courage, the current level of which is minimal in political and military institutions. I think that the motto for the situation is CYA ("'cover your ass").

It's a high-risk sector, and only a few of us know just how risky it is, having been in the line of fire. CSETI members have often been to see the President over the last five years, providing briefings and detailed reports. The relevant files were given to Tony Lake, head of the National Security Council, and to Dr. Jack Gibbons, a physicist who is a scientific adviser to the President. As I mentioned, I personally have met various congressmen, including committee chairpeople. On our website you'll see that on April 9, 1998, we provided briefings to representatives of 30 congressional departments, including certain committee chairmen, such as Indiana Rep. Dan Burton, the current chairman of the Government Reform and Oversight Committee, who could have held the hearings by himself! He wanted everything we had on the subject—he's one of the major players in the game—and it's interesting to note that even people at this level have been threatened and frightened, both before a public hearing and before a presidential meeting. The U.N. promised us a place for us to hold a serious disclosure conference where we could introduce all these hundreds of witnesses and evidence to the public. However, the participants withdrew, because officials from the Secretary-General's

Office—with whom we were collaborating—were approached by some U.S. intelligence agents and were advised to drop the commitment they had made and the subject in general. Something similar also occurred in May 1997, but in that case we got around it. It's an incredible story. One day I'll write a breath-taking book about it.

PH: It sounds like the start of an important investigation. I think that so far, there's been too much science-fiction in this area, which has obscured other investigations. There are too many amateurs in the sector muddying the waters.

SG: That's one of the problems, and it's intentional. For example, the abduction phenomenon is, above all, of a military nature, as everyone now knows. It's interesting that it's an uncontrollable phenomenon. One of the rules of counter-espionage operations is, as a matter of fact, to create a phenomenon which can be confused with the real thing, containing the message which you want to disseminate. The alien phenomenon is underway and is growing, while the world, through a succession of spasmodic changes—typical of the 20th Century—is undoubtedly on the path towards a future where there will be a peaceful civilization everywhere. Those who have mocked all of this will address the subject, discredit it again and exploit some of its aspects, thereby creating a distorted message, quite different from the original one. In our case, we have military personnel and military-industrial giants who have secretly used and copied alien spacecraft and then put incredible high-tech products on the market. But in doing so, they also learned a lot about alien technology, which is very sophisticated in electronic terms and directly interfaces with minds and thoughts.

In actual fact, humanity has been studying this technology for 60 years, ever since the '30s, when the Nazis acquired one of those craft in northern Germany. Eventually, you can simulate or hoax an alien event, making it seem ET, whereas it is completely of human doing. The purpose is to obscure genuine phenomena, which aim to transmit a kind of message or stimulus. In this case, the involved humans desperately want to replace this message, and transmit instead a sort of demonic *Independence Day* or *X-Files* scenario, because the intention is to initiate, in the next century, a phenomenon which requires a trillion-dollar military response. You need to understand that anyone with an IQ above 40 knows that given the proliferation of weapons of mass destruction—biological, chemical and nuclear weapons are easily produced—we have two choices: Develop a global, peaceful civilization, or destroy ourselves.

PH: How can we attain world peace in the light of the militarization of space, unless we have a common enemy?

SG: You are suggesting an important link. They are trying to replace international conflicts with an interplanetary conflict, which could enable them to unite the world in order to control it, but instead of uniting around the positive humanity which we all share, we would unite around something else to hate, another enemy to fight, in other words, another "Evil Empire." Instead of the Soviet Union, it could be something in space. By the way, all this is very lucrative, and the Cold War is small fry in comparison.

Imagine an agenda—a covert program—which, by inserting mass disinformation in popular communication media, spreads the fear of a sinister and frightening threat from space among the public, making the predictions Ronald Reagan made in the '80s inevitable. He said: "Wouldn't our task of creating world unity be easier if we had a common alien threat to unite against?" The President of the U.S. may have been manipulated at the time by those who wanted the alien issue to take a turn in that direction, insofar as this would have benefited several long-term programs, including the one—of no lesser importance—to engage the current American military industry in a trillion-dollar space mission.

PH: Thank you, Dr. Greer.

Insiders

Chapter 12

The Insiders

Sgt. Clifford Stone

I have visited Clifford Stone several times in Roswell, N.M., and have become good friends with his wife Hahn, with whom I shared a three-hour bus ride to Albuquerque in 2001. Clifford authored *UFOs Are Real*, and it is outrageous that he has never received any money for it. In his generosity, he gives away his books, tapes, and information in a sincere effort to inform the public, which is his passion. My colleagues agree that Clifford is a sweet man and very credible. He often speaks about his past experiences in the recovery of crashed UFOs, a job he began at 19, and for which he was not fully prepared. He has a wealth of information, a myriad of documents at home, and, as fate would have it, in 1997 I happened to photograph on his coffee table a movie canister that contained six minutes of a historic Holliman meeting between aliens and military. I never did see it projected, nor did I realize what was in the canister. It was not until my editor asked me about the old 1950s label on the canister that I was aware of what I had filmed.

Clifford did show the film segment to some researchers, but he said that the intelligence community took it from him when they heard him discussing it on the phone. In the case of Clifford Stone and Dr. Michael Wolf (see page 91), It was always clear that our phone calls were being monitored, so I purposely avoided "too-sensitive" material. It is more my intention to *connect the dots* than to find a "smoking gun." Clifford is a courageous witness, and his very personal testimony for the Disclosure Project brought people to tears in America as well in Italy.

He was willing to come forth to swear to "his Almighty God and to the members of Congress that we are not alone, that some races look like us, that some also have families, and feelings and are sometimes afraid when caught." In fact, he proudly announced that with the help of another soldier, he aided one alien being to escape. From Clifford's testimony and others, I realized that the problem may lie in a difference of perception, and our earthly policy toward the extraterrestrial reality depends upon this perception. In that particular incident, Clifford was accused of aiding and abetting what the military often calls "the enemy" but what he actually perceives as "guests."

NASA ground crewman Clark McClelland (see page 110) also discussed this difference in perception with me when he recounted an incident when military personnel witnessed some UFO activity around some nuclear missiles at Vandenburg AFB. When the missiles fell into the Pacific, the military proceeded to call it "an act of war," when in reality the containment of nuclear weapons on Earth is really "an act of peace" from an ET perspective. Therefore, the conflict still exists, but there is real proof out there, if researchers would just find the witnesses and verify their stories. This "living room debunking" that some experienced researchers practice only muddies the waters and reveals their ignorance. I suspect it is part of the cover-up process of confusing the public. Sgt. Clifford Stone, and the now-deceased Col. Philip Corso and Dr. Michael Wolf have all been prey in the hands of these publicity-hungry researchers, and the rub is that some of them are dead now and can no longer defend themselves.

Even Italian researcher Dr. Roberto Pinotti (Centro Ufologico Nationale, picture, page 27) came all the way to Roswell to find Clifford, who was open and generous with his home and his material. In my opinion, Clifford is part of the vanguard of insiders who are paving the way for the truth to be exposed, and who suffer intense ridicule just to open our eyes. Clifford is very courageous, and his story must become part of an archive, so he is collaborating in writing his memoirs with capable San Francisco journalist Leslie Kean, who has written many articles for the mainstream press. Where other journalists present at the Washington Press club ignored the story, she pursued it. Lately, Leslie and I have spent many a late night discussing strategy and how to properly support the Disclosure Project on an international level. Clifford's interviews below are part of this effort.

July 2, 1998, at the home of Clifford Stone in Roswell, N.M.

PH: Sergeant Stone, what is your background, and what events led to your book, *UFOs Are Real*?

CS: When I was seven I had my first close encounter with a UFO, followed by interactions with alien entities. I served in the Army for over 21 years. At first I was reluctant, then afraid, then disillusioned, by the way the government handles the subject. When I decided to speak openly about UFOs, I was still on active duty, and the Army only told me to always make consistent statements. However, when I was assigned to another detachment, I was categorically ordered *not* to discuss UFOs, or write or make requests to Congress without authorization or approval. I considered this to be unacceptable, especially since I was involved in the program without the knowledge of my commanding officer. Instead of being discharged, I was sent to Germany, then Belgium and then around Europe, and I found myself involved in the UFO situation again, though unwillingly. I heard about an incident in the USSR. The Soviets tried to shoot down a large unidentified craft and mysteriously lost three of their planes. So I decided to come out into the open, in spite of my superiors, who may not have been aware of my intentions and my links with various agencies connected to UFOs. I asked to be discharged, informed the structures not connected to the Army about this, and I left Germany.

PH: What year was this?

CS: 1989. I went home on apparently ordinary leave. Only one colleague, a Russian interpreter, knew about my involvement with the UFO program. My request to be discharged was denied two days before I arrived at Ft. Bliss, and they assigned me elsewhere for two months. They convinced me to stay and said I wouldn't be sent back to Europe but would be assigned to Ft. Belvoir. I was still set on leaving, because I didn't want to go through the same experiences again—experiences which can't be discussed. My family knew nothing about them, but they were used to my sudden, long absences and certain strange visitors.

PH: Were they government agents?

CS: Yes, but I didn't know they were. Here's an example: From 1969 until April 1998 I was in close contact with someone who remained anonymous and who called me "Colonel." He was an agent responsible for my protection.

PH: *UFOs Are Real* contains classified documents. What impact has the book had on public opinion?

CS: It contains a large amount of American government documents with a high-classification level. The government denies everything and doesn't even admit that top-secret documents on the subject exist, but it keeps them well hidden! My interest centers on Operations Moon Dust and Blue Fly, which are still involved with UFOs. The U.S. Air Force has an installation at Ft. Belvoir, Va., which is identified as Air Intelligence Group 696. It is responsible for the collection of UFO data and material. Names and programs are given pseudonyms. I was in the Army's counter-espionage service when the program covering these operations began. These missions are both run by the State Department. Well, that's a half truth. It's actually the Defence Intelligence Agency that really controls both projects. They use military attachés in every consulate and embassy in the world to send data about UFOs, while our military personnel was, and is, ready to go into action anywhere in order to obtain any prospective document and make it disappear.

PH: Such as documents about recovered UFOs, which the U.S. has always hidden, on the basis of certain agreements?

CS: I am absolutely certain that the majority of the foremost governments and intelligence agencies know the truth about UFOs. Don't get me wrong: We don't know how much has been disclosed.

PH: What *didn't* you say in *UFOs Are Real*?

CS: I didn't say very much about Moon Dust and Blue Fly. I got hold of certain documents, but when I tried to find certain information, I got nowhere. They told me that for the moment it was probably classified material and could not be divulged. I then went to certain members of Congress, who denied—through political channels—both the existence of operative units with these names and the role of Ft. Belvoir. I went back to the same Congressmen and showed them 23 documents which confirmed these missions and the Ft. Belvoir operative base. The Air Force intervened, first claiming that they were war missions, and then trying to make Moon Dust and Blue Fly out to be peaceful. In the three chapters devoted to Moon Dust and Blue Fly, I have not included letters that name members of Congress who stated that the relative documents had been destroyed. That's pure disinformation on the part of Defense. The Attorney General knew about the Air Force's cover-up but didn't follow up with an enquiry.

PH: Why not?

CS: For two reasons. Firstly, if we claim that life elsewhere is possible, then we should reach a technological level which can be applied and integrated into the culture in case of hostilities. Secondly, we'd feel the need to understand our visitors as much as possible, and this constitutes a serious problem. The Army repeatedly told me not to expect or anticipate that meetings with the so-called "entities" (the EBEs—but they called them entities because they didn't know where they come from) would be peaceful. Later on, they told us that they may even be hostile. Every now and again we shot at them, and they responded with weapons. There was an episode which took place in Brazil: Two military contingents opened fire from the ground on two UFOs, which responded, causing a 60% loss of material and an 80% loss of personnel. So were we capable of standing up to hostile action? Not at all. A lot of people believed an *Independence Day* scenario was possible. But in reality, an invasion of forces from space or from other powers is already under way, and I'm not talking about one race, but 57 different races.

PH: 57 different races?

CS: Yes, we have identified 57.

PH: Is this documented?

CS: Yes it is, but in documents that will never be published, unless they manage to force open the archives. Do you know how we know all of this? There's only one possible way: using so-called "interactions," or "interface exchanges." Anyone who worked in this field and revealed that they knew about these secrets was told: "You have a special mission to carry out." In any case, if I told you everything I've done, you'd find it hard to believe. I loved my country, I believed in the Army and in doing my duty in Vietnam, even if it cost me my life. It was destiny. So, even though I had been declared unfit for service, I arrived in Vietnam and realized that all the wrong people were giving the orders. My task was to gather together the children and help them. In the end we saved 1700.

PH: Do you know about particularly gifted children who are used by government agencies as interpreters or interfaces with aliens?

CS: That's a subject which worries me a lot. I was once on one side of a table and there were non-human beings on the other. No one in that room knew what was going on but me.

PH: Have you ever talked about it?

CS: No. I told my son that I'd take it all with me to my grave. Instead, it was my son who died, and I still have a lot of doubts about that.

PH: So, after your sighting as a child, the government monitored your interaction with aliens, using you, we could say, as an interface with other races in order to glean information?

CS: Exactly. It was the government that wanted to squeeze this information out of us. There are a great deal of things I have never said.

PH: So, if your job was to be an intermediary, do you believe that there will be contact in the future?

CS: We have already had contact.

PH: But openly in the near future?

CS: Definitely. Within 25 years. We are moving towards a militarized space, which will lead to the opening of new frontiers in research and development. We will become voyagers in space. We will go to other solar systems. Current technology doesn't allow us to draw our discoveries together and put A, B, and C together in order to get D. If space becomes militarized, it will be a threat to our visitors. It's easy to see why. We need to use technology responsibly for the betterment of our race, and if other intelligent species really exist up there, we have obligations towards them. We, as a race, are still not mature and spiritual enough to do this. Do I believe in God? Yes! And they believe in God, too. But our definition of divinity is probably in conflict with theirs, which doesn't mean that we have a different point of view. They might wipe out many races in order to better define the concept of God, and at the same time they might get themselves killed before taking the lives of others. But they are also ready to defend themselves. I think they will continue to monitor us until we constitute a threat, within the next 30 years. This (showing me a page in his book), is a document taken from an intelligence memorandum which was sent to the FBI. It should have been destroyed. I told the FBI that the Air Force had authorized its release. They didn't know that the Air Force didn't want the information to be released, and it worked.

PH: Your book came out in 1997, and by now they ought to know that you have these documents, don't you think?

CS: As far as the Air Force and the Pentagon are concerned, these documents don't exist, but I have shown the opposite to be true.

PH: Can you tell us the number of your work group?

CS: It was 4607.

PH: Is that a recovery team in the Air Force?

CS: Yes, it's based at Ft. Belvoir. There they train and look after people who have had—I hate the phrase "psychic phenomena"—who have had *experiences* as an interface. They tell you: "You are going to be an interface," and it's logical that your reaction could be very emotional.

PH: What do you think about Area 51?

CS: Do you want the truth? Area 51 is an expedient. However, there is a connection. We still use Edwards AFB in California. I want to make it clear though, that I am not saying that nothing associated with UFO phenomena happens at Area 51.

PH: And what do you think of alien corpses put in containers?

CS: It's science fiction. We have a "marker"—an identifier who acts as an interface with the fabricator. The fabricator then provides specific information, small fragments of the truth, messages which must appear to be very positive. So after managing to influence the identifier, the fabricator will disappear, and the identifier will carry out the task he has been assigned to do. If we want the UFOlogical community to believe certain things, it must know what we do. First of all, we give the fabricator the task of identifying what we define as "intelligence targeting," a target being an individual who will circulate—this is the marker—and start to spread...it's surprising to see how easy it is...

PH: ...to spread the partial truth....

CS: We call it disinformation.

PH: If the Roswell crash was covered up, does that mean that during World War II something similar had already happened? Why are you smiling?

CS: At 12:15 during the night of February 25, 1942, a formation of 12 to 15 unidentified craft was seen in the sky over Los Angeles, California. They were neither ours, nor the Navy's nor the Marines'. Not having established their identity or radio contact, we decided to attack, in case they were unknown enemies. Our coastal artillerymen discharged 1430 shots against the targets. There was no reaction, no bombs, no planes shot down, no damage to property, no victims, and the craft disappeared. General Marshall related the incident to President Franklin Delano Roosevelt the very next day. In 1943 in the Pacific, General Douglas MacArthur asked General Doolittle for news of an unusual object which had faced our fighters and bombers. At the end of 1943, Doolittle informed MacArthur that some "spectators" had followed the main military action. They were not terrestrial, and maybe they were hostile.

PH: "Spectators"—is that what they call them?

CS: That's how Doolittle and MacArthur described them. We didn't know much about it. All I know is that something happened in China based on events which led to the recovery of a craft, which convinced Doolittle, without a doubt.

PH: Some of your story coincides with what Dr. Michael Wolf has said. Let's go back to the children. I find it incredible how the government chooses some who are particularly sensitive and puts them into its service.

CS: Just think, I was declared unfit for service, and yet at the end of my service I received another kind of training, the so-called "AIT" or "Advanced Individual Training," and they sent me to the archives of the Post Intelligence Center, where I found a guy, apparently on special service from the Pentagon in Washington, D.C. I stayed quiet, and it was he who talked to me about UFOs. "Don't worry. It will all be OK. What do you think of this?" he said, showing me a document. I replied: "It's nothing I should know about," and he said, "I wanted your opinion of it." A couple of days later I told him I was worried because I had seen a top-secret document. He replied that he hadn't shown me anything.

PH: Why?

CS: I asked him the same thing, and he answered: "You'll find out in due time." It said on my file that I'd enlisted in the Air Force for three years, whereas the service period then was four years. In the end I was assigned to NBC—Nuclear Biological and Chemical Warfare—in the communications sector.

PH: Did they ever ask you about your experiences of contact?

CS: I believe they knew about it.

PH: In that case, they could have learned about it from two sources: your family or the entities themselves, aliens who decide which humans will work with them.

CS: It's likely. During the training, you go through a phase of indoctrination, where you find yourself face-to-face with a mountain of information which blows your mind—so much so that my legs once gave way and I I nearly fainted because of an extremely painful migraine.

PH: Are the people who are used as interfaces aware of it or not?

CS: Colonel Corso knew about this.

PH: Corso never directly implicated the whole government, but only five or six departments. No one knows their respective *modus operandi*. If this happens in the U.S., it's possible it happens in other countries, too.

CS: Yes. The situation is such that we are forced to reveal the information to every interested country. There's no doubt about it. In the U.S. a small group of people deal with this, not designated officials. You can't trust the government. Power is only apparently in the hands of the White House or Congress. It's a select group. For them it's always and only a question of "national security." They're interested in military application, as Corso said—in new technology. Anything else is secondary.

PH: In other words, the government gets everything it can out of this contact. In the meantime, no one worries about interior development or the spiritual side of the UFO presence.

CS: Absolutely, they don't give it a thought. But in reality, the spiritual aspect of the UFO phenomenon must be given the utmost consideration.

May, 2001, Roswell, N.M.

I contacted Clifford Stone in Roswell, N.M., after his appearance at the Washington Press Club at the Disclosure Project press conference headed by Dr. Steven Greer (see page 61).

PH: Hello, Clifford.

CS: How is it goin', kid?

PH: How is it going with you after that disclosure conference in Washington?

CS: Still hangin' in there. I went ahead in the news conference and spoke a little, but some took a little longer. I said, "This is me. This is what I did. I stand before God and my country and before Congress under oath to state that what I know is true."

PH: That took a lot of courage! On the Internet, you are listed as one of the chief witnesses and as a recovery team member of Project Moon Dust.

CS: There was a lot of inquiry on me. I broke down several times. I can't help that. When you are back there and you start telling, you are no longer here now. All of a sudden you see everything in your mind's eye. There are several things that they don't want me to talk about, but I covered some of what I was involved in. I thought I needed to let people know, so I went ahead. It's hard to eliminate some things, as they are part of the total story.

Well, there was not a dry eye when I talked. I gave Jaime Maussan an interview, and they talked to me from the *Dateline* TV show. I told them the impact it had on my family and friends.

PH: I read in Italy that there were 250,000 people that tuned into the audio on their computers. And at a times there was some jamming. But in any case, it was the largest audience the Press Club has had. When I saw you on the list, I was surprised. You have been threatened so many times. The last time I heard from you was when you were trying to get to Canada, but I heard you were stopped at the border. I want you to be safe!

CS: I was not going to go. But they insisted. They—the powers that be—said "Go! Have fun with this!" I thought, "This is good." But they want me to avoid bringing up certain things. How can I talk about it without that stuff being brought up? So, as it turned out on that night, I thought, "No holds barred!" I hoped Dr. Greer wouldn't get mad if I got emotional, but even he cried when I got up. No one had heartburn with what I had to say. As I've always said, "If I didn't live it, I'd find it hard to believe."

PH: What did you tell in your individual testimony?

CS: About my first recovery and the situation where we helped one escape.

PH: Was that a long time ago when you helped an ET escape?

CS: This was in 1969.

PH: So was this part of Project Moon Dust?

CS: Yes, it would have been part of what I was doing, but I can't go into it right now. I am trying to tell more, but it is like when I spoke—I get physically and emotionally strained. I told Dr. Greer, "I gotta leave, I can't stay here. I gotta go out!"

PH: He understood, though.

CS: He understands.

PH: The media said Dr. Greer asked older people. They said "gray-haired men." Were there mostly older people there?

CS: Mostly. Ya gotta understand. There wasn't a whole lot of younger people. Larry Warren was there. He is 40. I am 52.

PH: I heard George Filer was there from MUFON.

CS: Yes. One of the colonels there said "We never did any of this other stuff." I said, "Well, I can show it to you in writing. I was there." Finally we decided there, that what they did back then and what I did when I was "in" were two different things. Well, I will tell you a little secret: When I talked about my experiences in front of the media—about how we communicated—I thought it was only about five or ten minutes. I thought, "I'll try to get through this real quick. I won't break down." Well, I broke down.

PH: You are still emotional about it. It is coming out slowly, and someone wants this to come out, right Clifford?

CS: Well, I think there are people who want this to come out but don't know how to do it. I've always said, "Don't punish those who have kept the secret." There was positive free-energy discussion. We have this technology that should be available to the peoples of the world.

Focus forward with charity toward all. Seek out the truth so that we can go ahead and be doing those things that are right for the future. We will be able to build a more caring and loving future, and the world can come together representing the planet Earth, and not be divided, representing various theocracies of this planet.

July 19, 2001, at the home of Clifford Stone in Roswell, N.M.,

PH: Let's talk about your testimony for Dr. Steven Greer and the Disclosure Project!

CS: I have documentation to prove a lot of the dynamics! What I really wanted to do is tell it one time, and this is it.

PH: You should. It is a really important legacy to leave behind for humanity.

CS: Remember I have post-traumatic stress syndrome...like in Vietnam, we get it from other things, too.

PH: Clifford, give us four reasons why you think they are letting you talk.

CS: Remember I still hit stumbling blocks. One—Most of the people that I interacted with like me. Two—I think many agree that it should be coming out. Three—They know that there are facts about the things that I am saying that can't be proven, so they don't have to think about effective counter measures. Four—They are not sure how many people will believe me, and, for those who do believe me, what end results are going to happen. I think they are trying to find a way. They've pinned themselves into a corner, and the question is, "How do you get out of that corner and minimize damage?"

PH: The corner you are describing is not telling the people the truth. So you might be saying that they might be letting us do all the work. Right?

CS: I believe it has reached the point that much of this, if not most of it, should be coming out. The ridicule needs to stop! And once and for all, the people need to be told the truth and that is: *UFOs are real. They are inter-planetary*, and *we are not alone* in the universe. We have interactions with those entities, and these are things that have to come out. I think some of this is coming out slowly, but surely, and the way you do it is by chipping away, almost like with a small pick at a very large dam to try to break a hole in it. And once you break a hole in it, the water starts coming through, and then everything else will break.

PH: Thank you, Clifford.

May 10, 2001, Washington, D.C. Disclosure testimony of Clifford Stone

"Ladies and Gentleman, what did happen I am going to tell you tonight. There were craft that did not originate on the face of this planet. They have living beings in them—living entities—people, very much like you and myself. When I say that, I mean that they have a culture. They have lives, they have families. They have likes and dislikes. It didn't take me too awfully long doing "recovery" before I came to realize this, but then I could not tell my family what I was doing. I want to relate one incident to you, and that one incident is the incident that really propelled me on to that type of situation. It happened in a place called Indian Town Gap, Pennsylvania, in 1969...."

Stone continued to say that as part of what he thought was a Nuclear Biological Chemical unit exercise, his duties included UFO crash recovery. The Pennsylvania incident included four dead alien greys. In a very emotional recounting of this and other incidents of his life, Stone asked the people to understand the entire scope of these visitations. He is clearly an insider, but a courageous one, as he concluded his talk in May 2001 at the Washington Press Club Disclosure Project meeting with the following:

"Tonight, I come to you as a scared individual—a scared little man—telling you just a piece of what went on in my life. There were other incidents that you too might like to know, that this is the case. I said it yesterday, and I will say it again, that the "absence of evidence" is not the "evidence of absence." It is evidence that is just simply denied to the American people. I stand here to tell you, that before my almighty God, I am willing to go and stand before Congress and tell them what I told you tonight as being the *truth*, and I can relate more of the events that have occurred, because I have that moral obligation not only to my family but also to every American and every person on the face of this planet. I have that moral obligation, quite possibly, to our visitors. The situation is: *We are not alone in the Universe, and I thought you might like to know.*"

Chapter 13

The Insiders

Ed Fouché

I first heard about Ed Rothchild Fouché from my editor of *Dossier Alieni* and *Notizario UFO* magazines Maurizio Baiata after the book *Alien Rapture* had come out. My boss thought it talked about exotic planes, exotic technology like the TR3B and the Aurora constructed in Area 51 and back-engineering. It was known that Fouché had subcontracted to work on technology at S-4 at Area 51. Later he would talk by phone with Dr. Michael Wolf because I would put them together and they would find common ground. This was important for me, because I needed to cross-check stories, and I was curious what common experiences they actually had.

Ed Fouché is as courteous, kind and sensitive as he is tough. He has a broad view of the conspiracy and the reason for the cover-up. He also had had some conflicts as a consequence of his testimony, although his book was a fictionalized account in collaboration with famed author Brad Steiger. I recognized the same kinds of plots of intrigue, murder, secret black-ops programs and Bob Lazar insider-type disclosure in this fiction-alized plot as there was in some of Michael Wolf's book (see page 91). Ed Fouché included an interesting element of spiritual awakening that involves an underwater contact. The word "rapture" is biblical and pro-phetic. Ed told me he enjoyed the interview, and he sent me a great deal of technical material on the TR-3B and aerial technology. In this interview I asked him also about the alien presence and about any possible contact experiences he might have had, since I was struck by the "underwater" scene in the book, which resembled the one from the movie *The Abyss*. I thank Ed for trusting me and sharing his fine mind and his thoughts with me.

Telephone, 1999

Paola Harris (PH): During your talk at the Laughlin Conference in Nevada, you showed slides of a plane built using very advanced technology, similar to extraterrestrial technology.

Ed Fouché (EF): They show the development of certain craft which the government denies exist.

PH: Are the photos classified or unclassified?

EF: Some used to be classified, but they aren't anymore. Take the TR-3B for example. We had an old digital image where it was impossible to make out the shape of this craft. So I took it to a friend, a graphics expert, who enhanced the details by enlarging it. That's how we managed to accurately recreate its characteristics.

PH: Is this material in the public domain?

EF: No, we may have restored a photo, but the TR-3B is still the most secret craft in the world. The government has many covert programs, and at least half a dozen of them concern top secret planes— the most highly classified objects in the world—and the technology behind them.

PH: When triangular objects are sighted, as in Belgium in 1990, are they actually craft built by the government?

EF: They aren't alien. They have a flat, triangular shape; we call them *mantas*—a kind of TR-3A with bat wings, totally different from the TR-CB. A friend of mine, "Gerald", worked for NASA for the whole of his career. We met at the end of 1976. According to him, there are three prototypes of these craft measuring about sixty meters (200') across, and the operational model is about 180 meters (600') across. He saw them with his own eyes. The copyright on this information dates back to 1994.

PH: Did he tell you what year he saw them?

EF: I think he saw the first prototype in 1991. There were triangular planes before then, but this was the first triangular craft with an Magnetic Field Disrupter (MFD), a magnetic propulsion system. It's a plasma accelerator which somehow disrupts gravity around the craft, thereby reducing its mass and weight by 89%. In practice, this was the result of reverse engineering from UFOs, but it didn't fly like a UFO, as it had an operational efficiency of 89%. If you've got a craft which can't reduce its mass and weight more than this, the only logical thing to do is to build a triangular-shaped craft with three multiphase rocket engines mounted at the corners, which is precisely what people see, both in the 200' version and in the 600' one. The photos, which are very dark and are posted on the

Internet, were taken at night, and you can see three bright lights which correspond to rocket engines. The large glow in the center is due to the energy generated by the MFD.

PH: A friend of mine who works in Intelligence told me that you had come into possession of MJ-12 documents. What did they contain?

EF: Part of the documents concerned the autopsy of some supposed aliens, similar to those described by Col. Corso in his statements, and also some things that came out of Santilli's alien autopsy, broadcast in the U.S. on Fox, which in my opinion is a reconstruction by the government in an attempt at disinformation.

PH: Are you referring to the Santilli footage with the alien with six fingers?

EF: Yes. The aim of the reconstruction, based on the original footage but showing an alien with six fingers, was to confuse the public. Anyway, an MJ-12 autopsy document also talks about a removable lens, like the one seen in the Santilli footage and as described by Col. Corso. But note that these MJ-12 documents were filed a long time before Corso wrote the draft of his book or before Santilli had seen it in the footage.

PH: That's interesting. And did the aliens have six fingers?

EF: No, four. Why did they film aliens with six fingers? Think about it for a moment. If everyone believes that four-fingered aliens are roaming the Earth, and all of a sudden footage appears which corresponds exactly to the real film but where the being has six fingers, then it's clear that the footage is not genuine. The aliens in the video aren't real.

PH: There may be more than one race, given that they are allegedly biological entities created in a laboratory.

EF: I disagree with Dr. Wolf's view here. Initially, there was a UFO crash in Germany and the aliens there were grays. The second crash happened at Roswell and another then occurred in the U.S. In between the two incidents, there was a UFO crash in Russia.

PH: Some alien races are believed to be very similar to human beings. Col. Corso said that it was worrisome that some of these races may be so human-like that they could walk along Pentagon corridors without being recognized.

EF: As I mentioned, one of my key informers, an NSA investigator, swore that there was an alien race of this kind. We knew of their existence but had never managed to communicate with them. This is why a massive technological race began in order to equal them, so we could protect ourselves. Although these aliens have never shown hostile tendencies, they were so technologically advanced that they constituted a potential threat. You know how the military thinks: if they can't control something, they prefer to kill it.

PH: That's absolutely true!

EF: So it was all part of the rationale; it was a question of secrecy. At that time the Strategic Defense Initiative (SDI), or the so-called Star Wars program, was launched, and following a new Majestic 12 Charter, various technologies were developed, basically to defend the atmosphere, which forms our external barrier.

PH: Have you ever heard of luminous aliens, or beings of light?

EF: Quite the opposite. The reason why this race uses EBEs (Extraterrestrial Biological Entities), going back to Roswell, is because they are neither humanoid nor sentient beings. In the autopsy document, EBEs are described as absolutely identical to each other, that is to say, they are manufactured beings. This is logical, in my opinion. Indeed, there is no reason to send a living being to explore the universe on a one-way journey when your scientific knowledge is advanced enough to create an EBE which can do it for you. Today, we have moved closer to this type of technology: Beings are being designed with higher perceptive capabilities, for example better visual abilities, where the bodies are programmed for a mission and then they are sent into space. While considering myself to be a rational person and not agreeing with many aspects of UFOlogy, everything I wrote in my book is completely logical, in my view and in the view of those who know me.

PH: So in other words, they are robots or androids. Do you know anyone who has communicated with them?

EF: According to Gerald, at the site of the Roswell incident a "body" was found still alive. Everyone denies that Secretary of Defense Forrestal was at the scene. On the contrary, it seems that everyone had a good false alibi. Well according to Gerald, Forrestal was right there, and communicated telepathically with the alien. As you know, Secretary Forrestal then began to show signs of a mental and emotional disorder, and was admitted to Bethesda Hospital, where he threw himself out of a window on the sixteenth floor. In my view, there aren't any holes in the story. They have never sent us an alien ambassador, and there are no underground bases where military personnel work alongside aliens. If we had had some sort of technology-exchange program with them, why would we have to invest billions of dollars in Research and Technology in order to do everything on our own? We could give them hundreds more human beings in exchange for their science.

PH: In your opinion, do these androids or manufactured beings have a program? They must have, mustn't they, seeing as too many people continue to talk about their abduction experiences?

EF: I'm not so sure, and this is part of the current diatribe. According to Gerald and another two people I have talked to, there have been some abductions, but only a limited number. Most abductions are carried out by the government.

PH: Why on Earth would the government be involved in abductions and insert screen memories in people's minds, making them believe they were abducted by aliens?

EF: There are several reasons. TMK is easy to use: it's a mind control technique first used in the '30s and '40s, when the CIA used to give people large doses of marijuana extract (THC), heroin and mescaline, altering human behavior via brainwaves or ultrasound to create screen memories or to put false memories into people's minds.

PH: In other words, you are saying that the manipulation of human beings is being carried out by the government, and not by aliens.

EF: Three people I trust swear that they are absolutely sure of this. Think about it—one of the reasons which comes to mind is that if there were some alien germ which could infect us, we could alter human genetics through injections. But what would happen if aliens came to Earth and released microbes which could modify our atmosphere? We would have be able to adapt. In other words, maybe we know that aliens are coming and they will settle on Earth. How can we protect our race?

PH: Is this how you explain the reasoning behind abductions?

EF: Exactly. It's for the protection of the species. Or maybe they've learned how to improve our species from genetic engineering.

PH: But why abduct people, Ed? Why do we have to do it in such a violent way? Can't we find another solution? For example, say it's being done to fight a disease?

EF: But how would you harvest eggs?

PH: But these people truly believe that they have passed through walls and been in spaceships. Why would the government create all these false memories?

EF: Disinformation. If you plant half a dozen different versions of what is going on in people's minds, no-one will ever believe anyone else, and that's exactly what's happening.

PH: It's a worldwide phenomenon. In Italy too, really strange things are happening to people who live both in cities and in remote areas. How can it possibly be a government conspiracy?

EF: It could be a cross-section.

PH: They would have to have made agreements with Italy and all the other nations.

EF: I have never believed in the theory of aliens or the New World Order controlling minds for financial reasons. The New World Order exists for a different reason, it's part of a Majestic 12 plan to unite the world under a single government. Supposing there's an alien threat, how could we unite the world under one power? How could we all agree? We would never agree, not even through the United Nations. Not unless a pre-existing authority imposed the terms of the future new order.

PH: So you believe that convincing people that we are threatened by aliens will unite everyone in a single world order?

EF: Yes. It would also happen in the event of a crisis. Y2K is a prime example. The world now relies on computers. There is no easier way than to crash all the computers in the world to take control and overcome those who possess all the computer-based and military power.

PH: Why would they take control?

EF: To rule the world under a single government.

PH: Made up of...

EF: Whoever these people are.

PH: So, as far as you are concerned, the UFO phenomenon is in reality a major conspiracy devised by the people of the New World Order, who may be acting exclusively for their own benefit? We blame aliens for abductions, but in actual fact it's the government's doing?

EF: Put it like this: we are under threat. Whoever has sent these genetically designed androids or robots (EBEs) to Earth has transmitted a return signal. These beings have found an inhabitable planet with intelligent life forms, and sooner or later the real "striking force," the real aliens, will arrive. So we have embarked on this massive program; we have eggs from all these people. We have created special, genetically modified children, and we have placed them in all areas of society through adoption, including placements with individuals connected to the government.

PH: Just a minute, you may be right! They have given these children to people connected to the government. I think I have met some of these children. But why would they do this?

EF: OK, I'll tell you. A microbiologist friend of mine is a great believer in junk DNA; that is to say, the potential of our DNA has never really been grasped. In reality, it can form a third DNA helix, which is an important evolutionary change. Once the One World Order is established, all the genetically modified individuals will be injected with another DNA element. Imagine, for example, DNA capable of sparking off an evolutionary process inside them: these individuals will be able to control the world and not be influenced by aliens, even biological entities which communicate mentally. They will all be placed in key positions, and obviously their seed and eggs will be used to make more human beings, who will also be endowed with these abilities.

PH: Have you ever as a child had anything strange happen?

EF: When I was small, my mother says once when we were riding in the forest, we saw a forest fire which came right into the car but my mother does not like to talk about it. I have a vague recollection of it. It is funny that you are the only person who has ever asked me that question.

PH: I am curious sometimes why people are interested in this field, Ed. Sometimes it could be they are chosen or given an invitation. Thanks for the interview.

Chapter 14

The Insiders

Dr. Michael Wolf Kruvant

"People need to be willing to accept the unusual," Dr. Michael Wolf Kruvant told me in one of our 70 or so taped phone conversations over the two years I knew him. I didn't realize it in 1998, but I was the only journalist to fully inquire into this story. I had forged a strong bond with him, and I visited him four times in his apartment in Hartford, Conn. Michael Wolf died in September of 2000, of pancreatic cancer. His real surname was Kruvant. He was a Russian Jew who first described himself to me on the phone as a "Buddhist Jew." He had an eclectic spirituality encompassing several schools of thought. He said that by using "Wolf" as a pen name, he was protecting Russian relatives named Kruvant who worked on the MIR.

Some of my colleagues called him totally "crazy." "Crazy like a fox," he would say, laughing infectiously. Few people could follow his complex mind when he talked of quantum mechanics, judicial law theories, or a "third DNA helix." Many times he lost the listener. He would often say to me, "You can't put the universe in a box, honey." Then he would laugh and tell me to read about "super-string theory."

As synchronicities would have it, in 1998 what I first noticed and recognized as I walked into his living room was the old faded photos of Fellini, Claudia Cardinale, and Marcello Mastroianni on his wall, along with several photos showing studio technicians as they wrapped a very young, handsome dark-haired Michael in a white sheet as part of a movie stunt.

I might add that he was still a very handsome gray-haired man, who stood about six feet tall, but due to the fact that he had also contracted diabetes, which added to his list of many ailments, he was extremely thin and had lost his teeth from radiation poisoning. He had suffered very much in his personal as well as his professional lifetime. Dr. Wolf then told me he worked undercover with Federico Fellini as an extra on the film *8 1/2*, and he had once lived at the "Sporting Hotel in Parioli" (which does exist). He spoke Italian with my friends via the speaker phone, and he talked of having coffee at Doney's when he occasionally lived at the Excelior Hotel in Rome. He said he had many passports with different names from his undercover work, and he hated being away from his wife and child in London.

I always wondered why debunkers never researched his counter-intelligence life in Italy, where we were able to verify pieces of his story from the details he provided us. I even saw an angry letter in his files from the famous "Charlie" character from his book. Charlie was a young actor, son of a British director whom Michael knew in his younger days, and he and Michael had known each other well. For those who say he was never married and never had children, he had family photos and constantly provided me details of his relationship with Sarah, whose photo was on his bulletin board. His book recounts how his family had been killed on Christmas day in a car bomb accident while he was driving. In truth, Michael would go into a depression crisis every Christmas. During that period, he was unapproachable, because he was re-living something terrible. I spent much time trying to take his mind off these tragedies and talking about *hope*.

It is hard to research this man's life, but one criterion that I use to determine a person's credibility[1] is that when these men repeat themselves, they tell

---

1. I learned this technique from Col. Corso and other military figures whom I interviewed, including my own father, who served under Mussolini as a cavalry officer in 1943

exactly the same story. In the case of the colonel, I must have heard his war stories at least 20 times, and he never changed a detail, because he truly seemed to enter that realm as he retold the event. Wolf also repeated himself often, never changing the details in the slightest way, even if I repeatedly questioned him intensely, asking for more details, dates, etc.

In these 70 taped conversations, Wolf was crystal clear about events. He got very irritated and did not hesitate to correct me if I made the slightest mistake about any of his experiences, such as when I said he had worked at S4 "Indian Lakes Facility," instead of "Indian Springs," as it is truly called. But then Dr. Wolf's philosophy—his third commandment—was "forgive people before they injure you, because they are most surely going to do it." Dr. Wolf used a precise scientific vocabulary, and he assumed that the listener was intelligent and knowledgeable. He was also "cultured," as he often spoke about his love for the Italian painter Modigliani, whom he imitated when he painted a nude on his laboratory door at the age of ten. He assumed the listener or reader could easily follow his logical connections because our minds should work like his —but he had a 200 IQ. The truth is that few of us are wired like he was, and such geniuses wrongly assume that we are on their level while they try to communicate with us. Michael once told me that, in his capacity as diplomatic interface for the U.S. government with the extraterrestrials, he found that ETs do not possess a duality and take things quite literally. They do not try to confuse us, as our government often does.

It was impossible to look into the jet-black, green-pupiled eyes of Dr. Michael Wolf and not coin a totally new term for this extraordinary man: "meso-alien." *Notizario UFO* Staff writer Adriano Forgione and I flew to Connecticut August 8, 1998, to see for ourselves what this scientist with a most unusual blood chemistry looked like. It was then that he took a flashlight and showed us his dark green pupils. Dressed in doctor's scrubs, which to some mistakenly appear as pajamas, Dr. Wolf is indeed a medical doctor, and a neurologist. In his house are medical encyclopedias, two electron microscopes, several computers, glass chemistry tubes, an oscilloscope and other various and sundry articles.

Wolf had an M.D. in neurology, a Ph.D. in theoretical physics, a D.S.C. in computer intelligence, a J.D. in international law, an M.S. in the electromagnetic fields' (EM) influence on organisms, and a B.S. in biogenetics. Most of these degrees were earned in the government's secret "black operations" program, and the participating universities have erased him from their records. Previously, Dr. Wolf had served as a scientific consultant to the President (we saw the "Thank you" letter from President Clinton on the wall), consultant to the National Security Council on extraterrestrial matters, a member of the Majestic (MJ-12) Special Studies Group, and director of its lead agency, the Alphacom Team. He was a respected, long-term member of the New York Academy of Sciences and American Association for the Advancement of Sciences (AAAS). He served as an Air Force Colonel, pilot, flight surgeon and counter-intelligence officer for the CIA and NSA. He had a great sense of humor and an enormous love for "humankind," especially the children of planet Earth.

So how does one speak with an alien or even a "meso-alien," a scientist with an intense sensitivity for his fellow man? Wolf possessed a genuine emotional love that Adriano and I truly felt in his presence. He was a man who understood the workings of atoms, particles, subatomic physics and galaxies of the universe and who saw everything as connected, created and manifested by the Creator Source, which he called "The Forever." Perhaps this marvelous creature, this Michael Wolf, this "meso-alien," this man who always spoke of "a gateway treatment" to other dimensions was also evolving, perhaps creating more synapses in his brain from the connections he kept making, as he conversed for hours upon hours with people on the phone. He was a self taught genius who mixed art with quantum mechanics, science with metaphysics and who saw the connection to everything. When I was at his apartment, I saw letters from all over the world—one in particular from a French physicist who recognized Michael's expertise and genius and concurred with him on his quantum-mechanics findings.

He spoke often about the split between science and spirituality—a dichotomy between the physical and metaphysical worlds. We humans have split ourselves in two, and now it is time to get it back together. We are able to both kill and love intensely. He said we will have to fight to join again this dual nature as we leave the Fourth World of advanced technology and enter the Fifth World of spiritual growth, as the Hopi prophecies tell us. The answer is love, says Michael, "the greatest power that the Forever has put into this universe!"

It is quite ironic, and certainly not surprising, that the Lakota shaman Standing Elk (now Golden Eagle) invited Dr. Wolf to speak at the Sedona Star Knowledge Conference, an event that united many Indian tribes and UFOlogists in a continuing dialogue about the forthcoming Earth changes. Meanwhile, the outside world continued to deny that Dr. Michael Wolf existed. I

DR. MICHAEL WOLF KRUVANT   95

once asked Wolf's friend, clinical psychologist and UFO researcher Dr. Richard Boylan (see page 48), how Dr. Wolf can stay loyal to his country and be so intensely committed to saving the planet by being a supposed insider. He responded, "Dr. Wolf saw no intellectual contradictions here. He excels at straddling difficult boundary lines."

I am pleased to include in this book Michael's story, which was very time consuming and expensive. The transatlantic telephone calls alone cost hundreds of dollars. Because of his Italian connections, it was quite fitting that I convinced my editor Maurizio Baiata to translate Michael's book *Catchers Of Heaven* into Italian. I have never seen a book have such a profound effect on young people. As an introduction to these interviews, I will reiterate his claims. According to his book, Michael was abducted as a child, did communication experiments with non-human intelligence as a teenager, was an intelligence operative, worked at S-4 in Area 51, cloned a hybrid soldier named GI-JOE, and worked and lived with alien scientists and visitors there.

He was an international diplomat and interfaced with extraterrestrials for the government. He claimed to have been invited to work in many black-ops science programs, including particle-beam weapons technology in the Reagan years and earlier in remote viewing. He maintained that he—and many others—have been slated to provide a slow, processed release of information to humanity at large.

Later, when I verified many things Michael Wolf was talking about, I asked German researcher Michael Hesseman, who spent a entire day with Dr. Wolf, to help validate some information about the artifacts he gave us. Dr. Wolf gave Adriano Forgione and myself two pieces of extraterrestrial craft metal material and asked us, as he asked Michael Hesemann, to whom he also gave a piece, to have it tested (see page 102). Wolf predicted it would be 99% silicon and 1% extraterrestrial, and that is what the studies at the University of Pisa and in Germany both showed. Our samples wreaked havoc on a cellular phone and disabled it, and allowed my colleague Adriano to go undetected through a metal detector that earlier had balked at his enormous metal belt buckle. These fragments also gave out quite a bit of energy, which we both felt when we touched its surface.

Someone who is hiding something is unlikely to go to such lengths to contribute so much to the body of UFO knowledge. After having been in this field a while, I can truly say Dr. Wolf knew a great deal—not from reading it, but from living it! The details are too much for this book and will await an authorized book about him that he insisted I write. When he would call me late at night and I was too lazy to tape the conversation, he would say "You will be sorry if you don't do it, because I will not be here someday, and you need to be my spokesman. You need to write a book." It was somewhat like the charge Col. Corso gave me, and it has been an enormous responsibility.

I can verify that Adriano Forgione and I had seen enough documents, photos, and credentials to convince us that this was a serious story. More importantly, that was the only time both Adriano and I had a contact experience. It scared the living daylights out of Adriano—who had always bragged about wanting to be contacted—and confused me totally, convincing me that Michael indeed had an ET connection! He claimed his real home was Altair 4, and he yearned to return.

Because of my interviews with Dr. Wolf, my good friend and airline pilot Max Poggi and his wife Gabriella also flew to Hartford to visit Dr. Wolf. They found him to be extremely credible, especially when he remote-viewed their home in detail. It is hard to fool Captain Max. Their additional testimony adds to Wolf's veracity.

During the period of gathering information, Dr. Wolf was probably monitored occasionally, because there were times when he was so terrified of breaking some oath and being taken to "Danbury prison" that he would call me and complain. But he was too sick to leave his bed, so he was going nowhere, and it was never my intention to expose the entire "cover-up" per se. He gave that detailed information to Dr. Boylan, who has placed much of it on his web site (see page 85).

I remember how excited he was when a British reader contacted him because some fraternity at MIT was looking for him after his records had supposedly been erased. He talked enough about being at Magill, Georgia Tech, and MIT to convince anyone who bothers to listen. The stories were personal and as secret as those black ops programs that trained him.

For the unbelieving —those who never bothered to talk to him or visit him since 1996—Dr. Wolf remains a mystery and an enigma. His life was complicated, and it is unethical to believe only those who try to debunk him without ever having known him. I was very moved to see that Michael is akin to John Nash in *A Beautiful Mind,* because of his fragile mental state and his enormous love for mankind, especially "the children of the planet." Unlike Nash's story, people have not recognized, nor been kind or respectful to him. His health-care giver called him a "noble man who had a lot to share with humankind." All three of his health-care givers in Hartford fell in love with his gentle spirit. I long realized that too many things in this story do not fall into neat little piles, especially with Dr. Wolf's physical and medical records.

The fact that right after his death, his apartment was cleaned out of all documents, computers and databases tells me something, and the fact that the big guns are out to debunk him years after his death says something as well. History will surely show that Dr. Michael Wolf Kruvant was one of the top players in the disclosure process via his novel *Catchers of Heaven*. Like many others such as Jacques Vallée's *Fastwalker* and Ed Fouche's *Alien Rapture* in particular, he mixed fiction and non-fiction, probably to maintain "official deniability." Luckily, Dr. Wolf will not disappear in history if only because we, in Italy, translated his work, and it is now widely read. Today Michael still inspires! It is all part of his strange destiny!

March 8th, 2000

Paola Harris (PH): Michael, there is a growing consensus that the public is being gradually conditioned for eventual disclosure of UFOs and extraterrestrials. Do you think this is an accurate perception?

Michael Wolf (MW): This will be true because the group that I am still advising is using the Learning Channel and the Discovery Channel to get people acclimated to the idea that "We are not alone." These channels do not produce fiction. This is an accurate perception. It is all factual.

PH: Is the public ready for it, in your opinion?

MW: Some are. Some are not. Those who believe that they are the center of the universe are never going to change their minds 'til one lands in their back yard, then they'll say it might be a Disney thing. The same people who don't believe in UFOs believe that man never went to the moon.

PH: Are the lawsuits by Peter Gersten of CAUS having an impact in the intelligence community?

MW: No. They are not considered an important problem.

PH: There have been many sightings of extremely large triangular craft, over Belgium, Phoenix, and Illinois. What can you tell us about their origins, their agendas, or who is flying them?

MW: Well, the very large ones are not being flown by humans. There may be some triangular experimental craft, but they are not completely silent, and we are years away from recreating anti-gravity vehicles, to my knowledge. We are years away from duplicating UFOs, as far as I know. Some triangular vehicles are said to be like three football fields in length and width, and there is nothing to keep them up there. They are defying gravity. They are coming from all over. The Phoenix lights were huge, and there was a blatant cover-up. They said "Oh, yes. We were putting up flares." Flares fall. These Phoenix lights did not fall. They put flares up to try to confuse people.

PH: There is a division in the field of UFOlogy as to the alleged benevolence or hostility of ETs, which include allegations that many violent abductions are staged black ops meant to propagate fear and suspicion against aliens. Do you concur, regarding these violent abductions?

MW: There are minimal negative abductions. John Mack's *Passport to the Cosmos* does point to a transformation of most abductees—and to multiple abductions by aliens alone. And yes, there have been some sloppy abductions by humans parading as aliens or "human-form aliens" wearing human uniforms; and yes, there is a part of the anti-alien forces that is trying to confuse people about abductions. Military abductions are not as widespread as a lot of people think.

PH: How would they do that? Are they cloned aliens or are they like holographic images?

MW: They are more like holographic images. As a matter of fact, I know of several cases when they were able to put their arms and fingers through these so-called aliens, which weren't aliens, and then occasionally they would see a uniform and a human. They made errors in the holographic program.

PH: What is your opinion on the benevolent/hostile ET issue?

MW: Most are benevolent. Occasionally some get through the alien barrier, but they don't generally come back. They don't come back here once they are spotted and identified. Once they have hidden agendas, once they are identified, they are barred from coming here

PH: Who does this? Do we do this? Do the benevolent aliens?

MW: Benevolent, (laugh)...they are not goodie-goodie. But they don't want negative interference, for the most part. The negative ETs might get through occasionally, and that is what anti-alien UFOlogists point out. But those are out of a myriad of races, and they are few and far between.

I think John Mack is possibly one of the best experts on this subject. I completely go along with him, and he has read my book, and he does agree completely with me. He is telling it the way it is. He does not interpret data. He collects massive amounts of data. He says that these so-called "negative abductions" are 0.01 of 1% of all the rest of them. It's those who misinterpret deliberately who have anti-alien agendas, and who—we all know who they are—write in their books that they are robotic. No grey is robotic, unless it is a holographic projection by *humans*. Next!

PH: Can you expand on the dual nature of man, and how you see it relating to the Hopi prophecies regarding the fate of our planet for the year 2012?

MW: I don't think we have anything to worry about. Gradually the whole world is going to know that we are not alone. Two channels—The Discovery Channel to discover the truth, and The Learning Channel to learn about it—have been producing positive evidence of "alien intervention in human affairs" to try to keep us away from such prophecies. Prophecies are not written in stone—they can be changed by man.

PH: They can be changed by man?

MW: Why do you think God gave man "free will" rather than making us subjects of "one" reality? All the goodness has already been planted like trees and is sprouting. Read read the truth in *The Catchers of Heaven*.

PH: What's next for you?

MW: I am going to be very busy working on "enlightenment programs" to let people know that most of the civilizations are just passing through like tourists, and the majority of those who are interested in us have plans for us that are "good" plans. They don't want us destroying ourselves. I'm working on "The Bright White Light Quartet." I am also ill.

PH: We have heard that you are suffering from numerous maladies and complications. Do you have any requests for prayer and light in that regard, for those who support you?

MW: I'm already receiving it, and I am very grateful. Don't forget that for 48 years from the age of ten, I was exposed to toxic substances. That was part of my work, just like the people in Area 51 who have suffered working on "black programs" and want a class-action law suit.

PH: That's pretty clear.

MW: That's as clear as you're going to get.

telephone, April 2000

MW: I'm not severing any relationships with people I care about. The book will tell people intimately what I am all about. If they want to know me, I *am* the book—the book *is* me.

PH: I know.

MW: I care very much, otherwise I would not be running myself into this darn debt by calling you. I'm not a rich man. I don't appear on television. You understand that sometimes I underestimate myself. Space is layered, and in my concept of the universe all bodies are affected—moving planets, all life-forms. This space is universal. You can't have an atomic bomb or a war on this planet without it affecting other worlds, other cultures. I'm not speaking "if they are there." I *know* they are there! Most people on Earth are beginning to believe we are not alone. So, if we are not alone, what kind of an example are we telling them that we are like? It's awful!

PH: I know. That's awful!

MW: But believe me, there are more good out there than there are bad. Yeah! There are some bad, but they are under control. There are some savage races, but there are also good ones who are more advanced. But if you are more advanced, you are not putting all your resources into fighting wars. You are putting them into peace; you are putting them into love, and love is one of the strongest powers of the universe. I got to figure out how to pay these phone bills.

PH: Thank you for calling me.

MW: No! Thank you for the opportunity to spread the message. You are a wonderful, wonderful message spreader. It is needed! You do it in other languages. My book is not too tough to read. Maybe they will have a few questions, but if they keep reading it, they will gain something, and if they keep reading it more, they will gain more. I have over a hundred letters, and some have read it multiple times. At the time, I thought it might be my first and last, so I put everything in it.

PH: Michael, don't say this!

MW: No, at the time I thought it might be. People are already asking me for my second book without ever reading the first one. Please help me. I need the world to see that there is a beacon. There is a place to learn how to "hear" with your eyes and "see" with your ears. There is a place where you can look toward that beacon and see *light* and walk in the truth of that light. I'm not giving any speeches here, but I need people to walk in

the light with me. Believe me, if I can walk in the light, anyone can. This
is over an hour-and-a-half conversation.

PH: I know I changed the tape once. I know, Michael. You have my word. I
am working on it!

MW: If that farmer learns some of the principles and he has an open mind, it
will forever change his life, and maybe he will stop killing aliens. Unfortunately some of them may be mortal, and they die, and they are willing
to die, because they believe in the good things in the human equation.

PH: You are one of the good things in the human equation, Michael.

MW: Thanks. That interferes with my sense of humility. All these politicians—all I hear is *blah blah blah*! Why does a man like King Hussain of
Jordan have to die? That is wrong wrong wrong! I had tears in my eyes. I
prayed for his soul. I prayed that his son be a leader like him.

PH: Let's hope.

MW: No. Let's pray! Praying can't hurt. You don't have to pray to aliens. You
pray to God. You can pray to "the *Forever*" as they call God. Guess
what? The universe is listening in. The universe is listening in to us.
What we say and what we do is what they will find out. They will hear it.
They will see it! They will visualize it. It will move them if it is good. It
will give them more reasons to want to help us. We need help! But we
also need to help ourselves. God bless you and all of those beautiful children. All those beautiful children all over the world that don't deserve the
future that they might have. I just don't want them to have an nonviable
legacy. I want them to have a very good future. And I believe it is possible. I haven't given up hope. And those who have given up had better re-
examine that, because that's all negative energy, and *I won't stand for it!*
I will not stand for it. I've stopped defending myself. I don't have to. The
truth is in what I write and what I say, and if they can't see it, then they're
living in the dark. But there are a great many people in this planet who
are living in the light.

Michael Hesemann Report
Tested by "Federal Institute of Metallurgy" - Germany -
2000 FILM Productions Verlag M. Hesemann
Ms. Paola Harris
13 April 1999

Dear Paola,

It was a pleasure meeting you in beautiful Rome during the Holy Week. Re. our Conversation, please let me confirm,

1. I met and visited Dr. Michael Wolf and was very impressed by him. He certainly is a highly intelligent, brilliant man He *is* an M.D., and he showed me his credentials, proving this, as well as his friendship with Federico Fellini, proven by several photos. Of course, there is, and was, no way he could prove his ALPHACOM/MJ 12 membership.

2. He gave me a sample of his "metal," which, as he told me, he retrieved from a visit at Wright-Patterson AFB, We got it tested here in Germany, at the Federal Institute of Metallurgy, which came to the conclusion that it is very pure silicon—99% pure with 1% "unidentifiable" elements. They did not go into detail about the latter.

3. The sample he gave me is highly conductive, which is unusual for silicon. It does melt through ice.

4. The same characteristics were evident for silicon samples found in 1993, in the Israeli crop circles of Kadima after five cases of observed UFO landings/humanoid encounters. I do have a sample of the Kadima silicon. It is "the same stuff" as in Michael Wolf's sample. If you quote this statement, please do it in full length.

Sincerely yours,

Michael Hesemann

Chapter 15

The Insiders

Guy Andronik

The Hidden Truth

It never ceases to amaze me how blind people can be. At a recent conference in Rome, some high-level speakers were exploring the *hypothesis* of extraterrestrial visitations. It is totally incredible that some people still consider this phenomenon as a "hypothesis." Some of us are well past the hypothesis point and have progressed to the implications of the reality that "We are not alone."

A man seated in the midst of this mundane presentation raised his hand and asked to be heard. He said that he was part of a group of French geophysicists stationed in French Polynesia during 1966-69, and that on two separate occasions during the nuclear bombs tests, he witnessed a flyover of three luminous objects traveling at impossible speeds. He said that an alarm was sent out on the base because these craft were considered "intruders."

"Well," he said. "I asked myself the obvious: What exactly are these craft doing over the Polynesian base of Fangataufa, and how many people have seen them?

"It is eminently clear that they did not attack Planet Earth, but they made their presence known! They observed, I imagine, the formidable effect of these explosions, and France made 200 tests, not counting those done by the U.S. and other countries. Someone is watching! Someone is taking note!"

As I watched this distinguished Frenchman, I realized that he had quite a story to tell, and so I approached him. Later that week, I called Antonello Lupino, a brilliant young UFOlogist and director of CUI from Padua to assist me in cross-checking and corroborating his story. All too often, UFO researchers research from books and thus miss the real core of witness testimony like Guy Andronik.

Andronik, like military witnesses Col. Philip J. Corso (see page 3), Clifford Stone (see page 72), and Sgt. Major Robert O. Dean (see page 16) show us that UFOs are no longer a hypothesis but a *reality*. Many of these star witnesses have lost children under strange circumstances, as did Clifford Stone, Dr. Michael Wolf (see page 91) and Guy Andronik. Such experiences motivate them to go beyond certain specified boundaries of secrecy.

I herald them for their courage, for they are anxious to speak, providing us researchers with a formidable base of evidence. Guy sees in us a seriousness of purpose and professional support which he needs in order to continue to publicly disclose his entire story of contact. What follows here is merely the "tip of the iceberg," believe me!

Rome, Italy, February 16, 2003

Paola Harris (PH): You speak perfect Italian. Are you French?

Guy Andronik (GA): I am French, but I have been resident in Italy since 1969.

PH: What is the exact work you do? Can you explain in what capacity you worked in Italy?

GA: I am a geophysical prospector, now retired from the French corporation Companies General de Geophysique, which sent me on an assignment to its branch in Rome in November 1969, where a group of Italian geophysicists from various oil companies in Italy were placed side by side with us to research geophysical sites throughout the country, including the Adriatic Sea

PH: You said that you have had some UFO sightings while working in French Polynesia. Can you describe the circumstances?

GA: My destiny is odd. My assignment in Rome was programmed for three months, but in the end I lived there for more than 30 years. In July 1971, I married the secretary of the General Company of Geophysics in Rome, branch of "Companies General de Geophysique" of Paris. My two daughters, Nadia and Natacha, were born in that period; unfortunately Natacha died a little after birth because of serious malformations. My wife and I are now retired. Between 1966 and 1969, I performed my military service for the "CEA" (French Atomic Experiment Centre) and at the same time Pacific CEA had assigned me to Hao's Reef (Atoll), which was the support area for the whole civil and military staff employed by CEA. In 1960 the CEA was situated in Algeria, Sahara, where France performed 17 military nuclear explosions. Hao's Reef was around 430 kilometers from the atomic polygons situated in Fangataufa and Morurea's Reefs.

PH: How many nuclear explosions were performed in Polynesia?

GA: France, from 1960 until 1996, firstly in Algeria in the name of "Force de Frappe," and subsequently in Polynesia, had performed 210 nuclear tests, of which 50 were in the atmosphere and 160 underground.

PH: Where you there at this time?

GA: Yes! During this period thousands of civilians and soldiers, including me, had participated in this nuclear testing. In January 1996, France finally has decided to stop nuclear testing and to close the sites of Fangataufa and Moruroa (now declared interdicted zones to whomever) by signing an international non-proliferation treaty.

PH: How did you feel about this decision? Did you know then how dangerous it was?

GA: Certainly. We, "les vétérans des essais nucléaires français," are glad of this government choice. However, many veterans had been witness to various accidents. I was one of them. Without realizing it, all of us had been working in contaminated zones without the simplest precautions. A considerable number of these persons who are still alive today have serious health problems; many of their children have some handicaps at birth or some time after birth, as in the case of my second daughter Natacha.

PH: You mentioned at the conference that you saw UFOs on these islands while working. Is this true? Can you explain?

GA: Why of course. I will recount to you a curious fact that happened in those years but still today is considered extraordinary. About a week before the first H-bomb (thermonuclear) explosion, I was on Hao's Reef when suddenly other colleagues and I were ordered to participate in a general alarm. Someone had violated the military borders of Hao. The objects, sighted first by radar and afterwards by the general alarm, were three bright globes that suddenly appeared in the horizon. We received the orders "to establish a contact with the intruders and to chase them out of our borders."

PH: Did you follow them?

GA: Yes! We took off with a plane equipped to search for submarines. After around half an hour of flight we noticed the three bright globes on the horizon! They went past us, seriously damaging our navigation instruments, and disappearing afterwards at high speeds. This strange phenomenon (strange for me in 1968) reappeared in November of the same year at the Fangataufa site, precisely two months after the explosion of the H-bomb during topographical surveys that were performed in the daytime with a Zeiss T5.

PH: Did any of your colleagues see UFOs on the other islands?

GA: In December 1968, I was released from our base of Mataia, Tahiti. On August 28, 1968, I met two other colleagues of mine there who were employed in the mission at Fangataufa Reef. This was four days after the explosion of the first French H-Bomb. Their story petrified me! They told me that when they arrived on the Reef, the airport runway was completely covered with layers of many kinds of putrefied fish, and their first assignment was to restore the runway. Besides this, they had seen dozens of rats still alive (blood still visible), burnt only on the one side exposed to the explosion, and they had seen swarms of flies whose flight was considerably slowed down. I later saw the same on my return from Tahiti at the Fangataufa Reef. During the same topographical surveys, they also sighted on the horizon of Fangataufa bright, circular, luminous objects flying at insane speeds.

PH: Can you contact these witnesses now?

GA: We have never received news from them since. There were one sergeant, one lance-corporal, one first-class soldier, and two second-class soldiers. There was never any other communication from them. During our nuclear campaigns, we were constantly surveilled by the Russians, Americans, Dutch, English, and Australians and even by UFOs.

PH: Doesn't this present you with a problem. Why were they there?

GA: In these last 30 years, I have thought about what I have seen and experienced personally. I don't have any doubts about the existence of UFOs. Years have passed, but I still don't doubt their existence. But I have only one question: Why, after the Roswell case in 1947, has no one had any official contact with them?

PH: Maybe there has been, and we do not know. What is your assessment?

GA: Well, If you think about it, the answer is very simple: the only message of peace we transmitted into space was in 1898 through radio waves. From 1945 through 1998 we have sent into space about 2,050 explosions of atomic bombs throughout all continents. Remember there exist three types of civilization: the one of the *Homo sapiens*, the one of animals and the one of the military establishment. Even today, this last one, always denies, in the name of national security, to the others the freedom to express themselves!

NASA, Mars,
and Underground Bases

Chapter 16

NASA, Mars and Underground Bases

Clark McClelland

Exposing A Legend In The Shadows

http://Stargate-Chronicles.org

Just after Michael Wolf died in September, 2000, I went through a period of not wanting to deal with any part of UFOlogy for awhile. I was tired of becoming friends and supporting these wonderful people and then losing them. I kept asking myself, "Why can't I live a normal life like other people, just read magazines, sit around, go to the mall, and let this subject go?" It was then that I got a most unusual e-mail from Florida. NASA ground crew astronaut Clark McClelland had been moved by my article on Dr. Michael Wolf in *Nexus* magazine. He wanted me to take on his story and I found myself involved again.

I went to Clark's website and found that he had a wealth of information on the NASA-UFO connection. It interested me that he had known and spoken to Wernher von Braun, who said he was at Roswell, and who I don't imagine was picking up weather balloons. Von Braun was interested in all aspects of space not just rocketry, as I've written in the psychic connection section. Clark told me that he had been in MUFON for years. He originally spoke with Donald Kehoe because he had sightings of UFOs, even at the Cape. He believed that this led to his being laid off from his NASA contracting work as an engineer. Clark is fully cognizant of the role he played in the history of space exploration, and he is bitter that his career ended the way it did since he lost much money on litigation. Somehow we need to treat retirees as well as our space pioneers with much more dignity than was given to someone like Clark McClelland. I am happy to add him to my personal list of courageous heroes.

Clark and I corresponded for six months and it is my policy is to meet these disclosure witnesses "eye to eye," so I waited. His story sounded too valuable to pass up, so I decided to meet him in person. I needed to verify for myself that I was not being led down the garden path.

He was somewhat nervous during my visit to Orlando in 2001, but I was beginning to understand that my easy way of dealing with people opened them to telling me more than they had to other journalists. People seemed to trust me. In Clark's case I was told much more than I could ever print because I respect "sensitive material" — if the person asks me to keep a confidence, I do. I tried to calm him and asked him to trust my judgment. I cooperated with Clark, who approved this interview. I was very grateful to him because he gave me an extremely nostalgic, personal tour of Cape Kennedy.

Paola Harris (PH): Clark, as we sit here at Cape Kennedy, I can see that you have many moments of nostalgia. Tell me how your career began.

Clark McClelland (CM): I arrived at Cape Canaveral in the 1950s at the very start of the space race with the former Soviet Union. My father Clyde, mother Betty, and brother Robert had arrived at the spaceport area several months before I did, and my father was already working at there. He was educated as a structural designer in the former steel capital of Pittsburgh, Pa., which made him much sought after in the fledgling space program. His first assignments were to assist in the design and erection of the important steel missile-service towers. Each missile under development required a service tower, and the Cold War was actually hot and heavy in the development of IRBMs and ICBMs by the Soviet Union and the U.S.

PH: What about UFOs and the rockets that were launched? What do you know about this? He looked across the table and stared for a moment.

CM: Well, Paola, upon my arrival here, I was more than a steel designer. My associates were oblivious concerning my U.S. Navy ONI (Office of Naval Intelligence) background and my connection with the National Investigations Committee on Aerial Phenomena (NICAP) in Washington, D.C. I'm certain you realize that it was the leading scientific civilian investigation agency concerned with alien visits to Earth at that time.

PH: Did its director, Maj. Donald E. Keyhoe assign you to the Cape?

CM: Yes, I was an associate of the major, his associate director, Dick Hall, Stuart Nixon and others. Yes, he assigned me the responsibility to create the first (and only) NICAP subcommittee at Cape Canaveral. He did not send me to the launch base. Paola, I also served a two-year assignment as the Assistant Flor-

ida State Director of the Mutual UFO Network (MUFON) and created and directed their investigations unit at Kennedy Space Center in the early 1990s. I don't believe anyone else has ever served as director of a NICAP or MUFON Unit at KSC since. At first, I was hesitant to accept such a NICAP responsibility because I realized it was possibly going to cause conflict with my aerospace assignments and the top-secrecy level the other members of such a unit would be under regarding our various Cape assignments. The Cape was a highly secured USAF Base, and in other areas, the U.S. Navy and U.S. Army had authority at their development launch pads. I did specifically ask that Major Kehoe or his staff not disclose any of my Unit members in any documents, books, newsletters, reports, etc. He agreed and only mentioned our Unit-3 once in his book, *Aliens from Space*. The book was published in the early 1970s. The word, UFO was a no-no at the Cape. Later my NICAP, APRO and eventual MUFON Unit involvement did come back to haunt me.

PH: It's obvious that you were taking a big chance that your career could be shortened by a connection with NICAP.

CM: Absolutely. It eventually destroyed my career in 1992.

PH: What happened?

CM: I was at that time assigned to a top-secret area on the fourth floor of the LCC (Launch Control Center) building and responsible, with about six other team members, to monitor all activities with the space-shuttle fleet and other special orbital activities. We heard and saw everything that happened in orbit. I experienced incidents that have never been released. My being a member of the team educated in astronomy and aware of UFO mysteries made me a rare expert in LCC. I was there during the

STS-48URAS mission that has gained much notice due to swift and strange objects that were filmed leaving the atmosphere of the Earth. Many within the ranks of NASA and some outside those ranks have been quoted as saying the objects were nothing but ice particles. I tell you here and now, Paola—ice they were not.

PH: What were they, Clark?

CM: Let's just say that they were not ice crystals for now. OK? I'll add one note. Have you ever heard of ice crystals travelling 70,000 to 100,000 miles per hour? Or ice crystals escaping the launch of SDI weapons which were attempting to destroy the ice crystals?

This was a pretty amazing statement from a credible witness. What else did Clark know? We left our lunch stop at the center and began a tour of the full-scale field of rockets on display. Clark made comments about them and told me about his involvement with each one of the huge rockets. The Saturn 1-B, the Atlas Mercury, Explorer 1 Redstone, Jupiter C, Titan Gemini, Thor Delta, etc.

CM: I have observed or worked on every space program that the U.S. had developed, including the International Space Station now in orbit. I believe I was a part of this history.

PH: What other UFO incidents were you involved with here?

CM: We had several occur during the early days, up until I left the base in 1992. One that was very impressive to me was when an object was hovering at a significant altitude almost over a Saturn rocket that was in its last few minutes of countdown. I and many other space workers saw it as plain as day. It appeared to be a globe or saucer. The size was impossible to determine because there was no known object of that size for comparison near it. I called the Patrick Air Force Base Weather Station at Cape Canaveral, which was the weather control office for such a launch. The USAF officer said they were tracking no unknown objects in the vicinity of the launch. I was a bit puzzled, because it was obviously there. As the Saturn-1 reached "T minus 0" in its count down, it ignited and roared off launch pad 34. The object disappeared almost instantly. Where it went and what it was remained a mystery. All I can say was it was in the sky above the Cape and it just vanished. Was it alien? Was it a U.S. secret weapons system? We were not able to determine it. But it was there! In the early 1960s, the U.S. Navy was testing their Polaris IRBM that would later be placed aboard nuclear submarines. One was launched, and as it was rising on its plume of white solid-fuel vapor, a disc-shaped object of unknown origin was picked up by the telescopic tracking systems flying alongside the Polaris, as it headed downrange. I spoke with several theodelite-tracking personnel following the incident, and they verified the fact that it was tracked and observed It was not their imagination. It was real!

In June 2001, Clark told me a few other stories, including one incredible sighting experience he had had, but he asked me not to disclose these, because he is saving them for a book that he is passionate about. He desires to describe much more and set the record straight. Like most of the military and intelligence people I interviewed, Clark is extremely patriotic, extremely proud of his NASA service, and he loves his country. But he knows "We are not alone," and he invites the reader to see his graphically beautiful website. While I was in Florida I noticed that NASA was really pushing to go to Mars. I would so wanted to believe that it was going to be for "exploration purposes," but Cold War history shows us that most space exploration was—and continues to be—done for military purposes. I think a great deal will also be done for commercial purposes too; hence NASA's marketing of space.

Chapter 17

NASA, Mars and Underground Bases

Richard Hoagland

"To boldly go where someone has gone before!"

http://enterprisemission.com

One of the main disclosure films to come out—and which had a decidedly longer run in Europe than in the U.S.—was Brian DePalma's film *Mission to Mars*. It was relegated to second-rate theaters in the states and not taken very seriously. However, it should have been taken seriously, because it included the research of Richard Hoagland, who was very good friends with MIT researcher Bruce De Palma, director Brian's brother, who died of cancer, I believe. It is amazing to me how the efforts to discredit and ridicule controversial theories are so common in our culture. In Europe many people discussed this popular film.

I never intended to include Mars in my book, but when I was in Roswell in July 1998, I kept seeing the Hoagland's works at the UFO Museum's bookstore. The cashier behind the counter told me Hoagland had just moved to Albuquerque, and she only had his FAX number. I was leaving, having covered the conferences and completed interviews with Robert Dean (see page 16), Clifford Stone (see page 72), Peter Gersten, Stanton Friedman and the Roswell crew. I had a spare hour before flying back to Colorado, so I FAXed Hoagland, expecting no response.

As I was packing, I received a call from Hoagland's assistant Jackson Ellis, who said that I had to change my travel plans because Richard wanted to see me. Jackson would pick me up in a green car, if I sat on my luggage outside of the Albuquerque airport. My fellow journalists thought I was crazy, trusting a total stranger to pick me up and take me to La Placitas in the middle of nowhere. I had just done a stressful interview with Clifford Stone, and I felt paranoid—too many James Bond movies, I guess. I did not know then that my adventures—including an unexpected trip to the hospital with Richard Boylan (see page 48)— would be worse

Did I go? Yes! And soon Jackson drove up in a green car and took me to an A-frame in the mountains, where a very distinguished, gray-haired gentleman opened the door and greeted me with, "Do you know why you are here?"

I replied, "No."

He continued, "It is because my psychic friend from New Jersey said someone from Rome would drop by, and then came your FAX!"

I was pretty much in shock, since neither Hoagland nor Mars were in my plans, but only later did I realize that they turned out to be a vital part of the total picture, as anyone who has seriously studied this phenomenon can tell you.

The key is the Cydonia-Egypt connection and the sacred geometry that lies there and probably throughout the Cosmos. Hoagland maintains that NASA knows this and covers it up, as do most Egyptologists, who hide the true secrets of that mysterious part of the world. I can see why there would be a secret conspiracy about Egypt, because the real story would shake the very foundation of our planet's history. The film *Stargate* included the notion of a dimensional portal to other realms, which is an important clue. The Egyptians had an amazing knowledge of the Cosmos and the supposed after-life and what may seem like myth to many may indeed be fact! In my recommended books (see page 225) there is much to be learned, if the reader can weed out the fact from the fiction and disinformation intended to confuse us! Astrological and metaphysical aspects of Egypt are key ideas in the unraveling of the onion to get to the core of truth—a metaphor often used by Dr. Michael Wolf.

In the last several years I have been a personal guest of Richard and his beautiful lady Robin Falkov. Both treat me like one of the family, but invariably the visits become most interesting! Richard is the consummate researcher—he rises at noon and soon becomes absorbed at the computer, looking at images of Mars and teleconferencing with other scientists all over the world until the wee hours of the morning, a time when he can work in silence and total concentration. He usually turns in at 4:00 A.M. Sometimes, we all go out to dinner and then watch the New Mexico pink and blue sunsets. It is there that we often have stimulating conversations.

It was in Richard and Robin's home that we discussed NASA, Carl Sagan and the "Star Trek" connection with Gene Roddenberry. Richard connected me to Roddenberry and Arthur C. Clark, both of whom were present with Carl Sagan and Hoagland at NASA JPL  center when the Mariner was launched to Mars. So why does Richard name his site enterprisemission.com? Why can he see subtleties in the film *Artificial Intelligence*, which I see as just a Pinocchio story? Why does he see the big picture, when I get stuck with just UFOs? Why has he eliminated most noise from his life to dedicate himself to this research? Why does he watch Star Trek, NASA Select Shuttle mission broadcasts, and images of Mars on three different monitors simultaneously?

The answer is that he has been able to successfully synthesize information and connect ideas. He adds fact to science fiction, which he knows is derived from fact. He was there at perhaps the most historic moments of the space program. Someone who worked for NASA and Goddard and who has dedicated himself to science as he has should not be so easily dismissed, but then it is about "who publishes first" isn't it? The in-fighting in the scientific community as well as in UFOlogy is unproductive and merely distracts us from reaching the truth. As David Icke (see page 55) would say in a later interview, "It is separating the raindrop from the ocean that keep us under control." If more people would cooperate—and I have seen this with Richard's research with international scientists—then scientific research would make quantum leaps. He is perhaps the most serious and committed of all the researchers that I have interviewed, despite his having a normal personal life and surviving a heart attack.

Books that Richard suggested I read always play a significant role in my future research, although I never realize it at the time. It is there that I read *Fast Walker* By Jacques Vallée, which could be fictionalized fact and *The Truth shall set You Free* by David Icke, which could be the true story of world manipulation. It is there that I read the work of Andrija Puharich, which sent me in search of Uri Geller. It is there that I read *The Only Planet of Choice* about the entities who supposedly spurred on the New Age. It was there that I read *The Making of 2001: A Space Odyssey* and realized the genius of Clark and Kubrick. In the end, I realized that in New Mexico was a man who had already connected many dots, and it is from him that I learned "not to exclude what I could not understand."

I found that there were a whole group of people in the '70s who influenced each other and Steven Spielberg. One need only to follow Spielberg's tracks—Uri Geller, Stanley Kubrick, and J. Allen Hynek (his technical advisor for *Close Encounters of the Third Kind*)—to see that he began the ball rolling for some kind of acclimation program. This year Spielberg has progressed to the TV series "Taken" ironically always dealing with ultimate contact. Using Richard Hoagland's favorite phrase. "So what does that tell you?"

Well, Richard, it tells me that while I was looking at the books on Mars in that bookstore in Roswell in 1998, some unknown force was giving me a hand in becoming more informed in my research. I needed only to risk getting into a green car!

I hope the reader understands that the following interview was done at a historic moment. Richard had asked listeners on the Art Bell show, where he is a frequent guest, to bombard NASA and TV stations with FAXes to force NASA's cameras to photograph Cydonia again! He succeeded!

July 7, 1998, Albuquerque, N.M.

Paola Harris PH: Why has attendance dropped at the major UFO conferences? I heard the MUFON conference had something like 40, and I just returned from covering Roswell's 1998 UFO conference, and there was very poor attendance there. Why do you think this is happening in UFO Field?

Richard Hoagland RH: Something is changing in UFOlogy, because people at some level know that that's not where it's at.

PH: And I see this with UFOlogists who have become icons in their own right and are so concerned with their books and own images that they haven't passed where that is. They don't progress. What do you think?

RH: What I'm constantly trying to do when we find out something is to push the envelope. As soon as we figure something out, I try to figure out a way to tell the people but not lose them.

PH: Can we add "not scare them" too?

RH: I'm not concerned about "scare." To me "scared" should not even be in the English language. To me, "being fearful" is more alien than the stuff we are dealing with.

PH: Being fearful?

RH: Yeah! To me the art form is to not surpass their ability to comprehend—to encompass it as a possible reality. A lot of what we deal with—to me and you and a lot of other people who are researchers— is commonplace, yet very foreign and alien. It's not something that you will see on CSPAN, or CNN, and because of that, it has to be dealt with in a way that doesn't lose people, but the "fear factor"—I'm not sure that there is that much fear, because the fear is coming from official levels—is propaganda. It is manipulated. At the "grass roots level" it is much more open....

PH: Adults are convinced it is all science fiction, Richard.

RH: But which adults? It comes back to this idea of consciousness that is not bound by age level. There are people who are more aware than other people, and it has nothing to do with race, sex, religion, occupation, or age. It is "individual" signing on the curve. There should be terms like Hynek defined for contact—close encounters of the first kind, second kind, etc.

There needs to be a consciousness factor. Applied to the sociology of this, there needs to be some way to qualify the level of people's consciousness in their appreciation and approach to the subject. It really comes down to *Is there more to reality than we have been told? ...more than we are permitted to understand?* That is what this is all about. And then are a lot of people—more people every day—who are beginning to look around and say, "There is more than this." It is like water in the desert. They are thirsty, so they go to the outlets to find out who's going to give them a drink of water from that well and who is going to fill that thirst.

PH: So the strategy is to be in touch with this, so that people...

RH: ...can democratically appreciate this. What we (the Enterprise Mission) are doing is by the numbers, by the book, by a democratic process. This is not experiential. Experiential things are very private. They cannot be shared. What we need to do—I think—for the science, physics, psychology, and politics of this, is to create a common set of experiences that can be shared. And that means that you've got to go by a process that is available to everybody and which does not require that I tell you about my secret UFO experience late last Thursday night during an eclipse. That is irrelevant. But what I do talk and write about and present are things that anyone can duplicate and follow—things that they can share because they are experiences common to the whole of humanity.

PH: OK. Let's talk about a few.

RH: OK. Fifteen years ago, when I started looking at these pictures from NASA, what snagged me, what caught my attention was the eerie similarity—when you are looking down from the orbit—between the ruins of Cydonia on Mars and Egypt. Now that was a subjective emotional response. It just *looked* like Egypt. Now we have all kinds of numbers, math, graphs and equations that say on some level, it is Egypt or Egypt is a reflection of it.

My dear friend, Graham Hancock wrote a whole book called *The Mars Mystery* that takes off into the sunset expanding on what we had done, which is exactly the way the process should work.

There was a Russian, Vladimir Yvinsky, who did work on Cydonia simultaneous with our work back in '83. He called the face on mars "The Martian Sphinx." I eventually discovered his work in *Russian Life*. Now we know that it is more than a metaphor. The epitome of the Egyptian side of Mars—Cydonia—is that there is a dual message. The message of Egypt was that the Sphinx is hominid and feline. It was man, woman and cat. We now know —from the latest pictures of Cydonia taken by Mike Maitland's "little camera" on our Mars Surveyor—that the Martian Sphinx is man or a woman and cat. Now it's on two different worlds separated by 35 million miles, the closest approach. But in terms of the math of the locations on these two separate worlds, the geography—the geodesy of the two latitudes—is linked through this very particular geometry that we decoded again through Cydonia.

PH: Who is we?

RH: The Enterprise Mission—a whole bunch of people who are involved with the Enterprise Mission. We have experts, geolomorphologists, artists, photographic experts, cartographers. This is a very eclectic and diverse group of generalists who have an expertise with the ability to look over and say "Oh, what's going on over there is relevant to what I'm doing over here."

PH: Do you have NASA's cooperation?

RH: Of course not! Just the opposite, and as Graham Hancock said, "NASA's role is to suppress, lie, cheat, and keep us from knowing this," and he was courageous enough to simply stand up as a foreign corespondent and say this on stage in Albuquerque two weeks ago. And I've said it in various other ways, and I don't say it's all of NASA. I say it is a small, select group in the middle of this republic who have abrogated to themselves the absolute right to decide what our reality is, and no one else gives a damn, no one else should know, no one else counts. And my thesis is: "That's wrong! That's not the Constitution. That's not what I grew up with, and I will do everything I can and have been attempting to do to change that."

So NASA certainly is not in our camp. Now the honest part of NASA after the new photos of Cydonia is in a dither. Our sources are telling us that there is a veritable war going on inside the halls of NASA—in Washington, at NASA Ames, at NASA Goddard, at NASA JPL in Houston—because the honest people that thought that this was all nonsense are going "Oh, shit!" and they are at war with the guys attempting to suppress this. They say "Are you out of your mind? Are you crazy?" and there is a huge internal fight within the system, Because on some deep level—and this does bring in the concept of intuition—we kind of know, as a culture, where we need to be going, apart from the uptight suppressors who do not want us to go there. We, as a culture, at some level of the meaning of this experience—the United States of America—is to "boldly go where someone has gone before."

PH: You have just changed that.

RH: Of course. I was responsible, along with the help of 400,000 Star Trek fans, for naming the first space shuttle "The Enterprise." Of course: To boldly go where someone has gone before. That's what Cydonia is telling us. That is the motto of our Enterprise Mission. Very deliberately! Because when you look at these pictures, it is obvious that we're not the first. Someone was there! The point is that there are a lot of threads coming together. It's kind of like that old Mark Twain quote, "When the steamboat time, you steam. Well, it is steamboat time." It is time for this culture to get in synch, to explore the future which is really its past. This is where we are certainly going. This is the ultimate message of Cydonia. This is where we are all eventually going to wind up. We are looking at ourselves....

The following picture is of the Mars surface near a crater. Notice how perfectly shaped the object is. How about its obvious symmetry?

A PORTION OF NASA FRAME AB108505, SHOWING A POSSIBLE ANCIENT CRAFT POISED ON A CLIFF

July 23, 2000, Placitas, N.M.

PH: That UFO picture on Mars though—were you the only one who saw that UFO, and it is an artificial metallic subject?

RH: It was strategically placed in the photo, so...someone knew what photo to take. It seems to be a metallic structure. A third of the rim is over the edge of that cliff, which is approximately a mile above the ground level and a mile below the rim of this canyon, and it seems to be on a platform.

PH: Are you saying that this craft might be some kind of tourist facility?

RH: Yes. They would need something with big windows that would take people slowly so they could see these incredible canyons. It fits that model perfectly, and that's where it's parked. You can see the stuff falling out its window, if only you know how to interpret what you are seeing in the images. I'll show you these images—the close-ups—and I will show you the debris streams falling out the windows, which indicate that these things are rusting, like the *Titanic*, where things were corroding and sinking into the abyss. Well, with the atmosphere *on Mars*, there is not a lot to corrode right now. The primary corrosive agent is sand storms. I think it is pretty well preserved because it is sitting up there on a canyon, which is like a dead end, where the wind can't really get going. There is less abrasion, less sandblasting. You don't have much oxygen in the atmosphere of Mars. However, whatever rusting took place before the atmosphere disappeared, and now you have very slow degradation. So the craft still looks old. It does not look new. Superficially it looks new because it is pristine. The form is an oval. It is symmetrical. And yet there are people who keep seeing a crater. They are blind. There are people who are emotionally unable to get closer. They can't go there mentally.

PH: Is there somebody besides you "going there" mentally? Does NASA know?

RH: If you look at the odds of that picture being taken and where it is in the frame, somebody had to know where it is. The picture is so tiny and the area is so big, that Malin had no way to know where to take it. He was either told "just take the picture of these coordinates" or he was told exactly what he was looking for, and they put it out with no comment. It's all a game. NASA is in it for something else than what anyone will ever believe.

PH: Are you having success disclosing this? So many like Dr. Steven Greer have tried.

RH: The name of the game is who's published first.

PH: Who talks about it first?

RH: No, not who talks about it, but who publishes first.

PH: I understand.

RH: Dr. Greer during the Disclosure process revealed secret Pentagon sources who didn't know what to do about it. They are just part of the inner "in crowd," but they are not running anything anymore—not the important stuff.

PH: But nobody who is involved in the important stuff has a "need to know," from what I understand. It is the peripheral people who know. Perhaps it is better that they don't tell us. "You can't deny what you don't know." Is that how this works?

RH: Yes! So we are living under this enormous clouded hypocrisy so that the left hand doesn't know what the right hand is doing.

PH: Absolutely true!

RH: The big problem dealing with people who have no outside interests is that when they are totally sealed off from any outside input they become totally weird. They become infallible. They become their own universe. They make stupid mistakes and don't even realize it, because they are not getting any outside critique—if no one says, "Come on, that's crazy!" That is the big danger. It's not that they start out with evil ideas; it is just that they just don't have any new blood to give them a fresh perspective.

PH: That makes sense. What you are telling me is logical, but does it also turn out that they may become a secret society of some kind, a very restricted circle of people?

RH: Exactly! A very restricted source of new analysis and new information. And if they are making "world-shaking" decisions, they will affect all of us. And you've got a bunch of doddering old fools who don't know how to interpret what they've got, because it has been just handed down to them over and over again for so long. So we are all in trouble—not because they are evil—but because they are fallible like any other human beings.

In the real world, the way we handle these big decisions is that you get a lot of people looking at this; you get a lot of different viewpoints. But they keep talking about the isolation of the President, how he doesn't get enough input. The biggest problem is "not enough input." Well, these people have set up a system so there is never enough input, and if it's handed down as a legacy from generation to generation—selected priest-hoods—they have no outside input. So it means they're operating—if the situation has changed, and it has markedly—on information centuries old, if not thousands of years old, as dogma. That means we are in real trouble.

PH: Have some of these people secretly called you and asked for input?

RH: Who knows? I get people calling me all the time. Who knows who they are? I was hoping, by being very visible, that somebody would get curi-ous as to how we "know what we know" and engage in a kind of a secret dialogue and just get our ideas.

PH: In other words a "deep throat" kind of thing?

RH: In reverse. But there have been people who have called me over the years and "picked my brain," that sort of thing, and I'm hoping that some of them are connected with somebody who will do something.

PH: That is very altruistic!

RH: Look, I live on this planet, too.

PH: You don't know how many people support you outside this country. Your work has been discussed at USAC in Italy, an intellectual group of UFO enthusiasts comprised mainly of scientists who must have been "Buck Rogers" fans in their younger days. They do this as a hobby and remain home with their computers and put "two and two" together. They are computer programmers, university professors and even a meteorologist. Some work in the archives. They do not ridicule this material in Italy—no alien costumes with antennae. It is darn serious!

RH: How do they support it?

PH: They don't. They have other jobs, but in this club they look at your work and keep track of every single bit of it and add their own conclusions. There is no language barrier. English is the universal language of tech-nology. All software programs are in English. They run up to me at con-ferences and say, "We have been following Richard Hoagland's work. He is absolutely right on!" They wonder how safe it is for you to do this. They see it as imminently dangerous.

RH: Well, I think visibility is the major key.

PH: I am telling you that there are a nucleus of credible people in Italy who support your work. We have a space agency too in Italy.

RH: Did you follow what we were discussing on enterprisemission.com in terms of the Italian tethered satellite? About this whole shuttle experi-ment where they unwound this whole 12-kilometer-long cable, and it had this Italian beach-ball-shaped spacecraft at the end of it, and suddenly something broke the tether, and I wrote a whole bunch of stuff about "how" and "why" and how the physics interfered. They should follow that, because that is their own satellite.

PH: You have never had the desire to speak in Europe. I know we have invited you. Why don't you travel abroad? They are really into it!

RH: But the leverage is here. Unless we break the logjam here, nothing is going to change. This government—or the secret government really—is what's sitting in the middle of the "runway," preventing anything from happening. Unless it is changed here, it isn't going to change anywhere else. You can have umpteen conferences, and nothing will happen. We actually did something really cool. The question is, "Does anybody take it seriously?" You have to look at the timing of events. NASA has lost two space craft in the last two months. The Orbiter and the Lander. I go on "Art Bell" and I basically say that I think it is a put-up job, that there is something really bizarre about this. Who cannot translate feet to centimeters? These are adults!

PH: Thank you, Richard.

Chapter 18

NASA, Mars and Underground Bases

Dr. Richard Sauder

Dr. Richard Sauder is a good researcher and a most willing protagonist in the disclosure process. Although I had never met him personally, I had heard that he is one of the best researchers in the field, having worked for some very prominent figures. Dr. Sauder represents those behind the scenes from academia who are able to skillfully access data and analyze it successfully enough to put together many pieces to this cosmic puzzle. Sauder told me that much of what he writes about is in the public domain. It just takes skill to find it and analyze it. I first interviewed him in 1998 about his book *Underground Bases and Tunnels*, which gave us much sought-after information about the locations of the underground bases such as Area 51 near Groom Lake, Nev., and Dulce base, N.M., where some of these mysterious black projects originated. Since then he has written *Underwater Bases*, which completes the picture and lets us understand just how widespread the global tunneling network is. Richard is always very willing to be interviewed, but I find him very knowledgeable about all aspects of the UFO phenomenon. He is very spiritual, as is evidenced in *Kundalini Tales* where he talks about his own spiritual evolution via meditation.

Since I decided to include Mars research in this book, I felt it most appropriate to include another interview to complement that of Richard Hoagland. I interviewed Dr. Sauder by telephone about the artificial structures on Mars and NASA's involvement in the cover-up.

telephone, July 18, 2000

Paola Harris (PH): What got you interested in Mars, going from your first book? Why did you go from something like tunneling to Mars?

Richard Sauder (RS): Since I was five years old, I have had the firm conviction that when I was 45 years old, in the year 2000, I would go to Mars. I'm pretty sure how I got that idea. I grew up in Tidewater, Virginia, and, at that time, the Mercury astronauts were training there at the Langley Air Force base, as they had a choice facility for astronauts there in the '50s. My father was a newspaper photographer and knew these astronauts personally by name, because he would go out and take pictures of them. He also knew where two or three of them lived, not far from where we did. I remember well, as a young boy, maybe five years old, going for a Sunday drive past these astronauts' houses. And I was very impressed by that, as any young child would be. And, so, there was all of this excitement, as you may remember, back at that time. It was when the space era was still young, when the first astronauts were just training to go up. It was a very exciting time.

And, of course, you can imagine how this influenced a young boy's imagination about the blasting up into outer space. It really fired up my imagination then, and I was quite sure that I would go to Mars in 2000. Well, this year has come, and I'm still earth-bound, but if my body, as we speak, is not physically on Mars, I certainly cast my gaze on the Martian surface through the 27,500 photographs that have appeared on the Internet this summer.

PH: Do you do any remote viewing?

RS: No. I haven't done any remote viewing of Mars. I am not really a remote viewer, although I have had many experiences that might be characterized as paranormal. And I had a very vivid component that is similar to remote viewing.

PH: I downloaded your top 10 pictures from your web site.[1] Do you have an intuitive feeling of what they are? Are they artificial, for sure?

RS: I can't say for sure. On some of them I have an intuitive feeling—informed by what I perceive—that there is possible evidence of artificiality. I have no firm evidence that there are artificial structures on Mars, either ancient

1. *http://www.rense.com/general2/saudmars.htm* This is Jeff Rense's site, where the top 10 photos may be seen. At the time of publication, Dr. Sauder's web site was anomalously missing in action.

or contemporary. But I don't rule out the possibilities. So, when I look at photos of Mars, I keep an open mind. I don't go in with a set of preconceptions saying that we definitely will find life there or, on the other hand, that we definitely will not. The evidence will speak for itself!

By the same token, I don't say either that I definitely will see or definitely will not see evidence of artificial structures on Mars. I try to keep my eyes open and look at the Mars photos and see what shakes out, what falls out. What is there? What reveals itself to me? How does it unfold as I observe the image?"

PH: What is the strangest thing that you've seen there?

RS: The strangest thing that I believe I have seen is not so much strange as it is enigmatic. I would make that distinction. And that is this class of features that are ripple-like, dunelike, ridgelike, or damlike. You've seen them.

PH: Yes, I have.

RS: You've seen them marching in orderly rows across the bottoms, of these rills, these canyons, and ancient river beds. There are many of them, mile after mile of them. On the one hand, you can make the argument that they are a purely natural part of the topography, that they are nothing more, nor less than natural sand dunes. On the other hand, you can say, yes, but when you look at other photos of Mars, you do see single sand dunes marching across the surface. Those other fields of sand dunes do not have the orderly, tidy, regular appearance that the other ones do, that are on the bottoms of the rills, the canyons, the ancient river beds. So you can say, on the one hand, that they could be natural sand dunes, but, on the other hand, because of their regularity, their ordered appearance, and the very tidy type of arrangement that they have, it raises the question of a certain nature.

The question: Could they possibly have been constructed? And, if they had been constructed, of course, the following question is, by whom or by what? And, also, there is a related question: If they were constructed, and, indeed, are not just purely natural features, such as sand dunes, then might they, perhaps, have been constructed by themselves, or might there be some kind of living organism? And I don't know that I want to keep those questions open in the absence of any solid evidence that would say how these are constructed structures.

PH: Is your feeling that it could possibly have been done by "human beings" at some given point?

RS: Yeah. I want to say that in the case of these things in the bottoms of the rills and canyons, I'm inclined to say no. And for this reason: There is weather on Mars—winds, sandstorms, etc., so I believe that if it had been done by terrestrial humans, in antiquity or in remote antiquity, by this time, the erosion process would have blown them all away.

PH: So, if I understand you correctly, what you are saying is that because they seem to be intact, then whatever is there is there.

RS: Yeah. Whatever is there is fairly new or recent, on a geological time scale. It's a contemporary phenomenon.

PH: Now, the other thing that you noticed—and I took a few notes on the pictures that you have on your web site—is that you seem to think that some of these pictures have been altered, and are manipulated because of the shades of gray or because of the way they look.

RS: Yes, I do. Well, I'd like to say something about the quality of photos. First of all, Malin Space Science Systems (MSSS) have announced that they have put out 27,000+ photos on the Internet. But if you go and actually start looking at them, as I have, you find more and more URLs where there is supposed to be a photo but there is nothing at all, just a red X indicating nothing. There is no image there at all. Then there are other images where the photos are extremely dark and the contrast is very, very bad. And you can make out little or no detail. Or they are totally black, or, in some cases, completely blank. So there is a certain percentage of the photos that are actually not there at all, or they are so degraded that they are actually next to useless.

Now, there are also, beyond that broad class of photos, many photos where the quality of photography is poor. You can make out some detail, but you can't make out fine detail, certainly not enough fine detail like the cameras are capable of resolving.

And the question arises as to why, because the same cameras on other occasions take photos that are extremely clear with very fine detail in which you can make out features with great clarity. And, so, the question is: Why, on some occasions, are the photos so good and so excellent, and then, on other instances, the photos are so bad, so poor, and so degraded? I think this is an issue that is worthy of discussion.

After all, this is a public-policy matter. The missions to Mars are paid for with public dollars. The photos of Mars should be available for public inspection. And remember, too, that there was a long time delay in releasing these photos.

PH: You are right!

RS: It's going on three years, I think. And that raises questions, too, that the technology is there to download the photos virtually in real time—if not in real time, then within a matter of hours or days.

PH: Yes, but, you know, Richard, why that wouldn't be feasible, because, should there be something questionable on a photo, it would need to be confiscated for matters of national security, like all the other photos that had something questionable on them.

RS: Yes. But the long time delay does raise a lot of questions about why the data are being held back so long. And, that why, when they are finally released, so many of the photos—not all of them, to be sure, but many of them, a sizable fraction of them—are either very badly degraded, not as good as they could be, or not as good as other photos taken with the same camera.

PH: When were these photos taken? You said three years ago.

RS: If I recall, it arrived in July 1997.

PH: So, we are seeing some photos of two, three years ago.

RS: Yeah. I think in the latest stuff, some of the photos were going on two years old. And the reason I question the delay is: Why were they holding them back these months, in some cases a year or more? And then when they do put them out, some of them, the links are there and we need to go to the link, and when you go to the link...there's no photo there.

PH: Can you reveal any independent sources that have enlightened you on any of this, without mentioning names?

RS: No, I can't. I have just taken the data that they have presented on the Internet just as anyone can who has a computer and who can access the Internet. I simply go and look at the photos. I do a certain amount of reading on the photo at the web site. And they do provide detail for a few hundred of the photos and some brief, but not detailed, comments about what they think may be going on in the photos.

But, from what I've seen, for more than 90% of the photos, there is no commentary, or virtually no commentary. It's just like, here it is. Here are 20,000 photos. Look at them, and make of them what you will. Or here are 20,000 photos in theory; in practice, a certain percentage are actually bad, blanks, or black, etc. There's a real mixed bag.

PH: It takes a lot of detective work to see what it is. You said you wanted to go to Mars. Well, you almost got your wish, Richard, because, if you saw *Mission to Mars*, you could have been there vicariously. We know, for a fact, that the uniform used in the movie is verifiable. The environment is verifiable. They have a copy of it at the Kennedy Space Center. The whole entire environment is geared towards Mars. They are even doing surveys about Mars with the people that visit the Center. What do you feel is NASA's intention about Mars? Do they think it is the only place we could possibly colonize?

RS: Well, I think Mars is one place that could be terraformed and colonized. I do know from the reading I've done in the popular press that these ideas have been kicked around for some years now, and that NASA and some other agencies do have an interest in doing more investigation of Mars, probably leading up to a manned Mars mission and, perhaps, also a woman's Mars mission sometime within the coming years or within the next decade.

PH: They specifically mentioned the date when I was there at the Kennedy Space Center. They are planning that with public support. Now what do you feel about the movie?

RS: I saw the movie. From an artistic standpoint, I'd say it was about a C+ or a B-, a solid B- grade. But from the standpoint of trying to build a ground swell of support or contribute to creating a public mood where a manned mission to Mars would be politically feasible, it interested me. Of course, they made explicit mention and showed an artificial construction on the surface site (Cydonia), going inside and having a look at it....

PH: Right. I heard that that wasn't part of the deal, though. I heard that director Brian de Palma was supposed to edit that out later but didn't.

RS: Well, maybe. If it were part of the deal, I don't know whether NASA would publicly admit that or not.

PH: No, evidently. The article I read said that it wasn't part of the deal. I was curious about your impression about origins. Does that sit well with you? What about the talk of the DNA manipulation of the human race?

RS: I do know that the origins of the human race on Earth are pretty murky. I've had the traditional Western education. I've gone to university. I've had a couple of semesters of anthropology, physical and social anthropology. I learned about CroMagnon man, *Homo erectus,* the Neanderthals, and all of the other so-called hominid predecessors that we've had.

But I have many questions about the true origins of the human race. The best book I've seen dealing with the early origins of humankind from antiquity is a book by Michael Cremo and Richard Thompson, *The Hidden History of the Human Race.* They amass large bodies of evidence indicating that the human race on Earth goes back millions of years.

There certainly do appear to have been previous cycles of high civilization on Earth going back a long, long time into remote antiquity. And by remote antiquity, I don't mean 5,000 or 10,000 years ago. I mean way back—hundreds of thousands and millions of years ago.

And it appears that civilization on this planet, for whatever reason, goes in waves, from stages of barbarity to technological sophistication and then falling back into barbarity again, the causes for which remain obscure.

PH: What about extraterrestrial help?

RS: I don't know. I've seen enough, I've talked to enough people and I've seen enough inexplicable things in the sky and had enough mind-stretching inner experiences to complement my outer experiences, that I am fully prepared to admit the possibility of other life-forms in the solar system and even right here on Earth, both outer space and inner space. So that, for me, the question of the possible existence of extraterrestrials is something about which I have an open mind.

PH: OK. But I'm talking specifically about ET manipulation of genes and genetic experiments.

RS: I believe that the human race has manipulated its own genetics. We're doing that now, aren't we, with the genetic sciences? And if you read the details of the prophetic utterances of Edgar Cayce while in trance, earlier in the 20th century, he spoke explicitly about tampering with the genetic structure. He doesn't use the terminology in his readings that we have today because genetic science wasn't as developed then as it is today. But he clearly is making explicit allusions to breeding experiments and genetic manipulations that resulted in great harm to many beings in ancient Atlantis many thousands of years ago. Now, I'm not accepting every word of the Cayce readings as gospel truth, but I do believe that it's very possible that, in previous times, the Earth, and the human race, itself, developed a genetic science very similar to the one that's being developed today, and that it was used in a negative way to our mutual detriment.

PH: In other words, I remember a question that I asked you in a previous interview where we were talking about contact abductions, and so forth, and you were saying how this and a lot of other mysterious kinds of things are really more government black ops and humanly done. They're not all ET.

RS: Yes. Many of them are. I don't rule out the extraterrestrial activity. It's just that, by nature, extraterrestrial activity is even harder to investigate and to provide evidence about than terrestrial activity by human actors. I mean—for God's sake—it's very hard to find out what these various government agencies are doing in their clandestine projects and operations they are carrying out. I mean, they are human agencies that are carrying out projects right here on Earth. And it's hard to find out what they're doing. So how much harder is it, feasibly, to discover, what extraterrestrials are doing, who come and go and, if anything, are even more secretive and more stealthy than their terrestrial counterparts.

PH: Right. That's a very good answer. Do you have questions about the Mars Lander?

RS: I do. Because, you have to remember that since the very beginning of the American space program—and I think a lot of this is true of other space programs, too, definitely, of the Russian program— there's been heavy involvement in space policy by the military agencies and the spy agencies. And while they are separate from JPL/NASA/MSSS, the intelligence agencies of the Pentagon, and the separate spy agencies have separate bureaucratic turfs from that of NASA and the Pentagon. Nevertheless, there is some overlap in their respective areas. And many military officers have gone up in NASA spacecraft, and NASA has, from time to time, had clandestine launches of payloads, so there is overlap between the black/clandestine work that various government agencies do, and more—or purportedly more—public open projects that NASA has carried forth over the years. So I definitely think that it's very possible that there are black-ops components of some of the missions that we have seen over the years, including the recent state of the Mars missions.

And just because NASA and the JPL announce, "Oops! You know, it got there, but you know what? Just when it got there, it stopped phoning home. Sorry!" ...just because they trot out press spokesmen who say that, does not, in and of itself, mean it's true. It may be true. But, on the other hand, in recent years, we have seen so many examples of in-your-face-lying from the President on down that I think by now any rational person ought to realize that just because a government agency or official says something, that does not, in and of itself, mean that the statement is 100% true. We can look at the President for exhibit #A in that regard.

PH: Is it possible that there could be two NASAs, for instance? The one that says, "OK, the Mars Lander is not working, and therefore, everybody go home," and the other NASA that's situated in some remote island, or in

Australia or someplace, that is downloading all of the information from the mission…

RS: Like Pine Gap, among other places? There are other satellite facilities around the world. But Pine Gap could certainly be one.

PH: So is it possible?

RS: Yes, I think so. And we have to talk about how the black world operates. There are stealth operations in the black world, black not having anything to do with Africans or people's African ancestry, but black meaning that it's done in the dark, beyond, out of the know of those who are involved.

That world runs cut-out operations, which are operations that have two facets, two aspects. On the one hand, there is a publicly divulged, publicly acknowledged, project that is carried out. On the other hand, in the back room, out of sight, out of the limelight, another project is being carried on that is given no publicity, and it is kept covert or highly secret.

This is quite common. Spy agencies and military agencies carry out projects like this all the time. And I don't at all dismiss the possibility that this is happening here. Now, if it is happening, of course, then it would be very hard to prove that. I have no solid proof that that's happening. I can only say that there have been numerous examples of this in the world. Cut-out operations exist because they've become public knowledge, and these agencies, many intelligence agencies and military agencies, in some cases, operate this way. And so, I think that's a possibility. Now, you'll notice one of the photos that I feature makes reference to a radar-stealth region.[1]

PH: Yes.

RS: You must have seen that photo. It's a lava flow. The lava flow looks like a perfect and natural geological feature to me. I've seen lava flows that resemble it on Earth. And it's not surprising that lava on Mars would look something like lava on the Earth. But what did interest me about that photo was not the image, but the rubric—the caption which makes reference to a radar-stealth region. Now what in the world, does that mean in the Martian context? I don't know. No one has been able to tell us.

PH: The radar-stealth region was put there by the Malin (MSSS) people?

RS: Presumably the MSSS, because they are the ones who are putting the photos on the web.

---

1. http://www.msss.com/moc_gallery/ab1_m04/images/AB102406.html

PH: Why would they ever put that out, if it is so blatant for people to make comments about?

RS: Well, I don't know. Maybe someone wanted to leave a clue. But, of course, radar stealth is a technology the Pentagon uses to conceal war planes. And for many years, during the '80s it was highly classified, and it only became public, I think, in the early '50s

But, here, we have reference to what for many years was a classified military technology, which the Pentagon held very close, in a Martian context. What that means, I don't know. But it surely does raise a question doesn't it?

PH: Yes. For me it raises even more questions as to why it would be put there.

RS: It raises two questions, you're right. Number 1: as to the possible deployment of a very advanced American military technology on Mars, which in itself raises a whole slate of associated questions, a whole slew of associated questions.

PH: OK but why label the photo?

RS: Right. Another question is, if that's the case, then why put it on there?

PH: Why label it? Is it labeled to spread more disinformation, or is it a joke?

RS: I don't know. I doubt it's a joke.

PH: Tell me about Mars and your future plans. Are you putting together another manuscript, and is it mostly the same kind, about underground bases? I noticed that you were also interested in underwater bases, sea bases.

RS: OK. Mars first. What are my feelings about Mars? I have very strong feelings that the American space agencies are not divulging publicly all that they know about Mars, at this point.

I do suspect that there are life-forms on Mars, if only because the evidence of water on Mars is now so clear. And not only water in the past, but water in the present. And what we know about life is that it is very tenacious and resourceful.

And here on Earth, we find organisms—simple to be sure—but living organisms, nonetheless, living and flourishing under great environmental extremes and great depths in the oceans, in the coldest regions of the Antarctic, on the top of Mount Everest, in the driest regions of the Sahara Desert. Everywhere you go on this planet—from the highest height, to the deepest deep, to the hottest place and to the coldest place—we find life. Now, it's interesting that water appears to flow, even today, many places on the surface of Mars—springs gush out of sides of canyons and crater walls. I believe that there probably is life on Mars. I can't prove that, but I strongly suspect that's the case. I believe that NASA and MSSS/JPL probably also have the same strong suspicion, and maybe even have evidence in that regard. I believe also that there may be evidence of advanced life-forms in antiquity on Mars. I believe we may be seeing evidence of that in some of the photos.

PH: Are you talking about the Cydonia site?

RS: I'm not as high on Cydonia as some other researchers are.

PH: The Mayan city, in particular. I'm not talking about the face.

RS: Yeah. I spent a lot of time looking at the Cydonia images, and there is so much else to see on Mars. I think in the case of Cydonia, for many of those features you can say either it's natural on the one hand, or on the other, that it's greatly eroded artificial structure. Now, having said that, the face feature is highly interesting to me. The platform, to my eye, looks strongly artificial. It looks like it was engineered. I may be wrong, but that's the impression that I have when I look at it. I talked to other people about that, and many people get the impression that the platform looks too regular, the base looks too regular, the symmetrical type of beveling that's been done around the sides and the bottom were strong suggestions of being artificially engineered.

Now, in the photo that I looked at, I also see—to my eye—indications, here and there, of artificial features. So I am keeping an open mind as to the possibility of artificial structures on Mars. And I guess that NASA, JPL, and now the MSSS, have also seen features that they believe may indicate possible artificiality.

PH: OK. Now, of future books…

RS: My next book is almost finished. It's not anything like my first book, *Underground Bases and Tunnels*. I have since run across more information, found more documents, talked to more people, read more books, and found more source material that I am incorporating into the text. I hope it will be out later this year or, at the latest, next year sometime.

But it is not a repetition of the first book. It strikes out into new territory and has a great deal of new material.

PH: You only mention one undersea base in your book.

RS: Yes. I devote a good amount of space to that topic in this next book, whose working title is *Underwater Bases*.

PH: That will be very interesting to see. Thank you. This interview has been really wonderful and informative.

The Contact Scenario

Chapter 19

The Contact Scenario

Alex Collier

The Validity Of Witness Testimony

Included in the cosmic soup of the UFO phenomena is the "high strangeness" components of contact and crop formations. Probably 80% of those I have interviewed have had some type of contact. Monsignor Balducci stresses the importance of witness testimony (see page 42). Although I personally have never experienced *contact*, I'd better take heed. I am beginning to believe that we should look at the whole picture  from a different perspective, as now many "experiencers" are also giving first-hand accounts of this phenomenon. I believe some of these people are telling the *truth* here.

Alex Collier's name was given to me first by the Rev. Jean Holmes, whom I greatly respect, at Standing Elk's Star Knowledge Conference. I ignored it then, but later, a young Italian contactee chanced to suggest that I contact him! Since I go largely by instinct, I tracked down Alex Collier in Colorado. He has much to say that has been verified by my previous "nuts-and-bolts" witnesses. In his book *Defending Sacred Ground*, he frequently refers to Richard Hoagland's research, and it is no coincidence that I am researching Hoagland's Mars claims (see page 115). So *someone* must be leading me along this path.

I sat and spoke with Alex Collier for four hours on July 29, 2000. We had breakfast in Boulder, Colo. He is a devoted family man, and I liked him very much. He has an incredible story to tell. He spoke of the Reptilians, and their negative Earthly presence, as David Icke does (see page 55). His book, *Defending Sacred Ground*, is well worth reading!

July 28, 2000

Alex Collier (AC): How did you find me?

Paola Harris (PH): I think that I am a "bridge" that links people worldwide, and I am surprised that I am speaking to more contactees lately, because I have been dealing largely with military and government witnesses in my writings. I was asked to contact you by Rocco Maschitti, who is a young Italian guy who lives on the Adriatic coast of Italy. How could he possibly know of you?

AC: I don't know. I think this information has a life of its own. We get emails from every country in the world—India, China, Russia, even Albania— because a lot of people know there is something else going on, that we are not the only ones. A lot of them have actually seen the metal themselves, seen the crafts, or know somebody who has.

PH: Is your information channeled?

AC: No. I'm very suspicious of 95% of the channeled information.

PH: How did you begin then, as a child?

AC: It's all in the book. It started when I was eight at a family picnic in Michigan. I remember I was lying down in some tall grass and just hiding. I closed my eyes, expecting to be found, and the next thing I know I am lying on a table looking at two men—a short one, who was very old looking, very white skin and on the other side of him was a tall one, a huge man. They were hairless, but they were human in every sense of the word—even their eyes—but their skin was blue. It is because of their star. The frequency of their star is blue. The tall one is "Morenae." That is not his real name, but they are a telepathic race, and they use symbols for names, like mathematics. I knew them. I recognized them. It is hard to explain how I knew them. We are so much more than just this.

PH: Did they tell you anything that you could understand?

AC: Oh, yes! Basically, they had a program in place to re-educate me on who I was, which is one of the first things they did. They put something on my head which looked like a cap. But it had a hole in the center like a donut, and it fit my head. It was a metallic structure. Morenae waved his head over something on the table, and suddenly all these monitors appeared on the wall out of nowhere. They just weren't there before, so they just materialized, and when it was over, they disappeared. One of the monitors was measuring my heartbeat and all my physicality from this one little cap, on the right side. It was like it was reading my mind, because I got to see visually in space what I was thinking. That was very intense!

PH: Really?

AC: It immediately started showing me these scenes. It was like movie clips. And then I knew almost instinctively that it was past lives. They wanted me to know who I was and my relationship to them. They were showing me what was already in my brain in that other portion that we no longer have access to because of DNA alteration.

PH: So they showed you this. What did you do?

AC: They were basically educating me on who I was.

PH: So are you from Andromeda? Is that what they were telling you?

AC: That's right. My soul. They used to have an outpost here. Your soul wasn't born here either. Nobody's soul was born and hatched on Earth. Virtually, all of us have come here in some physical form or another. We have come back, or we have chosen to be back, or we were killed here during some kind of upheaval or a war. There have been tons of wars here. I was very open with my mom for a very short time. After that it scared her big time!

PH: I'm sure!

AC: Because of my relationship with them and the time I spent with them, I was able to hear their thoughts. I used to tune into them and scream "stay away from my head!" because I used to hear their thoughts.

PH: Do you do that now?

AC: Sometimes.

PH: Were there other encounters?

AC: Oh, yeah. There were a lot of others. They would come over the house at night and just take me out of bed.

PH: There has been a lot of discussion about whether it is a "physical taking" or an "astral-body taking." If your mom opens the door, are you still there? For instance, in the case of Michael Wolf, his parents saw him disappear, and he showed up later in the woods.

AC: It is a physical event. My dad experienced it, too. He had the habit of getting up in the middle of the night and getting a little snack. One night, as he turned around, he saw a light in my room. But he said he saw me about six inches off the bed as I was floating down. There was a little light like a Christmas light, flicking across the room, watching over me. Then he felt it looked at him as he opened the door. Then when I was down on the bed, it looked at me and flew out the window. We talked about it in the morning and he said "did you see your friends last night?" I said "Yes," and we never talked about it again.

PH: Does this still happen? Is there a blue light?

AC: There is a beam, like a laser pointer of light blue light that dematerializes all my atoms. What it does, it separates all my atoms and molecules so that I can pull through the light. It is light blue. I go up in the ship and I literally rematerialize.

PH: Do you feel good?

AC: I feel so free. You can't believe it.

PH: No physical problems?

AC: No, I never had any of that, and I don't consider myself an "abductee," and I resent that people classify me as an "abductee."

PH: There is a difference between abduction and contact.

AC: I know that, and you know that. I am willingly part of this process.

PH: If you are not at the intellectual level to accept contact, you will consider it a violation. It is too bad these experiences get "bad press." Was there a feeling that you had something to do and you had better do it and you had agreed to do it before you were born? Are we talking *mission* here?

AC: According to the A's, we—everyone on this planet—are genetic royalty, and it has nothing to do with where we are on a soul level. People confuse the two. It is like people don't listen as well as they hear. They say we are genetic royalty because we display in our genetics the subtotal of 22 different races. Many different races have been here, over millions and millions of years. They have genetically tampered with us, left us, and ended up mating with us while they were here.

PH: What does this mean?

AC: Some of us have chosen to be here at this time because the only way to make any real serious change here without direct intervention would be for some of their kind to come into the physical body and effect change as part of the race.

PH: We are not talking "walk-ins" here, are we?

AC: No.

PH: At what age did you learn all this? How old are you?

AC: I'm 44. By the time I was 16, I had all this information. Everything I had been taught was reality wasn't. At that time, I was then a hell of a football player and a baseball player. It took a lot of years for me to figure this out. To be perfectly honest with you, it wasn't until my son Nicolous was born that I realized what I should do and what I needed to do, and it all fell into place. Now I have an experience, I have a perspective other than Earth, and I'm looking at this planet and I'm saying "you know what? This is an asylum." The "inmates" are running this society. It drives me absolutely nuts, and nobody wants to hear it. I have been talking 11 years now to very small groups because I am a very private person. That is why I try to keep a very low profile. Provide the information and let it have a life of its own, whatever anybody has to do with it. I am not here to save the Earth, because I can't. It is not my choice. It is everybody's individual choice, and no one is coming to save us—not Christ, not Krishna. God helps those who help themselves. "These things I do, ye shall do greater, if ye have faith."

PH: Did the beings actually take you to their planet or to a ship?

AC: I was on a ship, and I had been taken to another ship, and I spent three months with them, but in Earth time I was gone 18 minutes because they don't have time.

PH: Was the ship big?

AC: They are 900 miles square and located just outside the asteroid belt. There are different races that they call the Consortium who are here, trying to figure out how to help us without disempowering us, and that's the trick. "How do we intervene without disempowering these people and without making them worship us?"

PH: Does this make you very dangerous because of this information?

AC: They told me to take my site down. I did. I think that the rogue government is scared, really, really scared. They cut a deal with one group. They could not trust them, but they did anyway. And now they have totally lost control of the situation.

PH: Who is the group that they cut a deal with?

AC: It is not just one, it is a consortium as well. Zeta-1 and Zeta-2 Greys, Sirius-B Humanoids, Lyrans, Draconians (otherwise known as Reptilian races, Regressives, or Negatives from Orion), a group who controls some Zeta-2 Greys, others from Rigel and Capella systems. It is the Regressives who have a negative agenda. They are controlling the situation. The Andromedans, Pleiadeans, and Zeta Reticulan Greys are waiting to see what we do and are generally positive races.

PH: The Nordics...?

AC: The ones on our planet are genetically modified. The Nordics are clones and are run by computers. They are not actually living souls. Here is the thing: The clones are enough aware that they exist, but they know that when they die it is over. It is like the movie *Blade Runner*. That is why the Greys are trying to genetically mix. According to the Andromedans, the third density will eventually implode and will cease to exist here, and much of the third density is going to be raised in frequency, and that which cannot be raised in frequency—or chooses not to—is basically going to compress itself, go through a black hole and create another space in which to continue to evolve. This is the natural progression. Apparently all this is supposed to happen between now and December 30, 2013.

PH: The end of the Mayan Calendar?

AC: Now these other races that are not real and don't have a "soul" realize that this is going to happen, because they are very scientific, but they can't make this leap because they don't have a soul. Now what is "soul"? The point of the Andromedans is that the "soul" is essentially a conductor of light—multidimensionally with total self-awareness. We are light!

PH: Do they believe in the collective unconscious or even mention God?

AC: They refer to it as "is-ness," the gods that they refer to. "The Sons of God married the daughters of Earth," and these would be extraterrestrial. There is this intelligence! We use only 15% of our brain matter. That's it! According to the A's we will only understand the universe to this level. That's it. Here we are, trying to understand something that is so infinite that we could not possibly deal with it. Here is what is happening: These races are trying to create "soul," and they think that if they merge with us and create our physicality, they will create soul. Here's the thing: The reason they are so interested in us on Earth, Paola, is that we are *genetic royalty*. Do you understand? That is why they are forcing us to shift. We have an extreme of emotions. We can choose to change frequency. We are amazing!!!

   This conversation then went into discussing different alien races, Earth history and advanced technologies and the "why" and "wherefore" of current UFO sightings, all of which can be found in detail in his book. I suggest that you decide for yourself what rings true by reading the book. I personally have chosen to touch on those points in his book *Defending Sacred Ground* that coincide or have been verified by other interviews I have done in the past.

Chapter 20

The Contact Scenario

Eltjo Haselhoff

I met Eltjo Haselhoff in 1999 at a
UFO Conference (USAC, Centro
Accademico di Studi Ufologici)
in Ferrara, Italy, and since he is
married to an Italian, he can
speak Italian very well without a
translator, so he became a very
popular speaker in Italy on the
subject of crop circles. He is a
charismatic young Dutch gentleman and is a credible speaker,
because he is first and foremost a
scientist who works for Philips
Electronics in Holland.

Eltjo is a dynamic speaker who transmits his enthusiasm and curiosity to whatever audience he addresses, and he illustrates his talk with
images and movies of the grain fields and the genetically altered wheat
stems. This method enables the entire audience to view the crop circle
phenomenon and see exactly how Eltjo professionally studies it. Many
crop formations, by the way, have also appeared in Holland. His new
book, *The Deepening Complexity of Crop Circles: Scientific Research &
Urban Legends*, is essential reading that everyone should digest before
drawing conclusions about the anomalous nature of this phenomenon.
The book is very accessible, but strictly scientifically based and beauti-
fully illustrated.

May 12, 2003

Paola Harris (PH): What is the source of the crop-circle phenomenon?

Eltjo Haselhoff (EH): Good question. I don't know. The simple round circles may be a natural phenomenon. Obviously, a part of them is man-made, by simple mechanical flattening methods. But many crop circles are not made by mechanical flattening, I know that for sure.

PH: How can you be sure they are not made by "mechanical flattening"?

EH: Try flattening a carrot field without leaving imprints or damaging the plants. Try making a circle in a snow-covered field without leaving footprints. Moreover, dramatic biophysical plant alterations have been discovered, and those are not induced by mechanical flattening.

PH: Colin Andrews, another prominent crop circle researcher, says 80% of the crop circles are man-made.

EH: That is 80% of the formations in the south of England—not world-wide. That makes a big difference. Colin reached his conclusion from magnetic anomalies he found in 20% of the investigated formations, and not in the rest. But perhaps these anomalies do not always occur, or they disappear sooner in some cases. Dr. Levengood, for example, finds biophysical anomalies in over 90% of the investigated cases. It's no use speculating about the accuracy of these numbers. We must first try to understand those anomalies better, even if they are found in just *one* single crop circle!

PH: I have spoken to people like Ron Russell and Dr. Simeon Hein, who claim that they have seen human circle makers and know them personally. But I think there is a great deal of proof that says there is also something extraterrestrial here also. Are crop circles made by aliens?

EH: I don't know about any clear evidence supporting the hypothesis that humans make *all* crop circles. But I have spoken with many people who claim they saw how a "flying saucer" created a crop circle, and there are also people who say they communicate with the "circlemakers," who—they say—are extraterrestrial or supernatural beings. The hypothesis is that aliens are making most of them. Although there is no clear proof for this hypothesis, either, it also cannot be refuted. "Who knows?" is all we can say at this point, and more research is needed before we can say something more specific.

PH: Hoaxers say they can bend stalks, that it only depends on the weather conditions, and that it is the actual design that causes the anomaly.

EH: I don't believe in the "bent vs. broken stems" rule. Now *that* is an "urban legend." Your skeptics are right here, you can bend stalks, or otherwise biological effects will do the job for you. Moreover, you can easily find stems that are bent, near their roots, in the standing crop.

PH: What is the best evidence supporting the hoax hypothesis?

EH: For me personally? The fact that I have made crop circles, and that they were declared "genuine" by self-proclaimed researchers [laughs]. It is obvious that some circles are man-made. Just for the fun of it, and for thousands of other reasons. People are capable of many things.

PH: What is the best evidence refuting the hoax hypothesis?

EH: The fact that none of the hoaxers—or anyone else—has ever explained the simple scientific observations, such as structured node lengthening, germination anomalies, and other physiologic anomalies induced in the plants. This is *not* an urban legend. These findings have been published in peer-reviewed scientific literature. Anyone can check it out. You can also verify these experiments yourself, quite easily. It is straightforward to show that the flattening methods, allegedly employed by hoaxers, would never induce these reported findings. If these crop circles are man-made, it is not done with ropes, boards or garden rollers, but with more sophisticated, high-tech equipment.

PH: What about "Doug and Dave"?

EH: [Sighs] I think too much energy has been wasted on Doug and Dave already. Anyway, you should know that a British newspaper offered a cash reward of 10,000 British pounds ($14,000) to anyone who could explain the crop-circle mystery. I think Doug and Dave were convinced that all crop circles were man-made, because they were as ignorant as many others about the true character of the phenomenon. But how could they prove their point? It was clear that just a phone call ("Hello, we are Doug and Dave, and we solved the crop circle mystery—they are all man-made! May we have the money now?") was not enough. So they decided to make some crop circles, fool some people, and get the media involved. Now *that* would prove their point. And it did, as we all know.

PH: Why is southern England the home of the crop-circle phenomenon?

EH: Why is the South Pole the home of the penguins? It's too early for that question. First we need to know *how* crop circles are made. More research will be needed.

PH: Do crop circles also appear in other countries?

EH: Yes, of course! They appear worldwide—in the rest of Europe, the U.S., Canada, Australia, Peru, China, everywhere! Actually, I believe that the best crop circles are the non-British crop circles, even though they are not as intricate and fancy. But in most other countries the phenomenon is not as "polluted" by commercialism, self-proclaimed hoaxers and uneducated skepticism as in England.

PH: What about the eye-witness reports of crop circles forming?

EH: Some say they are made in just a few seconds, by a "ball of light"' hovering above the field. I have good reasons to believe those people, sure.

PH: Why do you believe such a fantastic story? Isn't that unscientific?

EH: Oh boy, I really can't go into details here, but it boils down to the fact that there are very simple observations made in those crop circles, using straightforward scientific methods. In fact, you can find a sort of "fingerprint" in the crop, which corresponds perfectly to the radiation pattern of what scientists call an "electromagnetic point source." In plain English: a "ball of light." I explain it all extensively in my book. It is not hard to understand, but the story is too long to explain in detail here.

PH: Some skeptics say your methods are flawed by experimenter's bias.

EH: I have noticed that scientific work on crop circles is often attacked by other scientists, and—perhaps surprisingly—even more by non-scientists. There is nothing wrong with that, as that is the way science works. But any comment should contain solid arguments. Statements such as: "a method is flawed"—only because the results are remarkable—should not be taken seriously. But of course I'm always open to any serious comments or suggestions, or trivial explanations for my findings—or those of others. Regarding the experimenter's bias, all measurements are done by computers, so there is none.

PH: Why did you write your book?

EH: Because writing a book is a nice thing to do in your spare time, and because I have noticed that there exists a lot of erroneous information about crop circles. Many people think they know what crop circles are— but they don't. When I give lectures on crop circles, people always ask me, "How is it possible that nobody knows about all this?" I guess this book is the answer to that question.

PH: Is there anything more about the book you want to share with us?

EH: I hope people will enjoy reading the book, of course. That is the most important thing. I also hope my book will make people think. Think about who we are, about what we are doing here on Earth, and about what is really important in our lives. When you are confronted with such a big mystery as the crop circle phenomenon, it humbles you and seems to put your personal priorities in a different, and, I believe, a better perspective. If there are reasons for the appearance of crop circles, I think this is certainly one of them.

Chapter 21

The Contact Scenario

Derrel Sims

www.alienhunter.org

One specialization in the study of UFOlogy is that of removing apparently alien implants from people who claim to have been abducted. One of the few experts is Derrel Sims, whom I have known since he was invited by CUN (Centro Ufologico Nazionale) to a conference in 1996 in Italy with Travis Walton. The film *Fire in the Sky* had just been released in Italy, and both men and their wives were present at a sold-out conference in Rome. I was interpreter for the press. And also invited them to my home, which was then near the Colosseum. Later I saw Derrel at the 1997 Roswell anniversary conference. His research would qualify as "Close Encounters of the Second Kind," physical traces that can actually be examined. Although I do not always agree with the negative press given to the "visitors," I admire the investigative method used by Derrel Sims, because he looks for the "hard evidence." At the 2000 Oslo, Norway, conference, Sims said that "the abduction-implant phenomenon presents an enigma. It proves we are in a cocoon. We don't know all the answers yet. Researchers say they have all the answers, but that's just not true." Sims said he has some answers to pieces of a puzzle that is "something so big" that he does not know yet what it all is. He also says, "We have to use science, the medical field, spirituality, all of it—not 'some' of it but—*all of it*." I personally believe that he is correct, at least in his approach.

Jan 29, 2000

Paula Harris (PH): Please tell me about your abduction experience.

Derrel Sims (DS): It was terrifying. It started at four. It ended violently at 17 and lasted 13 harrowing years. It followed me from Midland, Texas, to the mountains and deserts of New Mexico. Many encounters were while I was fully awake and even armed, while hunting.

PH: Sometimes society calls people who are interested in the UFO phenomena "cultists," even researchers and journalists. What do you think?

DS: If a person is not a scientist, is he automatically a "cultist"? I certainly have no interest in cultists (in the intelligence community or otherwise) but *if* someone could "make contact," shouldn't the government be a bit interested in the technique(s) involved? After I went on the Art Bell radio show and spoke on this subject, I obtained 180 hits on my web site from NASA, CIA, NSA, ASA, and a NSA computer located *in the White House*. It makes you wonder who is watching whom. I feel like governments should be accountable to tax payers' inquiries. We are paying for this secrecy. Whatever the UFO phenomenon is, good, bad or something else, this kind of information belongs to the world at large. It should not belong to the U.S., Russia, science, or to an investigator. It is a world-class issue. It is an issue that should be solved once and for all. I am a registered hypnotic anesthesiologist who works full-time in UFO field investigations. I have spoken around the world, because the subject has garnered the attention of doctors, professors and scientists alike. It is not my interest to convince anyone of anything, but to question "any evidence" or the hint of it.

PH: Derrel, I have followed your work for years and you usually work with a team. Do you find it useful for validation, and why?

DS: I work with all sorts of professional people. We now have a special place on our web site for police officers and intelligence agents who are working with us to get their stories out

I have the advantage of being able to see in people the propensity to lie, because I am a graphoanalysis expert and can look at handwriting to see who is telling the truth. I have also assembled what I call the "Dream Team" of cardiovascular surgeons, doctors, scientists and specialists, some of whom come from a skeptical background, so they can be perfectly objective with the evidence and can document it in a scientific way. I have my own ideas of how and why (perhaps) the alien entities do their work. I often use our scientists and professionals to review the findings and evidence to see if I am coming to the correct or close conclusions. A team approach helps me hunt for those who hunted me, and later my son, and others of us.

PH: How did you arrive at studying this particular specialty of research in the UFO phenomenon? What interesting characteristics does it have?

DS: In 1960, I discovered an object that I called an implant, due to a conscious event during my own abductions at age 12. The procedure (if that is what it was) was horrific and painful. This conscious "remembrance" is what propelled me to investigate other people's cases in the late 1980s and do some private outpatient surgeries to confirm or deny my own event as real. The results were unsettling to say the least. Later I was paid to speak at a presentation to 250 surgeons at John Muir Medical Hospital on the subject of "Medical Complications of Alleged Human/Alien Contact: Implants." This was the first and only AMA-sponsored conference in which a UFO investigator presented medical evidence.

Researchers have found that some implants are made from a rare meteoritic material, and they can find you anywhere. It is unusual that 45% of the people I reviewed were of Native American/Celtic background. This may show some genetic manipulation

I have made several predictions:

1) If the object we retrieve from the public surgeries is in fact alien, then the objects will produce no inflammatory response, either chronic or acute, in the surrounding tissue.

2) The area surrounding the objects will also contain tissue not native to that area of the body.

In the first two public surgeries after that presentation, I was proven correct. The reason for this is "I remember" a lot from my own events. This enables me to do things proactively that others only "record" or write books about. I dislike it when anyone says that many people have alien implants. It is patently, provably wrong. In my world travels every year, I see hundreds of X-rays, MRIs, and CAT scans from bewildered people, and 99.9% of these individuals do not have implants—even though a number of these folks have had alien encounters. There is no reason to say folks have implants when they in fact do not. Misidentification of an "implant," psychosomatic, psychogenic and other phenomena can often account for "alien implants" and their "removal" under questionable conditions. There are some folks out there who will slice and dice (not my term, but a surgeon's description of some of the procedures occurring) you for a fee and remove your alleged "implant." Amazingly so, you won't get your evidence back, and you may pay a hefty price for some procedures.

Caveat emptor—let the buyer beware. Please consult professionals before you decide to do this or any other kind of "removals." Then make your decision.

PH: Can you then describe accurately what an alien implant is?

DS: The fact is that no one has ever established a baseline for what an "alien" implant is. No one has even yet to prove what an alien or a UFO is. I hope that my new book exposing and explaining the real implant phenomenon as it historically unfolded will put to rest some of the fringe aspects of this work. Most of what we do here at Saber Enterprises has little to do with implants, compared to the other physical evidence we have and continue to search for. For example, we have found 1-1/2" needle-like objects in people, objects in the skull the size of a life saver (and amusingly, it looks like one), and many other objects we intend to ultimately remove, if this is what the client wants. Currently we are studying the effects of the objects in situ (in the body). I show people slides of physical marks and implants, which are encased with the "wrong kind of nerve cells" in the body and show no signs of inflammatory response. Around these implants nerve propriocepter cells were present—intelligent cells. Ceramic and metal implants are old, almost fifty years old, but the "new" ones are biological implants and will be almost impossible to find. We find central-nervous-system cells around these new biological implants, maybe brain cells, like a mini-brain."

PH: Can you describe the kinds of implants you have helped to remove?

DS: Implant studies, and previous surgeries done prior to Saber's publicized surgeries of August 19, 1995, and my medical team's three surgeries on May 18, 1996, (including the first Milab surgery ever)

  o Surgically removed four objects from two people on Aug. 19, 1995.
  o Testicular implant story: noticed in early 1970s.
  o Occular implant: found in 1992.
  o Knee implant: removed 1988.
  o Jaw implant: removed on May 18, 1996.
  o Spontaneous combustion of brother of implantee.
  o Nasal implant; reported in 1989 by psychologist to me.
  o Ear implant removed in my home by alleged alien presence on an abductee staying with us, 1999.

These are just a few of the objects we have found, but finding objects in abductees doesn't make them alien.

PH: Do objects exist that are alien to the human organism, but not necessarily alien in origin?

DS: Yes. Do we have some we removed? Yes. Were the objects extraterrestrial? If lamellar projections from the Widmanstatten meteorite or the dendrites of the Yanshuang H6 meteorite are extraterrestrial, then the answer is a resounding "Yes!" Do all the surgeries we do suggest that these other objects are all alien? Absolutely not! There is no reason for folks to live in anxiety beyond their existing event-based trauma. I dislike misrepresentation and manufacturing of "evidence" to call something alien implants. It's your money! Do as you please. We do not charge abductees for our surgical, investigative, hypnotic anesthesia therapy, etc., or any other thing related to the UFO phenomena. We are philanthropic in our approach and do not promote anxiety. There is enough to deal with that is often horrific without adding to the burden of those in the throes of these events.

PH: Are we dealing with a real and concrete phenomenon?

DS: If aliens don't exist, then why all the fuss? NASA under the Extraterrestrial Exposure Law (circa 1980s) states that (ostensibly an astronaut) can be fined $5,000, imprisoned, and quarantined if this law is violated.) My question is again: *If there are no aliens, then why the law? Should there be a concern?* I think there is concern.

PH: What unique characteristics of abduction experience have you noticed?

DS: First would be our unique approach in research and development. Second would be our unique findings that are due to our medical setting. (We have a cardiovascular surgeon who heads up our medical work.) Some disturbing reports and evidence shows us that some reports by abductee women of molestations, artificial inseminations, etc., may in fact be true.

PH: Where do you find corroboration for your findings?

DS: I was surprised in San Marino over a year ago to find a physicist, two doctors, and others who confirmed to me that my findings regarding the implant phenomena were in fact correct. The physicist lectured on implants they'd found. He began by saying, "I just want to thank Derrel Sims and his pioneering work in the implant discoveries." Then he went into his brilliant presentation. I was, of course, delighted to hear of their work. I have also spoken in Turkey and in England to big groups.

PH: I am told that *Taken* had a lot of the elements of your research in it.

DS: Both Spielberg's *Taken* and the *X-files* have obvious connections to our research. It is all part of the abduction phenomenon.

PH: I know you are writing a book. What is the title?

DS: *Fluorescence: Looking at Evidence in New Light: From the Invisible to the Visible.*

PH: I know that you were one of the first, if not the first, to find the florescence factor in abductions. Can you explain it?

DS: I discovered that. "Brilliant green florescence" has also become permanent evidence of physical traces on a body, even on cattle, where an alien touched the human or animal. The government also knows this, therefore they send black helicopters and use infrared tracking systems. My research team also uses "infrared" and "black light" to track implants and today human-made implants are injectable with syringes

PH: That is a terrifying scenario, because it suggests that entire populations of people may be implanted and controlled by future governments. What conclusions have you reached on the alien "abduction" phenomenon?

DS: That "they," whoever they are, are vulnerable. They may not be as "advanced" beings as many have thought. They also function like an intelligence community. I know, because that is what I used to function in for a short while. As an abductee for 13 years, I noticed striking similarities between what they do and what we did in the CIA in covert ops.

PH: Do you think we are being observed or monitored from other worlds?

DS: If one looks at the U.S./Canada area from the satellites at night, the entire outline of the continent can be seen by the lighted cities. Did we think no one would notice? No one has expressed a definition of what an "alien" might be. It seems to me, we'd better be finding out what it is that the DSP infrared/ultraviolet and visual-range sensors are picking up. Interestingly enough, I am finding physical evidence findings with these light ranges on some alleged abductees. The DSP satellite system of 18 units, 22,300 orbit miles, is designed to detect the launch of ICBM and test-band monitoring. It is primarily infrared digital, multi-bandwidth, with "special" detectors. So what is a "special event sensor"? These two sensors are quite interesting in that they are made from relatively thick-walled aluminum (and therefore are *not* alpha or beta particle detectors) and are filled with crystals. Some think that these are the sensors uniquely designed to detect "*Fastwalkers,*" or UFOs. If so, the professional UFO chasers are already doing the job they claim doesn't exist.

PH: You have given us food for thought. Thank you.

The Paranormal Factor

Chapter 22

The Paranormal Factor

Ingo Swann

The Parapsychological Connection to The UFO Phenomenon

biomindsuperpowers.com

Most of my work deals with "nuts and bolts" interviews on UFO phenomena, so to completely veer off in this "paranormal" arena is highly unusual for me. It occurs to me now, that on some interdimensional level I am being led there, as I am being led to the "truth." All of us can access this information. It is a matter of quieting our minds, eliminating artificial stimulation—whether drugs or TV, not contaminating our bodies with what we put in them, and simply "looking up" instead of looking down. A special thanks to Israeli psychic Uri Geller and Belgian psychic Pascal Riolo, who tuned me into the strangeness of being "in sync" or "tuned in." It is ignorant to try to explain everything that has strange timing or is synchronistic as "coincidence." Time is a mystery thoughtfully discussed and explored by all those interviewed in this section. Strange timing and cosmic messages give all of us what so many are now calling "the chills."

International Remote Viewing Association (IRVA) Conference

June 14-16, 2002, I attended the 30th year reunion in Austin, Tex., of the original SRI (Stanford Research Institute) research team with government remote viewer Ingo Swann, physicists Hal Puthoff and Russell Targ and archeological remote viewer Stephan Schwartz. It was only at this reunion that I actually met Paul Smith, whose interview I did (see page 168) in 1999. At that time I did not understand what this technique does, how it works, or who the players were.

Remote viewing is about developing our psychic ability and viewing a target in the past or possibly the future. It can be mastered by all and through visible demonstrations, which I personally saw, it can be taught. Like most modern technological advancements, its original purposes were for military intelligence, as explained in detail in the Paul Smith interview. The timeliness of publishing both the Courtney Brown (see page 185) and Paul Smith interviews only comes because I now understand exactly what they are talking about after having been catapulted into this arena by Uri Geller (see page 203). Geller insists that we all possess this ability, and he is right. I watched intensely as ex-government remote viewer Lyn Buchanan taught people to bend forks, spoons and several metals at the psychokinesis party at the conference just by concentrating and yelling *"Bend!"* Although I did not try it, I saw at least 50 people do it over and over again. Under this organized and controlled environment, there were, what most people would have labeled as "strange goings on," but the skills were considered very normal, metal bending being a skill that all can learn with discipline and persistence, and the right technique. But, in the outside world, I overheard young people at the main desk of the Austin Doubletree Inn talk about the strange spoon benders in the ballroom the night before. This demonstrates perfectly the duality of this phenomenon, quite normal but considered "high strangeness." It was Ingo Swann who leaned over to me in the garden where we were sitting with several people and explained, "We all have this ESP programming in all our hard drives, but society does not encourage us to use it. It simply takes training and discipline and persistence." His procedures, those he first developed with CIA and NASA funding are delineated in his book.[1]

Of course neither our society, our governments, nor our institutions would encourage us to use these potential talents, because, besides being a potentially invasive technique, with possible mind control components, it would allow for these powers to access information that, if misused, could possibly be subversive, as well as manipulative. It would mean an *end to lying*!

---

1. *Secrets of Power* Vol. I and III. Ingo Swann Books.

ESP: the Double-edged Sword

It's remarkable that this type of convention could take place in 2002, giving scientific credibility to a skill that a few decades ago was shoved into the area of the occult and witchcraft. With the dawning of the New Age and healing movement, remote viewing is now categorized positively as part of

HISTORIC REUNION: THE SRI PIONEERS:
DR. RUSSELL TARG, INGO SWANN, STEPHAN SCHWARTZ, DR. HAL PUTHOFF

our "human potential." Classes in it are being offered by the same practitioners that were used by the military for intelligence gathering. The interview with Paul Smith (see page 168) explains the personal advantages of learning these techniques to enhance our everyday lives. But it was Courtney Brown (see page 185) who cautioned that the government says that this "must" not enter into the "mainstream" nor must "big money" fund it, otherwise it becomes dangerous.

My stance was to keep a low profile and observe, as this operational method of remote viewing "a target" was demonstrated over and over again. It was an honor to observe the pioneers, SRI's Swann, Targ and Puthoff, mix with the people and explain the history of remote-viewing research in the '70s. Russel Targ, with his sense of humor, said the decision to fund the SRI studies came after Werner von Braun told NASA and the government to "give these guys some money" because he had a psychic grandmother. "That is the basis on which many government decisions are often made—a psychic grandmother," quipped Russell Targ. Amazingly, his speech detailed his personal growth through the scientific study of ESP to a sort of metaphysical conclusion of the love and inter-relatedness principle of a totally connected universe. He was watched over by a fatherly Ingo Swann, who was afraid that Russell would fall off the podium because of his vision problems. Targ, Swann and finally Hal Puthoff, the consummate soft-spoken scientist who knows more than he lets on, forged the way for all this back in 1973. But knowing me, one might ask "Did they mention UFOs?" No, I did!

The Amazing Ingo Swann

"Ingo, is it true that in your spellbinder book *Penetration* you viewed non-human intelligence on the dark side of the moon?"

He answered, "*also* on the light side!"

Ingo also describes in his book *Penetration* being asked to remote view the alien presence, being taken to a possible landing sight under cover and finally identifying an alien while in California. He suggested strongly that the government knows something about this.

In his book he goes into detail about this and insinuates that we were told to stay away because we were invasive to these entities.[1] Today Ingo Swann gives clear messages: "Keep the power in your own hands"; "Access your inner 'ESP hard Drive'"; "Realize all is not what it seems, and we are living in an illusion." He sees humans as "energy-life-conscious-entities usually set in our own local environments."[2] He is very clear that "Societal conditioning flattens knowledge of individual will and dynamism in favor of subservience to societal power artifices."[3]

In conclusion, one thing is for sure, I have shifted my thinking to believe that ESP and these parapsychological events are truly of interest to science and scientists, but for better reasons than that someone "had a psychic grandmother," and I have a gut, intuitive and psychic feeling that someone, if not "big money," is researching this as well as funding it, and "Yes, it is science!" It does not take a genius to realize that if we are dealing with telepathic, interdimensional beings, we must know how to talk with them!

---

1. *Secrets of Power*, p. 53, "Psychic Touchdown on the Moon."
2. *Secrets of Power*, p. 115.
3. *Secrets of Power*, p. 162.

Chapter 23

The Paranormal Factor

Russell Targ

In my opinion Russel Targ has contributed a great deal to science, but he has even more to contribute to philosophy. Targ is a physicist and author who pioneered in the development of the laser and many laser applications. He co-initiated the Stanford Research Institute's

investigation into how the future affects the past, and he has profoundly influenced developments in modern physics such as nonlocality. He is the ideal combination of scientist and metaphysicist, and he is perhaps one of the few with whom I've spoken able to see the big picture. A scientific mystic with thick glasses and a perennial smile and an incredible sense of humor, Russell stands way over six feet. He is an very imposing figure, and if you engage him in conversation, he asks "you" the questions instead of pontificating on his own research findings. I find him one of the most interesting and enigmatic people I know, because he knows much more that he lets on, and he has "connected the dots" within his own research. He is co-author of five books on psychic abilities, most recently, with spiritual healer Jane Katra, *Miracles of Mind: Exploring Nonlocal Consciousness* and spiritual healing, and *The Heart of the Mind: How to*

Experience God Without Belief. He was my special guest at my 2003 Pescara, Italy, conference. He was mystified, after having given some remote-viewing tests to Italian women, as to why they are more psychic than their American counterparts in Silicon Valley, Calif. "Maybe they are more unconditioned by their society and more open to risk," he says.

Paola Harris (PH): I call you a "scientific mystic" because you seem to cross boundaries, cross disciplines and reunite what has become separated. What do the healer, mystic, psychic, and spy all have in common?

Dr. Russell Targ (RT): They are all in touch with our nonlocal (quantum-interconnected) mind and our community of spirit. If we extend our awareness to access information anywhere and in any time period, then past, present, and future are all one.

PH: Can you talk about the purpose of the CIA-sponsored research at SRI?

RT: SRI (Stanford Research Institute) conducted investigations into the human mind's capacity to envision distant places and future events and activities—a capability called "remote viewing." SRI's research was supported by the U.S. government for more than two decades. Its task was to understand psychic abilities, and to gather information about the Soviet Union during the Cold War. I was co-founder with Hal Puthoff of this program, which began in 1972.

PH: Can you talk about the underlying science as it applies to parapsychology, according to the SRI research and its surprising discoveries?

RT: We do not yet know the physics underlying psychic abilities. However, researchers in the field of parapsychology agree on the undeniable observation that it is no more difficult to psychically describe a picture or an event in the future, than it is to describe such a target in the present, when it is hidden from view.[1] It is as though our bodies reside in the familiar four-dimensional geometry of Einstein's space-time, while our consciousness has access to another aspect of this nonlocal geometry that allows us to find a mental path of zero distance to seemingly distant locations. This is how a physicist expresses such an idea, while mystics for the past three millennia tell us from their experience that separation is an illusion—and we are all one in spirit, or consciousness. From such experimentation in many laboratories, it is clear that we significantly

---

1. Dunne, B.J., R. G. Jahn, and R. D. Nelson, "Precognitive Remote Perception," Princeton Engineering Anomalies Research Laboratory (Report). Princeton, N.J., August, 1983.

misapprehend the physical nature of the space-time in which we reside. It is this knowledge, together with our experience, that drives our passion to understand and learn more about the universe and the transformational opportunities offered us.

PH: Can you talk about some of your work with government remote viewing?

RT: In 1974, Hal Puthoff and I carried out a demonstration of psychic abilities for the CIA in which Pat Price, a retired police commissioner, described the contents and activities inside and outside of a secret Soviet weapons laboratory in the far reaches of Siberia, given only the geographical coordinates of latitude and longitude for a reference. (That is, with no on-site cooperation from a person at the target.) This experiment was such a stunning success that physicists Hal and I were forced to undergo a formal Congressional investigation to determine if there had been a breach of National Security. Of course, none was found, and our research into psychic functioning was supported by the government for another 15 years. During these experiments, Pat Price made a sketch to illustrate his mental impressions of a giant gantry crane that he psychically "saw" rolling back and forth over a building at the target site. Later there was a satellite verification of this actual site at Semipalatinsk, Russia.

PH: I know Hal Puthoff and you worked together investigating Uri Geller. When I met you in Vicenza, Italy, in 2002, you were kind enough to tell me that Uri did possess some interesting abilities, but they were difficult to consistently reproduce in a laboratory. Now both you and Uri are saying that we *all* have some of these abilities, if not in Geller's intensity.

RT: We all possess ESP ability that can be enhanced by training, but not necessarily for the purpose of becoming a psychic spy or for doing something as simple as finding your car keys, but rather to know yourself better and maybe heal yourself. In my presentations, I compare the inflow of information that is the hallmark of remote viewing, with the outflow of intention that plays a part in facilitating distant healing, and the stillness of ego surrender, that can arise between these two. Spiritual teachers in ancient times have described paths and practices that a person could follow to achieve health, happiness, and peace of mind. A considerable body of recent research indicates that any kind of spiritual practice is likely to improve one's prognosis for recovering from a serious illness. Many of these approaches to spirituality involve learning to quiet the mind, rather than adhering to a prescribed religious belief. These meditative practices are inherent aspects of Buddhism, Hinduism, mystical

Christianity, Kabalistic Judaism, Sufism, and other mystic paths. What is indicated in the subtext of these teachings is that as one learns to quiet his or her mind, one is likely to encounter psychic-like experiences or perceptions. For example, in the Sutras of Patanjali, the Hindu master tells us that on the way to transcendence we may experience many kinds of amazing visions, such as the ability to see into the distance, or into the future; and the ability to diagnose and cure illnesses. However, we are admonished not to become attached to these abilities—that they are mere phenomena standing as stumbling blocks on the path to enlightenment. In our research, we describe the laboratory evidence for some of these remarkable phenomena of our unbounded consciousness, and their implications for science, mental health, and peace of mind.

PH: Under this aspect, the definition of ESP abilities becomes very spiritually oriented. Have you and healer Jane Katra done much research on this?

RT: In our book *The Heart of the Mind*, Jane and I felt that whenever any one person demonstrates an ability beyond the ordinary, it is an inspiration to the rest of us, as an indication of our immense and still largely undeveloped human potential. Recent research in areas as different as distant healing and quantum physics correlate with the oldest spiritual teachings of the sages of India, who taught that "separation is an illusion." This concept suggests that there is no distance for consciousness, and we have an intuitive inner knowledge that transcends the conceptual limits of time and space. In fact, we now know that information from the future regularly filters into our dreams—one could reasonably say that these precognitive dreams indicate that the future affects our past. That is, our dream tonight may sometimes be caused by an event which we will experience at a later time–strongly violating our ordinary understanding of causality. In research by the authors, who are respectively a physicist and a spiritual healer, we have been exploring how our mind's ability to transcend the limits of space and time is linked to our now well-documented capacity for distant healing.

PH: You are using the scientific method to study the paranormal. What in the past has been in the realm of hocus pocus and alchemy is now part of the overall picture—part of our world, our reality and our dimension—but it has been discounted by conventional science. Can you elaborate on the linking of the scientific and the spiritual in your research?

RT: The scientific and spiritual implications of psychic abilities illuminate our observation that we live in a profoundly interconnected world. The most exciting research in quantum physics today is the investigation of what physicist David Bohm calls quantum-interconnectedness, or nonlocal correlations.[2] It has now been demonstrated repeatedly, in laboratories around the world, that *quanta of light that are emitted in opposite directions from a source at the speed of light, maintain their connection to one another, and that each little photon is affected by what happens to its twin, many kilometers away.*[3] This surprising coherence between distant entities is called nonlocality. In writing on the philosophical implications of nonlocality, physicist Henry Stapp of the University of California at Berkeley states that this quantum connection could be the "most profound discovery in all of science."[4] Psychic abilities and remote viewing are demonstrations of our personal experience with such nonlocal connections in consciousness. Mind-to-mind connections, which transcend our ordinary understanding of space and time, allow us access to expanded awareness, which is entirely consistent with life in a nonlocal world. This connection is what a physicist means by nonlocality. Psychic abilities and remote viewing are demonstrations of our personal experience with such nonlocal connections in consciousness. To the healer, it gives rise to what physician Larry Dossey refers to in his book *Reinventing Medicine*, as Era-III healing of a distant patient through the intentionality of the healer.[5] Our knowledge of these remarkable abilities allows us to awaken each morning in wonder at the fact that our expanded awareness is not limited by either time or space.

PH: Incredible! It is almost the answer to a lot of questions I have always had about paranormal phenomena, of which UFOs are a part. We navigate in a sea of "awareness," and you keep telling me there is no separation.

2. Bohm, D. and B. Hiley, *The Undivided Universe*, London: Routledge, 1993.
3. Freedman, S., and J. Clauser, "Experimental test of local hidden variable theories," *Physical Review Letters*, 28, 1972, 934-941; A. Aspect, *et al.*, "Experimental tests of Bell's inequality using time-varying analyzers," *Physical Review Letters*, 49, 1992, 1804-1907; W. Tittel, J. Brendel, H. Zbinden, and N. Gisin, "Violation of Bell inequalities by photons more than 10 km apart," *Physical Review Letters*, 81 (17), 1998, 3563-3566.
4. Stapp, Henry, in Menas Kafatos and Robert Nadeau, *The Conscious Universe: Parts and Wholes in Physical Reality*, New York: Springer-Verlag, 2000, p. 70.
5. Dossey, Larry, *Reinventing Medicine: Beyond Mind-Body to a New Era of Healing*. Harper-Collins, 1999.

Russell, how can we achieve the ideal conditions to go inside, to do remote viewing, to heal ourselves and to expand our ESP abilities?

RT: Whenever we sit peacefully and quiet our mind, we have an opportunity to experience an oceanic connection with something outside our separate self. To many, that connection is experienced as an overpowering feeling of love, and it may well constitute part of our evolutionary process as a species. This feeling of universal love, without any particular object, is often associated with the realization that we reside within an extended community of spirit enveloping all living beings. Such feelings of unbounded interconnected consciousness have been described by many as an experience of God. The gift of a quiet mind allows us to understand what it means to be in love, like being immersed in loving syrup, as contrasted with being in love with another person. It is possible to reside in love (or gratitude) as a way of life. This experience is the source of the often-heard expression that "God is love," which in an ordinary context is easily dismissed as a simple cliché, or worse, as not even comprehensible.

PH: Being "in Love"! What a beautiful metaphor! Thank you for joining us here at my conference in Pescara, Russell. I believe we all were quite moved by your presentation.

Chapter 24

The Paranormal Factor

Paul Smith

Vice President of International Remote-Viewing Association
Former Government Remote Viewer

www.rviewer.com

Just as I became interested in the paranormal as a piece of the UFO phenomenon, something very interesting happened. As I was walking down the street in Boulder, Colo., I noticed a flyer announcing a lecture by Paul Smith, a retired military and former government remote viewer. I called him in Austin, Tex., and he kindly granted me this interview, which describes in detail the remote-viewing procedure used by the military.

October 11, 1999

Paola Harris (PH): I don't know if you know how I got your name. This summer, as I walked past the Boulder Bookstore I discovered a poster on the window advertising a talk you were giving. It piqued my interest, so I pulled it off.

Paul H. Smith (PS): That must have been after I had spoken there?

PH: Yes. After you had spoken there, in August. What do you do?

PS: I teach people remote viewing. That's my job.

PH: That's become a job now? Is it a spin-off from your military career?

PS: Yeah. I was, of course, in the remote-viewing unit for seven years from 1983 to 1990. I retired [from the Army] in 1996. About three or four months after I got out of the Army, I set up a business teaching people how to remote view. Actually, I have several things going on at once. One of the things I do in order to raise money for my other activities is to teach people to remote view. I also do a fair amount of lecturing. My main goal in doing this is not to make money, but to try to correct the misconceptions in people's minds about what remote viewing is. Unfortunately, some of my former colleagues have fostered some of those misconceptions. Another reason I teach and lecture on the topic is to introduce people to remote viewing who have perhaps not heard of it or don't know much about it. So, my current career with remote viewing is a kind of public outreach. I am also in a graduate program here at the University of Texas working on a Ph.D. in philosophy. This degree and remote viewing sort of cross walk with each other, as they are somewhat related.

PH: Do you make money at private remote-viewing?

PS: Yeah. I just make myself available to people who want to learn how to remote view and...

PH: ...they pay you privately?

PS: Yes. I no longer have any official connection with the government.

PH: Let's get a definition of remote viewing. If you extended the definition, could it be extended to psychic ability?

PS: Yes. Remote viewing is a form of psychic ability. Perhaps, remote viewing is a bit stricter in its meaning, but, nonetheless, it's a part of the psychic domain.

PH: You mentioned that you wanted to change misconceptions people have about remote viewing. You know the magazine I write for is UFO oriented. I've got to tell you what my stance is. I'm not interested in the government cover-up, as I think the government cover-ups are a foregone conclusion. I think that we know that's the way it is, and there is nothing that can be done about that. So, it's not my goal to get any kind of secret information from our interview. I am interested, however, in the Stanford experiments and in Hal Puthoff and Ingo Swann. Those were before you started, weren't they?

PS: Yes. Hal and Ingo got together in 1972. Before '72 they didn't know each other. What happened was that Hal was doing some fundamental physics research for SRI (Stanford Research Institute) and he got interested in tachyon particles, which are theoretical. But if they do exist, they have a potential of going faster than the speed of light, and there is some discussion about them being able to retrograde in time, as well. So, Hal wanted to find out about that, and he'd heard about a guy named Cleve Backster who was doing some experiments with plants. You know, hook up a lie detector to a plant and then cut off a leaf or something and see how it reacted. Cleve thought that maybe there was some way—if that effect was real—some way of using a laser to distress one plant, and then five miles away have a sister plant on a polygraph, and see if there was any effect. And, maybe, if there was, it could be explainable with this tachyon theory.

So he sent a letter to Cleve Backster outlining what he wanted to do. It just so happened that Ingo Swann and Cleve Backster were friends, and while Ingo was over at Cleve's house one day, an errant gust of wind brushed this letter off the desk onto the floor, right in front of him. And Ingo stooped over and picked it up and said, "What's this?" And he read Hal's letter to Cleve and wrote Hal a letter back saying, "Why bother with plants? Why don't we try doing this with human subjects or at least some similar experiments?" Hal agreed. And Ingo went out to SRI and had a very spectacular session on a scientific instrument they were trying to use as a subject. They never did experiment with any plants. They did all of their research from that point on with human subjects. That was how they got started.

PH: But Ingo is exceptionally sensitive.

PS: Well, Ingo says that he is not psychic. What he says, in fact, is that his history suggests that he just sort of stumbled into the psychic arena. He was there in New York working for the U.N. as a translator and interpreter while he was trying to establish his art career. And he just happened to make friends with a bunch of people who were involved in parapsychology research through The American Society of Psychical Research there in New York.

PH: So, in other words, he was working on this idea earlier? He had some idea about this before the two of them joined their research?

PS: What happened was he met these people. He found out what they were doing and they, for a while, were asking if you want to try being a subject, and he'd say, "No, no, no!" But he started reading about it, because he found it interesting. Finally, he agreed to be a subject, but he said there were probably better ways to do this. He proposed some modification of the experiments which amount to, I guess you would call them "pre-remote viewing," or something like that, before they actually refined the process. Those experiments were very successful and got a lot of notoriety. Ingo said it wasn't because he was a gifted subject. It was just because he opened his mind to a new approach and, you know, like any outsider coming in, often times the specialists can't see the forest for the trees, because they are so immersed in what they're doing. An outsider can come in and make one suggestion that changes the whole landscape. That's sort of what happened here. Now, anybody who works with this is bound to develop some capacity, and so that's what Ingo says. He wrote that he's not a gifted psychic; he just had some ideas and a lot of practice.

PH: I understand that. I don't understand Uri Geller, though. Because, you know, I know Uri Geller went to Stanford, and I know he did some pretty amazing things, because I remember hearing him talk in the '80s about his projects.

PS: Well, Geller says one thing, and the people at Stanford say something else. He did some things that impressed Hal, but he was never able to do them under controlled conditions.

PH: OK. [Point of clarification: Geller demonstrated remote-viewing ability in the SRI lab, but failed to demonstrate PK abilities under controlled conditions. —PH]

PS: Hal says that he thinks that Geller has some abilities, but he's just not quite sure about how they manifest, because they, sort of had to do it according to Geller's rules in order for it to work.

PH: I've got to tell you something, though. I took pictures of Uri Geller, and he completely erased my film. I was really upset. The lab called me and said there was radiation all over my film, and they were so sorry.

PS: "We'll replace it for free," right?

PH: Yeah. Exactly. I still have that film, by the way.

PS: When I talk about Uri Geller, people ask me questions about him. My standard response is "I really think he does have abilities, but as with any psi ability, it isn't always readily accessible; you can't always access it for whatever reason." And if you go on the lecture circuit, and you're on the *Tonight Show* or whatever, you've got to perform, you know.

PH: That's right.

PS: And so if it doesn't happen to be working that day, you've got to come up with something that does work.

PH: You got it, now. Exactly. But that's just logical. But getting back to you, how did you get into remote viewing? Were you in the Army, and you volunteered to do this?

PS: Sort of. I was in the Army. I moved to Fort Meade through some rather kind of convoluted circumstances. I didn't originally intend to be there. And it just happened that I moved in next door to Skip Atwater who was the training and operations officer and across the street from one of their newly recruited sources, as well. My quarters were, maybe, a five-minute walk from the office, you know. Of course, I didn't know any of this stuff at the time, as I had been in a Middle East analyst position.

PH: Were you in Vietnam?

PS: No, there at Ft. Meade in Maryland. I had come into another intelligence organization, just to work on Middle East issues.

PH: OK. But you were in intelligence then?

PS: Yes. I had been in the Army for about six years by then. I'd been an Arab linguist and had gone to officer candidate school and various things like that. None of this had anything to do with parapsychology, obviously. So I moved in, and they were, at that time, unbeknownst to me, looking for people with a certain set of criteria, because they had [three] positions to fill. And they were just about to embark on this new training program with Ingo Swann that Ingo called "coordinate remote viewing" back then. They were looking for people who might work, and I moved in. Their criteria were: successful in career, well regarded by their supervisors, and other related characteristics. Normal people, basically average to above average intelligence, that kind of thing. Plus, one other factor they were looking for was someone who was involved in areas that were a little unusual for an Army officer, such as, art, music, creative writing, those kinds of things.

PH: That's very interesting.

PS: Right. They figured an interest is the arts indicated a right-brain propensity, and even though that wouldn't necessarily guarantee the person would be good in their program, that was a screening factor. And they would then give them some evaluations and tests to see if they did come close to what they were looking for. So I moved in, and it turned out I was interested in art, languages, music, and creative writing—all of those areas at once. When they got to know me, the light went on. So they said, "Hmmmmm." And they continued, "Listen! We're in this black program that does some interesting things that we can't tell you about, but we would like to give you some tests to see where you fall, you know. We're recruiting, and if you measure up, we'll offer you the opportunity to volunteer." I said, "Well, OK. What the heck." You know, you're always looking for something interesting when you're in the Army. So, I took the tests and fell within the parameters they were looking for. The tests were basic personality tests. The program leaders were just looking for certain personality traits that research in the past had shown were useful.

PH: Were any of the questions "Had unusual things happened in your childhood?" or "Did you have strange dreams?" or that type of questions?

PS: Yes. There was one test which did ask those kinds of questions, but the goal was not to find out if I had weird things happen to me or if I did strange things. That was just part of the personality profile test.

They gave a lot of different tests. They were all personality and psychological tests. It turned out that I fell within the parameters they were looking for. And so they invited me in, and said, "OK. We are going to take you on, and if you decide not to join the organization, you cannot tell anybody that you ever heard about this!" So, I said, "OK." They said, "We use parapsychological means to conduct intelligence operations against foreign threats. And we want to know if you want to sign up?" And I said, "OK. Where do I sign?" I didn't even have to think about it. You know, once I understood what they were talking about, I knew it was something I wanted to do. But, in anticipation of your next question, up to that point, to my knowledge, I had never had any kind of psychic experience or any kind of near-death experience or out-of-body or any of that stuff. I just had a pretty much normal life.

PH: But, see, you didn't interpret it that way. You told me on the e-mail that when you were young, you were...

PS: ...able to find things. Yes.

PH: You know that I don't believe in coincidences. I do believe that people are sensitive, and that probably your ability to find things could also help you later on.

PS: Oh, yeah. I think that correlation you just made is probably true. I would like to add one other thing, though. I think everybody has that ability. Some people can just, sort of intuitively, tune into it. You know, some people are more aware of it, or, you know, it's more sensible to them.

PH: I agree 100%. Everyone has that ability. And this is a very good thing. This intuitive ability helps people in their everyday lives, if they would consider it a viable lesson or a viable training. I don't think our society considers it that way yet.

PS: Right. I'm glad you said *yet*, because one of the things I'm working towards is to make it more acceptable.

PH: You know, that's why I pulled the pamphlet advertising your talk out of the Boulder Bookstore window. Ah, yes! Because I am very interested in remote viewing, too. Now, to go on, you said that you were in a black ops program and you can't talk too much about any kind of operation that you were involved in?

PS: Let me correct something here. It wasn't a black ops program. There are two facets to the military world—that covert military world. One is operations, and one is intelligence collection. We weren't responsible for the operations part, which falls under an entirely different department in the Army. The two words they use are covert, (operational) and clandestine, which is intelligence collection.

PH: Right. Is there any particular incident or anything you *can* talk about that you were involved in then?

PS: There's actually a fair amount that we can talk about. One story that I do tell many people about is the attack on the U.S.S. Stark, because it's very interesting. It's really not sensitive any more, either. I'll start from the beginning with this story. We have this thing we called a directed search—an open search, where we would be given a coordinate and, of course, we didn't know it was an open search. But they'd give us a coordinate, which might stand for something, like "Tell us something important that is going to happen in the next 24 hours," or something like that. We'd go over it. We'd think it was just a regular session, which was usually directed against the facility or something. They'd give us the coordinate, and then we'd just describe the impressions we got.

PH: And the coordinate was like 32° left, 42°, like that kind of coordinate?

PS: That was the way it used to be. We used to use geographic coordinates, which were, like you said, latitude and longitude. But we discovered there were a couple of reasons not to do that, a couple of problems with that process. One was that the critics said that we would just memorize the places which the coordinates represented. This, of course, in itself, would be a pretty magical thing, anyway because there are billions of possible coordinates.

PH: That memorizing would be too much trouble.

PS: But there was a problem in that once we had gotten enough coordinates, we sort of did get the feel for where in the world we were. So, it might be that we would get the coordinates for the Soviet Union, and we would automatically think of snow and ice and blah, blah, blah. That knowledge would actually get in the way of the viewing. That was the main reason that they started using random numbers that stood for the actual mission target or mission. And, of course, it wouldn't be made known to the viewer what the mission or target was. The remote viewers would be given the number that stood for a particular target or mission. And then, in some magical way, their subconscious, the viewer's subconscious, would know where to go.

PH: Yeah. Wow!

PS: So, the coordinate is really just a random number that is assigned as an address for that mission.

PH: That's interesting. OK, go ahead.

PS: So, anyway, I went over to the office, to the operations building where we did all of our remote viewing, and I sat down. The monitor gave me the coordinate, which I don't recall; it was just some random set of numbers.

PH: You said the monitor gave you the random numbers?

PS: Yeah. There were two people involved. There was the viewer, and then there was the monitor. And the monitor was just to give us the coordinate and make sure we stayed within and followed the proper procedures as we were going through our remote-viewing task. There is a set protocol that must be followed.

PH: Is any of that a briefing?

PS: No, there's a different catch word for that, actually. The monitor is there to kind of keep an eye on you, and you sit there and go through and describe what you've got. And, in this case, I started describing this vessel going through the water at night. And it was very large. I identified it as some sort of warship. I even had this impression that it was a U.S. destroyer, but I figured that was what we called "analytical overlay"; it was just mental noise getting in the way. So I kind of discounted it. But the happening was definitely at night. I also got this impression of an aircraft flying along, a long ways away. And the aircraft dropped something that was cylindrical and pointed. It had little fins on it and made a kind of roaring, guttering sound. And this thing, kind of flew around aimlessly after it left the aircraft, until, all of a sudden, I had this impression of it coming together with this vessel out in the water. And then there was smoke and fire and flames. I got the impression of people screaming and yelling, and there were fire hoses and the fire.... Then I got this kind of a sudden flash of fire and fire hoses snaking all over the deck of this thing. Somehow the structure of the thing was leaning to one side. I went through all of the details about what I was seeing. I even described where the aircraft came from—a land that was flat and sandy and was being directed by people who were a long ways away, in a city that had flat-topped houses and was kind of third world. That was the impression I got, with domestic animals in the streets and stuff like that. I had another impression that the people in this place spoke Arabic, but I discounted that as well, because I've got an Arabic linguistics background, and I thought that I was just making that up, you know?

PH: You were using your brain, your logic?

PS: Yes, exactly. You have to be careful of that on remote viewing.

PH: I know.

PS: So, anyway, I gave this whole picture, and when I got towards the end of doing this, the monitor was kind of losing patience. And he said, "Oh, we had better quit here. You're obviously off." Because that wasn't what he was expecting to find out, you know. So we called off the session. It was Friday, and I went home and spent the weekend not thinking about remote viewing. Early Monday morning, Skip Atwater gave me a call and said, "Hey, Paul, where's that session you did on Friday?" I said, "Oh, you mean that one I blew?" "Get in here and get it. Didn't you look in the paper this weekend?" he asked. "The paper?" I said. "No." So I got the newspaper, *The Washington Post*, opened it, and on the front page I read the headline: "U.S. Frigate Attacked by Iraqi Missile in the Gulf," or something like that. The U.S.S. Stark had been sailing along when an Iraqi Mirage had fired a missile at it. It turned out actually the missile hit the frigate, which then was on the verge of sinking. Thirty-seven Americans had been killed and all kinds of terrible stuff happened. When I went back and matched the session with the actual event, I was pretty amazed. It wasn't until several years later that I was actually able to see the after-action report. I had not reported one single false statement in that entire session. It was one of the cleanest remote viewings I had ever done. It was very surprising.

PH: What year was that?

PS: It was May of '87. The interesting thing was that I had reported this event about 50 hours before it actually happened. It was quite an impressive sort of a thing.

PH: You weren't remote viewing, though, Paul, when you did that. You were predicting.

PS: It's still called remote viewing. It's just precognitive remote viewing, "*just*" precognitive remote viewing.

PH: Another word for it is clairvoyance, in a funny kind of way.

PS: You have to understand. Remote viewing does involve clairvoyance. Remote viewing is kind of like a cocktail of different things. It involves clairvoyance, clairaudience, clair-smelling, if you want to call it that. All of the senses are involved in remote viewing.

PH: No, I understand. You were saying how a person could be trained to do this, but I'm not sure that everybody could be trained to know ahead of time. They could probably be trained to report like radio signals what's happening simultaneously, or whatever, but, in advance?

PS: Well, here's the catch: You can't think about this in terms of radio receivers and senders and radio waves and stuff. Because there's evidence to indicate that it can't be a send-and-receive kind of a thing.

PH: OK.

PS: It's somehow tapping into the fundamental basis of reality. Exactly how that is, I'm exploring. But I don't know if I'll ever come up with an actual answer to it.

PH: Does it have to do with time?

PS: Oh, yeah. In a way. For example, we do past viewing all the time. Accessing the past is the same as accessing the present.

PH: Right.

PS: The future is a bit harder to do. In fact, the Stark session was a little unusual.

PH: It really was unusual.

PS: People argue with me all the time, but my theory is that the future does not actually exist yet. What we have are various possible futures out there, any one of which can be activated by certain decision nodes being tripped, you know?

PH: So you have a Richard Bach type idea here? (The author of *Jonathan Livingston Seagull* and *Illusions*.)

PS: Could be. I don't know. I know [the general idea is] not original with me, but, as far as my experience goes, it makes a lot of sense.

PH: There are several possible futures Bach talks about in his books. But, that's a time problem. That's just what I asked.

PS: Yes. And what happens is, the farther out you go, the less likely you are to get the right one. It becomes kind of problematic. Right? Now, if you're lucky, you may pick up the right [future], or if it's an event that lies across a number of time lines, you increase the possibility that that one will be what happens. Right?

PH: Right. The future can be changed by changing decisions.

PS: And, also, the closer in you get, the more likely you are to be accurate. So, when you get people trying to predict the future of 30 years out, they're almost certain to be wrong, unless they are remote viewing some major event, some major thing that covers a lot of time lines.

PH: What do you mean by the closer in?

PS: The closer in time. For example,...

PH: It's easier to remote view events of tomorrow than it is 30 years out?

PS: Exactly. It's more likely that you will get it right, if it's tomorrow, than if it's 30 years out. But, you know, I don't know. There are still a lot of unsolved issues with this. The fact is that the future is, to some degree, accessible. A trained remote viewer will be on target somewhere between 60% and 80% of the time in any given session he does. And of that 60%-80% of the time, he will be very accurate about 50% of the time. OK?

PH: OK.

PS: But, if you go to the future, that percentage goes down. I figure that only about 20% of the time, do you get valid information about a future that actually materializes. And it might not even be that good. So, it just happened that I beat the odds on this one event—the U.S.S. Stark. Now, there are exceptions to this; there are ways of remote viewing where you remote view your feedback in the future, and that's a closed feedback loop, and that is accurate, quite accurate, in fact, that's very, very accurate.

PH: A closed feedback loop? Will you explain that to me?

PS: For example, there is this technique called associative remote viewing, or ARV is how they abbreviate it. And Hal Puthoff and his crew out in California used it actually to raise money for a non-profit school that they wanted to fund. They went for the silver futures market. OK? So, all they needed to know was whether it was going up. Was the silver futures market going to go up or go down? And they had an investor who was going to buy if it was going up and sell if it was going to go down. Now, in order to make remote viewing assist with this, they might pick two objects. One stood for the market going up, and one stood for it going down. So, let's say a pencil and a hammer. I think that's usually what Hal uses as his example. So, a remote viewer is supposed to describe what object he is going to be handed the day after the silver futures' transaction takes place. OK. So we're on day one, when the viewer is going to do the session. Day two is when the investor is going to decide whether to buy or sell. And day three is when the remote viewer is going to be told the results of his session. So, then, now, it's probably a little confusing. But I'll talk you through it, and we'll see how it goes. On day one, they say, we want you to tell us to describe the object that we're going to hand you on day three. And so the remote viewer, let's say, he says, "Well, it's long and yellow and wooden and pointed." And, so, obviously, he's describing the pencil rather than the hammer. Right? So, they have decided the pencil stands for the market going to go up. And so you want to buy. Pencil means buy; hammer means sell. OK? He described the pencil, so they purchased silver futures on day two. And, sure enough, the market went up on day two. And that's what the pencil stood for—the market going up. So, on day three, see, the remote viewer so far doesn't know anything about any of this stuff. He just knows what he described. On day three, they hand him the pencil and say, "This is the object, that's your feedback." And he gets the pencil, and it matches his description. He now has his closed loop. Right? So, he's basically sending himself information from the future.

PH: Right.

PS: Are you confused?

PH: No, I get it. It's just using representations for what really is.

PS: Well, it's only a symbol to indicate whether it's going up or down.

PH: Were they pretty successful?

PS: Yes. Yes, they were. They made $25,000 in 30 days.

PH: Oh!

PS: Actually, they made more than that. What happened was that this investor said, "I'm going to invest. I'm not going to donate money to you. I'm going to invest according to what you tell me, and then I'll give you a percentage of my profits." So, they got $25,000, which was, I don't know what percentage, but if it was half, then, actually, they made $50,000 at that time.

PH: You just mentioned this particular incident you were involved with. Were you involved also in finding out if people were guilty or innocent, in any kind of incident?

PS: No!

PH: For instance, who the terrorists were in a certain situation?

PS: No, we didn't do that. What they wanted us to do in terrorist situations was to do some prediction on that. And it didn't work. Well, if it did work, it worked too well. But, you know, if you predict something and they do something about it, it might stop the event from actually happening. Right? And then...

PH: Yes, but that's more than predicting. I am using the word predicting, because you are using the word predicting. It's really verifying. For instance, verifying who shot the Pope, for example.

PS: No. We didn't do that kind of stuff. One thing we did with terrorism was prediction, which didn't work very well, and another was trying to locate, like hostages and stuff, which sometimes worked, sometimes didn't. No, we didn't get into verifying if someone was guilty or not. That's very problematic, because, first of all the courts wouldn't accept this as evidence.

PH: I know. Never. All that's a whole other world and a whole other area.

PS: Right. And, you know, plus, it gets so subtle at that point, you know, trying to discriminate one human being from another that...

PH: The next obvious question, and I have to ask you this, but you don't have to answer it, is "Is there mind control involved in remote viewing, too?"

PS: No, no.

PH: I know I've heard stories like the famous summit conferences where there were many people working on remote viewing or mind control in the other room, trying to get the important dignitaries to sign peace agreements.

PS: Yeah. There is some substantiation to the rumors that the Soviets were doing that kind of stuff. But, we were not doing that. Remember I told you about the difference between ops and intel collection? That would be an ops responsibility, an operations responsibility, and we would not be doing that stuff. Now, there have been people who claimed we did. In fact, I think Dave Morehouse in his book claimed that we did that. But we didn't. We did not get involved in that. That was not part of our charter, and, in fact, we felt that there were ethical problems with it.

PH: Yeah. There are. Because you are controlling someone's decision-making process.

PS: Yeah. Well, I don't know. In an operational setting, somebody might have tried to do that, but that would have been an entirely different domain than the one we were in.

PH: It could be for the benefit of mankind. Many things can be done for a "just" cause. You know, the end justifies the means, type of thing.

PS: Like any kind of technology, remote viewing has two edges—very positive or very negative, depending on how people apply it.

PH: Exactly. Now, say more about the remote-viewing training you do. How does this training enhance people's lives?

PS: That's actually a question that often gets asked. In fact, on my web page, I have a paper way down deep somewhere that discusses why people learn it. I explain it this way: I compare it to parachute jumping, to a free fall, or whatever. There are uses for parachute jumping: you can put military people into a situation; you can use it for para-rescuing; you can use it to put people into forest fires to put them out; you can drop supplies in some area that's been hit where there are no bridges. You can use it for a lot of practical reasons. But, by far, the largest number of people who jump with parachutes are people who do it just for the heck of it. And that's the way it is with remote viewing. It could potentially be—and has been—very, very useful, in solving crimes and finding missing people and all that kind of thing.

PH: Do you get this kind of feedback from people that you train?

PS: I really haven't had many who wanted to learn remote viewing for what you would call practical uses. They do it because it enhances them personally. They do it for self-realization, self-actualization. After they have taken the training, they're more than they were when they started; or, at least, they realize more about themselves. They have done something that society claims they can't do, and they prove to themselves that they can do it.

PH: That's a good enough reason. The self-awareness one is the obvious one, especially with today's New Age thinking. Going on, I was going to ask you specifically about Italian earthquakes and volcanoes. We've had two little earthquakes around Mount Vesuvius, in Naples.

PS: Oh? That didn't make the news in the U.S.

PH: Can this volcanic activity be examined with remote viewing to see if there is a problem coming?

PS: Well, you could. Of course, this is a future viewing, so you won't know. You could move to Switzerland.

PH: I thought about Switzerland. How would such a viewing be done?

PS: This is how you would set up a remote viewing on whether a large, harmful event was going to happen or not. First of all, it would be best if you had two or three viewers, none of whom knew anything about the project. If the first thing you say to them is, "We want to know if the volcano is going to erupt or not." Bing! Everything they know about volcanoes is brought back into their mind by memory. And this prior knowledge by suggestion really contaminates what they're going to do. One of the prerequisites for remote viewing is that the viewers cannot know, up front, what the target is.

PH: Then the remote viewers can't and don't put their personal experiences or conclusions on the present task.

PS: That's exactly right. If you ever see anybody doing a remote viewing, and they claim something is going to happen, be sure you always ask, "What was the task?"

PH: Give me an example.

PS: OK. Let's work with your volcano here. Of course, this is future, and so there are two difficult problems with remote viewing, what we call "Search" and "Future." Both of those are nearly intractable, but they can still be successfully done. For your volcano project, I would get, let's say three viewers, none of whom know what the target is. I would take a number, let's say, take today's date and then add a project number—991011329. Let's say that stands for the mission, which is to describe the condition of Mount Vesuvius on, let's say, a week from now, say on Oct 18. The remote viewers are given only the number, and then they will start describing what they see. Let's hope they will say: tall, hard, rocky, mountainous, mountain peak, flame, smoke, heat, hot. You know? If you get that kind of response from the viewers that suggests fairly strongly that the volcano is going to erupt.

PH: Only the person that is training the remote viewer knows what the actual subject is?

PS: Right. In fact, the person who is working with the viewer should not know what the subject is either.

PH: The monitor?

PS: Yes, the monitor shouldn't know either. We have three levels—the viewer, who does the work, the actual viewing; the monitor, who helps direct it;

and then the tasker, who knows what the project is and assigns the number. All the tasker does is to give the monitor the number, not telling him what the subject is. The monitor then takes that number and goes to the viewer; together, they work the session. The monitor will take the results of the session back to the tasker and simply say, "This is what we reported." The tasker might say, "OK. You are on the right track. Go ahead and tell some more." And that is all he would say.

PH: I never knew remote viewing was conducted that way. I honestly thought that a task was given. This procedure you explained makes the process of remote viewing more valid, because there is not any contamination.

PS: Exactly.

PH: Is this what you do with the audience?

PS: Yes. What I do is, I have four targets, sealed in opaque envelopes. I know what those targets are, but I don't know which one is in which envelope.

PH: So, you are holding an envelope?

PS: No, I let a member of the audience pick one of those envelopes and keep it, and I have him/her write the coordinate on it. And what I do is, we go with the date. Again, we use the date—991011, for example. Then I might say, "Write OA on that to designate that particular envelope and the target that is represented in it. So I don't know what the target is either. I know it is one of four, but I have no idea which one of four. The person in the audience continues to hold the envelope. I then put the coordinate up, and they all write it down. Then they give their impressions of what they think it is.

PH: And it works pretty well?

PS: It works pretty well. Of course, in that setting in the audience, I don't tell them this up front, but that's one of the worst settings in which to do a remote viewing. It is in a group setting, they have been sitting there for an hour-and-a-half, and they are tired. You know, all of the members of the audience have all this stuff going on and through their minds that I've been talking to them about. Thus, clear, accurate remote viewing is harder to do. They are neither relaxed nor in a good quiet setting.

PH: With this private practice you have, do you do one-on-one training?

PS: Yes! I train up to three people at once, but I lecture to all of them in a group. Then I take them one at a time and work through sessions.

PH: Do you do this training anywhere but Texas, now?

PS: If there is enough interest, I will go somewhere else.

PH: How long is a session? How long is the training?

PS: The actual training in remote viewing I was given by the Army took us 18 months to get up to speed. Following some of Ingo's lead, I managed to get my program down to three, four-day sessions: basic, intermediate, and advanced. The training days are very intensive. When they are finished, people come out of there shell shocked.

PH: I understand. Why do people take remote-viewing training classes? Is it all for self-realization?

PS: For the most part. There are people who wish to use it in the civilian sense and operationally. But, in order to really get good at that, people have to go all the way up through the three levels. Most people are satisfied with the basic course, because it gives them successes and a consistent skill level at which they can continue to practice. But, to really get all the bells and whistles which allow you to do remote viewing more reliably and to get the real details, you really have to take the intermediate course and the advanced course.

PH: Can UFOs be remote-viewed?

PS: First of all, I accept, obviously that there are UFOs. Whatever they are is something that's on many people's minds. I actually do believe that there is life on some other planets and that the beings from there are probably interacting with us in some way. I am cautious about what portion I accept, because there is a lot of baloney out there. But I have participated in a number of remote viewings, some credibly done and some not so credibly done, looking at UFOs. I was a sub-contractor, actually a contractor for Psi Tech, Ed Dames's outfit, for a number of years, until it just got so weird I just had to get out of it.

PH: Have you ever remote viewed an extraterrestrial being?

PS: No, not to my knowledge, although I have remote viewed what seemed to be alien artifacts, like space ships.

PH: If some extraterrestrial races look like us, you wouldn't be able to say whether you were remote viewing them or us, could you?

PS: Possibly, but not superficially. You might not be able to determine whether it was another human or not unless you really went into it.

PH: Your degree in philosophy should allow you to tie together some of these pieces to the puzzle, which is probably where you are going.

PS: Yes. That's why I'm doing an advanced degree in philosophy.

PH: Thank you so much for taking the time to talk to me and for granting me this interview.

PS: OK. Great! I enjoyed talking with to you.

Chapter 25

The Paranormal Factor

Courtney Brown

Cosmic Explorers Scientific Remote Viewing, Extraterrestrials,
and a Message for Mankind

---

www.farsight.org

Remote viewing had become interesting to me, but remote viewing aliens, even more so! I read Dr. Courtney Brown's book *Cosmic Voyagers* and decided to call him in Atlanta, Ga., for an interview. Intelligent, soft spoken and very open minded, he was very willing to talk about his research. Courtney's interview will fill in a few blanks about the use of remote viewing other worlds or maybe other dimensions. He is a university professor who includes serious research on his web site and invites the public to participate.

April 17, 2000

Paula Harris (PH): Your book was given to me because I'm really interested in remote viewing. I had been interested in Ingo Swann when he came out with his web site and his book *Penetration,* and I wondered how did this work, which I thought was top-secret, become public so people can talk about it?

Courtney Brown (CB): There are actually two sides to it. Ingo's stuff is very, very up front. I don't see any remote possibility for him to deceive anyone for any reason. He states that he's tried to clear up things on record as he's getting older, and he wants to get on with other things. I can't see any reason, or at least any profit motivation, for selling *Penetration.* The first 70 pages are riveting. I don't think he intended to write a spellbinder or anything like that, so I find him very credible. I've only spoken to Ingo once for five minutes on the phone. We've exchanged only one letter, and I wish I had been able to know him better. Anything I say about Ingo is only third-hand information, but it's always great, great positive stuff.

PH: Did you ever work with Hal Puthoff at SRI?

CB: No, we have our own institute here, The Farsight Institute.

PH: Did you develop The Farsight Institute?

CB: Yes, what happened was that SRI International, which used to be Stanford Research, part of Stanford University, were contracted by the government to research remote viewing. Apparently, the luminaries in the field are very up front about the CIA's involvement in terms of the funding, but also there was the Defense Intelligence Agency (DIA) as well, the intelligence wing of the Pentagon. And that more recently has become very up front. The DIA really had operational purposes for this. It was a very new phenomenon. The government wanted to know how to use it for espionage purposes right away, and the scientific luminaries such Russell Targ and Hal Puthoff wanted to do basic science. You just can't get something like this and throw it immediately into operation.

PH: I know.

CB: What is the mechanism? How does it work? Can it be reliable? What's going on? They were always under tremendous time pressure and funding for sure. I get this from published sources.

PH: Hal Puthoff and Paul Smith talk about the original SRI....

CB: This is the legacy of this whole thing that the Stanford group started, how the first initial investigation started, under tremendous financial stress and personal pressure, because the government always wanted results within months. They wanted operational information out of it, and so it's sort of a two-edged sword. They tried to get as much basic science out of it as they could, given the fact that their funding was going to run out soon unless they got some practical stuff out of it. So they had some remote-viewing scenarios that were very successful in getting target information, and then the U.S. government worked with those people, back and forth. But with these results, the U.S. Army came into it strongly. That's where the DIA came in. They developed a remote-viewing squad that was trained in techniques that Ingo Swann predominately developed—new methods of accessing this information—and when the U.S. Army came into it, Paul Smith was part of that. There was another Special Forces (again, U.S. Army) remote-viewing group as well that worked with a different noted psychic, Dr. Richard Ireland. He trained Glenn Wheaton, who now runs the Hawaiian Remote Viewer's Guild (*www.hrvg.org*), and their very effective methods are much different from the Ingo-Swan-derived methods.

PH: Was your involvement military work? Can you talk about that?

CB: I'll get to me in just a second. What happened was, after a while, the U.S. Army, the Pentagon, realized that the information about remote viewing was going to become open. They allowed a few of these people to go out and teach it. This is information that was told to me by two of those who were in the original RV/DIA unit. There's a lot of information that goes back and forth that eventually gets back to me. So what happened was that the government really wanted the remote viewing stuff to stay in the New Age community, and to stay out of the mainstream. Now I'm not putting down the New Age community. That's how the government saw it. As they saw it, in the New Age community RV would hang around in New Age book stores and healing and metaphysical places and coffee shops, all these non-mainstream places. That's not how I view these people, but that's what the government wanted. They wanted it to stay out of mainstream science where it might get the funding, and possibly get a lot of attention.

PH: If they wanted it to stay there, why would they fund something they don't consider science?

CB: No that's not true, they have funded it all throughout, even now. They do two things. They say they don't fund it, but they do fund it.

PH: But it is science, isn't it?

CB: Yeah. It is science. We are strictly a scientific institute.

PH: Yeah, I understand. I always believed this was scientific, but I have problems with the people that put it in the goofy New Age category.

CB: The whole idea was to put it in there and then never let it get out very far. I have been told this by people formerly in the military, actual people sitting in front of me talking. I won't tell the names of those people. I don't want to get into it; they didn't want their names published. Point blank, they were told by their upper-ups, that the remote-viewing stuff could only be let out only so much; anything beyond that would be shut down, and nothing would stop them (the DIA) from shutting it down. There would be no holds barred. It would all be oriented around disinformation. They knew it was going to get out, but they thought they could control it better if it was out and was laughed at, or at least marginalized, than if it got out and was taken seriously, because you really don't need too many experiments before you realize it's real. So they had to make people afraid to do the experiments that would put most scientists on guard because they don't want to risk their reputations. So the big money won't go after it.

So, really what happened is that remote viewing is very real, but it's still very marginal in the scientific community. So what happened was that these Army guys went out to teach, and I'd made friends with two of them, and one in particular. I paid cash to learn and to be professional at it. But I looked at it from an academic's point of view.

PH: Are you still working at Emory University?

CB: Yes. You can always get my whole academic and professional background at *www.courtneybrown.com* When I'm at Emory, I do nothing related to The Farsight Institute or remote viewing.

PH: Have you had problems at all like Harvard professor John Mack and other people with this material?

CB: The president of Emory University is very, very good. He understands that these things are separate, and that the scientific community has not yet put the stamp of approval on what I do. He understands that it's separate, and people are allowed to pursue their separate ideas as long as I don't do it in my political-science classes. It's separate. It has nothing to do with what I do at the Farsight Institute. What I do at Emory University is teach political science.

What happened is that I originally learned the Ingo Swan version of RV from one of these ex-military guys, then we parted company, and I founded my own institute. We've trained over 175 people to do remote viewing. I redid the RV protocols from my own "professor of science" perspective. I realized this stuff (as it was coming out of the Army) was very operationally oriented rather that science oriented, and so I changed it. I modified it. I adapted it. It wasn't just me, we had all of our researchers doing it. But our own procedures clearly evolved from Ingo Swann's procedures. They have a historical connection to them. And if you look them over, you can see how they evolved from the Swann procedures. But we have evolved our own procedures and vocabulary/language for it. We also publish our own web site, *www.farsight.org*, which has a huge library of free stuff. We are formally a IRS non-profit research and educational institute, and we do only basic science in remote viewing. We publish our basic science on our web site.

PH: I know. I noticed you have tapes to learn these procedures, but do you have classes to where people can attend?

CB: We don't have classes, at least right now. But we still teach lots of people RV, as I will explain. We formerly taught a whole bunch of people in personalized classes here in Atlanta. Like any college or university, we did not do this for profit. But it was taking too much of our time. We could not get our research done. We were interested (just like Puthoff and everybody else) in doing basic science research. So we decided to stop teaching, and, for a year and a half, we just didn't do any teaching. But so many people asked us about training that we decided to come out with a large free downloadable audio course (plus a free printable text) that was just perfect with nothing omitted, and we have been giving it away freely to visitors to our web site. But we really have a very active research agenda. We have some real advances that we've discovered, problems that have been around for a couple of decades, and we're right now in the process of writing them up, getting them out, getting them published. And that's what we're really focusing on. There have been some problems that have plagued people doing research for a long, long time.

PH: Do you want to go into any of them?

CB: Towards the end of the original SRI days, Ed May and those at SRI used a method for evaluating this remote-viewing process which was supposed to be scientific that went like this: You have a remote-viewer view a target "blind," in the sense that they're not supposed to know anything about it in advance. Then the RV data are given to a panel of judges who compare the data to a list of, say, five targets, one real and the others decoys or false targets. They're not told anything about what the correct target is, of course. They are given all the possible targets to try to figure out which one it would most likely be. Basically, they would say things like, "Okay that's clearly a sketch of the Empire State Building and it's certainly not a sketch of a desert." In situations in which they would be dealing with a number of possible targets on a shelf, they might observe that the RV data really looks like a vase and not a pen, or a cup, or plate. They would have five, say, different possible targets. So, they would be trying to remote view one target out of the list and then they would take the RV data and try to determine which was the correct target.

And the problem was that while sometimes they would get the correct results, other times they get results in which a very nice picture would show up, or a nice bit of descriptive information of one of the targets on the list, but it was the wrong target. It was very clear that the description wasn't of the correct target, but it was a description of one of the possible targets. It was correctly describing one of the targets, but the wrong one, meaning that target wasn't the one that was picked by the random throw of the dice, or whatever. These targets were chosen dynamically, meaning some event like throwing dice or something else was done to determine which target was actually going to be used. So the instructions to the viewer would be to remote view the correct one.

PH: But wouldn't he be given the coordinates?

CB: Well, sometimes they'd be given coordinates, but that's another aspect of the whole process. We don't need to get into technicalities. The basic idea was that they would be told there was a target, and there would be a set of procedures they would be using to do this. Thus, a viewer would be told to describe the target. Let's say the possible targets were a plate, a cup, a pen, and a basketball. The person would say the target is a pen, and then the random procedure would decide the correct target. The correct target was the plate, but the description was of the pen and so the blind judges would say this person is describing the pen. But really, which was the correct one?

PH: The plate.

CB: The plate, but this person is describing a pen. What actually makes one target the correct one and the other targets incorrect? Does the randomization procedure really do this? The pen is chosen as the correct target. And low and behold, it turns out that the random procedure picked the plate instead. But, you know the viewer had no idea that the pen was one of the targets when the viewing was done. I mean the person giving the instructions just says there is a target, and so the remote viewer would just describe one of the targets, and they had no idea which kind of target would be there. But they would end up describing one of the five targets. So the real question was how could a person accurately describe one of the wrong targets? What make a target a target? Is it because a random number procedure picked that spot on the shelf and said it was correct? Or is there some other process at work? So we spent two years investigating this problem. We first duplicated all SRI and SAIC (Science Applications International Corporation) results. And we found that indeed there was a problem. When you have targets on a list, you often get very good results of the wrong target. Very good results. Everything is correct. But it's not the one you want to get.

PH: At least it was a scientific exploration.

CB: Ed May moved the program to SAIC when he was the last director at SRI. He moved the program from SRI when they closed down the lab. So we invested two years looking into that research, and we have research under review right now which we think resolves the issue. We really think we understand the issue.

PH: I liked your first book.

CB: Actually, *Cosmic Explorers* is my second book. It reports my own personal application of remote viewing. It's also in paperback now, originally published by Penguin Putnam. It is a much different book than *Cosmic Voyage*, my first remote-viewing book. It's more recent, and it has 100 pages of methodology in it describing the remote-viewing procedures used at Farsight. It also has updates in the sense that it continues the information presented in *Cosmic Voyage*. But it's a better book because every book I write is better than the one I did before.

PH: I know where you're coming from, but we're at ground zero here with remote viewing. Nobody ever considered remote viewing scientific or valid. I've been fighting to get my article on remote viewing published in two Italian magazines with the possible titles "Government Remote Viewers: The Psychic Connection." Well, the response from the editors is "This isn't science." Well, I said "If it isn't science, why is the government funding it?"

CB: Well, the best place to get any information on remote viewing right now is our web site. There's no place you can get more, and it is all free. The information is not necessarily about the history of it, but about the science and mechanics of it. If you go to the resources section you'll find SRV Learning Area. That has the free downloadable audio course, a printable text of *Scientific Remote Viewing*. The audio course and text have all the procedures. They're pretty clear. You don't have to pay a dime, and you don't have to buy tapes or anything like that. Everything at the site is free.

PH: Don't people have to have the ability before hand to be as good as you are now, a little bit of intuitive ability? There must be some way of testing those who are more apt to be a good remote viewers. Is that true?

CB: We haven't found any limitations like that. What we have found is it really takes a lot of hard work and determination, persistence. Just like playing the violin. I mean if you play it, you'll make squeaky sounds at the beginning, but if you keep at it you'll eventually get it.

PH: Yeah, but there's some better people who play the violin, the people who take lessons...

CB: I understand. There is a level of talent.

PH: Do you have that?

CB: Well, people have said I have that. I've published all of the stuff so people can make their own judgments. We don't know the limits of the training process right now. People often take a few classes and then try to evaluate themselves. But we really don't know how far you can push this. So, people look at my work and say, that's what I do, and they see all this stuff published on the web and say "Oh, you must be just really gifted at this." But the reality is I work hard at this, and I feel deeply that others can be as good or better than me.

PH: Oh, I realize that you work hard at it.

CB: But I remote view at lot, meaning a number of times a week.

PH: Do you do it with other people? You use monitors, right?

CB: No, no we don't. None of us at the institute use monitors anymore. We just do solo sessions.

PH: Why?

CB: Monitors are good for training. That's when *Cosmic Voyage* was written, when I was still a baby at this stuff. *Cosmic Explorers* is also all solo stuff. And all the stuff we have on our web site is also solo stuff. All of us just do solo stuff now. And we have gotten to the point where we don't like monitors. There are some very good reasons for using monitors for research, but those are very commonly encountered. When you're good enough, you can just do solo stuff. Again, we have an entire manual available for free, which is extensive. It's like 100 pages of material. We have a library of remote-viewing sessions that people can look over, and we even also have the RealAudio, so you can listen to some sessions recorded live. For example in my area of the Institute's web site, found from the resources area of the web site, there are three of those recorded sessions. We've recorded them live so you can actually hear what was going on in the room. You can actually hear words spoken. Also, for six months we carried on a public demonstration on remote viewing, which you can also see on the web site. We had a tenured associate professor of medicine at George Washington University, Dr. John David Berman, pick the targets for us. He's head of their ethics committee. The really interesting thing about it was that we did "time" experiments for the demonstration. We would do the sessions first and then put typed and encrypted transcripts of them for people to download from our web site. You needed a password to remove the encryption. Lots of people downloaded them onto their computers. And while they were downloading them for a week or two, John—he likes to be called David— would then decide on the target that was he was going to choose. Again, the sessions were already done in the past. And he would say, "OK, I've decided the target is, let's say, 'the Eiffel Tower.'" Actually, for one of the targets in the public demonstration he said the target is the Eiffel Tower when it was being constructed. So that would be the target and he would then send us the target via email. Then we would post the password to unravel the transcripts and everyone would see how well we did.

PH: How did he send you the target?

CB: He would actually just e-mail us that the target is the Eiffel Tower, plus other aspects of the target, like the time.

PH: Do you use target coordinates?

CB: Sometimes we do use target coordinates, and I explain all of that in *Cosmic Explorers*, but they're only an aid, a crutch for the remote viewer to get started with. They aren't essential. The person who writes the target doesn't need to know those.

PH: So what now?

CB: Let me go back a little bit, so you will understand it. We do the sessions first before the target has been determined. We post the session, typed and encrypted transcripts of those sessions, which have been encrypted with PGP, which is a publicly available encryption program. We post the typed and encrypted transcripts up on the web so that anyone can download them. And so then they have a copy of what the transcripts are, so they know we can't change them afterwards. Then we need a target. Only then does John David Berman pick a target for us. He can't see the transcripts either, because they're encrypted.

PH: He picks the target after you've already done the remote viewing?

CB: That's exactly it. See we're a scientific institute. We were doing "time experiments."

PH: So, in other words, you're doing the remote viewing before you ask somebody to pick a target, but you've already done it, because you're going into the future. Are you going into the future? If so, we've got some serious problems with time here!

CB: I'm actually collaborating currently with a physicist, a retired physicist from a major research university, and he has been very clear with the all of this. Physicists do not understand time right now. No one really does.

PH: Okay, you went ahead and did this remote viewing, and after that you asked this gentleman to pick a target.

CB: Yes, all this information is still up on the web site. You can go to it and follow everything exactly as it happened.

PH: I have a million questions here. So when the gentleman then gave you the target, for the most part, was it usually accurate?

CB: We completed 13 experiments with that six-month demonstration, and there was only one time out of 13 that I didn't describe fairly well what was there. Often the results were exceptionally clear.

PH: Oh my God! So you RV something that he had not chosen yet? I have been trying to figure this out for myself.

CB: The thing is, most people would be confused. All you need to do is go to our web site. You can actually click on every experiment. Start with the most recent and go back.

PH: Where is it?

CB: On the home page there is a big graphic of a hurricane, and a person's face, the Parthenon, the U.S. capital building, and so on. And down in the lower left you can see the public demonstration. It's there. Click there, and then you will get to a page that has all the stuff for the public demonstration. You get to see the whole thing for all 13 experiments.

PH: You were doing it, and how many others?

CB: We had two viewers for each experiment. All experiments that we put up followed exactly the same format: two viewers using Dr. John David Berman (the medical professor) who would pick the target after the sessions were posted in encrypted format.

PH: That's incredible...

CB: We would then post the passwords to de-encrypt the transcripts together with the scans of the sessions after Dr. Berryman chose the target. If we didn't have the transcripts available in advance so people could download them and later de-encrypt them, then they would have said "Oh, they faked the sessions." But having the transcripts stored in advance is very convincing.

PH: I know what you're telling me, but it's just unbelievable.

CB: When we put up the scans of the sessions, you then compare the sessions with the transcripts. And then people would say, "Oh lord, my gosh. This is the exact thing I downloaded two weeks ago."

PH: That's incredible. Okay there's two people, you were one and somebody else was the other?

CB: Joey Jerome, and later Matthew Pfeiffer. For the first ten experiments it was myself and Joey Jerome. After a while, he got a little tired and then Matthew Pfeiffer was the second viewer. And then we all got a little bit exhausted after six months. We had to do some other research. We were all doing some other stuff that we had to get back to, and so we stopped the demonstration.

PH: Tell me about time.

CB: What we know for sure is that *time does not exist*, and I do not mean this as New Age metaphor. Time is nothing more than a limitation of perception.

PH: You call it a "limitation of perception?"

CB: Perception—that's all it is. It has nothing to do with the way we live in our physical bodies. Somehow in regards to this three-dimensional plus one (time) universe, time anywhere outside of this three-dimensional plus one (time) universe just simply doesn't exist. That means that when we remote view something in the past or the future as we did with the 13 successfully completed experiments in the public demonstration, the future already existed. The past also still exists, meaning that we were remote viewing a target that was already determined: It was already there. It hadn't yet been chosen for two weeks, but this didn't matter. It was still there. We just couldn't see it yet with our physical eyes. We had to wait in our bus ride through the street of time. We had to wait 'til we got there when our physical perception could actually see the real target that we remote viewed correctly two weeks or more prior.

PH: Is it all fixed, or are there places where we can change the future by jumping in?

CB: I've had extensive discussions with physicists on this. The remote viewing results clearly show that there is a definite future for any particular time line going out, but if you remote view the future and receive some information and thus change your current behavior, then you can veer off into another future. And no one really knows what to call that, a time dimension, another dimension, another time stream. Even the physicists are arguing what word to use for it. But there is only one sequence of events that brings us to our current time stream. You would be talking right now and only one sequence of events has brought us here. However, that doesn't mean there aren't many other possible other histories, but there's only one sequence of events that brought our current perspective to this point in time, this moment where we're having this conversation. We just don't perceive, we don't remember anything that happened in alternative past times. In the future, it's a little bit more variable.

PH: Okay, but do these "past time streams" exist? Do these streams all go at the same time? Can you jump from one to another?

CB: I can use an example. There was a time, and here I'll mention one thing that we did in the past—we don't do this anymore at the Institute. I just thought that I'd tell you. But we had some inkling of information that suggested that there might be something that could be happening, some terrorist event that could occur. Some people had some sort of vague vision, and we just decided to explore this as a target. The secret is we sent all of our viewers out to look at it. And they all came back with the same thing. This happened several years ago, right after the Soviet Union broke up, and so many of the viewers came back with some terrorist type of personality shooting a tactical nuclear weapon from some location near New York City, a suitcase-size type tactical weapon, with some type of portable vehicle to transport it to the United Nations. Most viewers were coming back with this person being a Russian or a Slavic person. We got all this information at the Institute. Now we don't have any project like this any longer on the web site. We did this in the old days of the Institute. And this is one case where we sort of said "Oh my goodness, what are we going to do with this information?"

PH: What year was this?

CB: Approximately 1997. And so we asked, "What are we supposed to do with this? Are we just supposed to file it away? Nobody's talking to us." The intelligence people weren't talking to us. We decided to just let "them" file this. So we took a risk and just put it up on our web site. When we got this information, you know, we knew we were going to be laughed at. I knew we were going to be mocked. And I knew that people would think we were nuts. But what are were we supposed to do with this? If we got laughed at, what's the cost? The cost was only to ourselves. So, we just put it up any way, the whole analyses, the whole stuff. Well, we found out later, a couple months later, a general of the former Soviet Union in Russia (General Lebed), announced formally that there were approximately 128 small tactical weapons missing from the (former) Soviet arsenal, and that they might potentially be in the hands of some groups that are hostile to the United Nations. And then about a month after that, U.S. Security Forces arrested two Lithuanians for trying to sell really small nuclear capable missiles in Miami, and they had been trying to sell them previously in the East Coast and had some problem. But the main idea was that (1) the General himself had admitted that weapons were missing and (2) that Slavic types were actually caught a couple months later trying to sell nuke-capable small portable missiles because they couldn't use them for whatever they were originally trying to do. It was reported this way, but it wasn't made into a big deal in the press, yet it circumstantially supports the original remote viewing data.

But then we got a very strange communication after this from somebody in the intelligence community. He actually became very interested in what we were doing. The intelligence community was monitoring us very closely, and he sent us a communication that gave us a transcript of one of our important phone calls so that we would know for sure that he was from the intelligence community, because how else could he have a transcript of our phone calls? He gave us a transcript just to show us who he was, and then he basically indicated that he wanted us to know that while everybody out there was laughing at us, the government was taking what we were doing extremely seriously. Nothing's being missed, and then we got some information afterwards suggesting that something we did made a major difference. Then they would not tell us anything more. Now what were we supposed to do? So the point is, can remote viewing be used to determine future events? Well, we demonstrated for six months that it could be done.

In the old days we used to do more risky targets that were just fun. I mean in the old days, we used to think these things were fun. So we did that one, and it got us into a whole bunch of trouble, and to be quite honest, we probably won't ever do these things again. Now we just want to build up the Institute and focus on the scientific part.

PH: The trouble is you got monitored, right? That was the trouble?

CB: The trouble is that the whole world laughed at us, and we want to be taken seriously. It is hard to do risky application targets and more sedate science experiments at the same time. The unfair public response to the risky application targets makes it difficult to have people seriously consider our other work.

PH: Can you now address the ET question?

CB: *Cosmic Voyage* and *Cosmic Explorers* address my own personal interest in ET material.

PH: I was just reading this on your personal web site that you said there's a species that is antagonistic. Are they working with the government?

CB: That is my interpretation. There's nobody in the government who comes to talk to us about this. But the results of my sessions are very consistent, and there are so many sessions that I've lost count. *Cosmic Explorers* goes into this in great depth. Apparently, there is an actual conflict going on up there in the skies some place. The government is fully aware that there is a conflict, and that's one of the reasons they don't want any of the ET stuff to come out. It's bad enough that they'll say that there are ETs but, my gosh, they have ETs in a conflict! Which side are we supposed to align ourselves with? Then they are worried about the stock market, society....

PH: I know this, but isn't there a group of ETs working with the government? Are they good or bad?

CB: Well there's more than one. They're both trying to influence the government. My research clearly suggests that the Greys are good. They're better than benign. They're very good.

PH: They're very good?

CB: Yeah. The best test to indicate what is good and what is bad is if you openly acknowledge that they are ETs, and then tell one of the groups to go away. Would they go away? The Greys would go away. But the other group, and I wish there was a better word for them, are Reptilians.

PH: Oh, great.

CB: They would not go away

PH: They will not go away?

CB: And they are directly tied in with the government in one way or another, and the Greys are trying to influence the government the other way. But the Greys have been very evolutionary about their activities. They're asking permission to do what they do all over the place. But the Reptilians have a very interesting approach. You see, the Reptilians are willing to give technology, and you know how materialistic humans are, especially over small bits of technology. Some will call that group the best friend they've ever had.

PH: Because of the technology?

CB: Because of the technology. The little trinkets that they throw.....

PH: But these Reptilians, Are they also shape shifters?

CB: I have been told about such things, but I do not know.

PH: Have you seen a Reptilian?

CB: That is always a question on my mind. We have remote viewed them. Under blind conditions we were told to remote target them, and every time we have a Reptilian target, we end up drawing these pictures of scaly types, though they do look human, or at least humanoid. And the point is they're probably very beautiful. When I say scaly types, I'm not meaning ugly.

PH: I understand.

CB: But they just have this type of a skin that sort of seems like a reptilian animal. You know, who knows? The prophets were probably the very first remote viewers, and they even realized Reptilians have been around for a long time. Maybe that's the origin of the mythology of Satan and the snake. In the original Biblical text, the Serpent isn't a snake, a lowly type of creature, a simple reptile. Maybe that's the way it got translated. In the original text, the word they used for this Reptilian guy was a full blooded big humanoid-type fellow. We only translated it into a snake. It's *not* a snake.

PH: That's interesting.

CB: The prophets were the ones who were seeing this at first and sort of tried to figure out how to describe it in their own primitive remote viewings, and people later tried to decode the word reptile and ended up calling the guy a snake. But in fact, there is a conflict on a heavenly level going on between species that definitely have different agendas. I actually followed out an alternative timeline in the book *Cosmic Explorers* and explored the agenda for the Reptilians. In a future timeline, if we should side with the Reptilians, we end up in very dire circumstances. The blacks in South Africa under apartheid in the old days were better off than we will be if we align ourselves with the Reptilians.

But if we go the way of the Greys, or make an alliance with the Greys, things will be better. The remote-viewing evidence clearly suggests that the Greys will not solve any of our problems, meaning they allow us to evolve and make mistakes but...

PH: We're better off.

CB: We're better off finding our own way in the universe.

PH: What about the third type, which is the Nordics?

CB: I've never remote viewed them. They may exist, they may not. I do not know.

PH: You've never viewed the Nordics?

CB: You know, time is short, but maybe one day I will be able to get to it.

PH: When I went to do Dr. Michael Wolf's story, I flew with my Italian co-writer, Adriano Forgione to Connecticut and we were with Wolf all day and then, we left, closed his door, and walked to the elevator, and we heard these chirping sounds all over the place, and we couldn't see where they were coming from. We heard them in the elevator. We heard them downstairs when the elevator door opened. They only stopped when we reached the street. At night something very strange happened in the hotel room. The next morning when Wolf talked to us he said, "Well, you didn't see my little Grey Friends. They walked out with you," he says, "they were trying to understand the human love and bonding and," he said, "they walked right out the door with you." We only heard chirping—like dolphin sounds. You mention this chirping connected with the Greys in your book, and it struck me!

CB: That's sort of like a sound that they make. And I have heard that there's sort of a spicy smell sometimes, but I've never smelled it.

PH: No, there wasn't a smell. It sounded like birds, then kind of like dolphins, like a dolphin-bird sound. And your book just hit a note with me. I said, "Oh my God!—it really happened," Could I hear and not see?

CB: Oh yeah, definitely. They have a way of making it so you can't see them. You won't see them; you'll just see right through them.

PH: We couldn't get rid of the sounds. We thought it was the elevator. We opened the door, and we walked out the front door, and we didn't hear them anymore.

CB: I don't have anyway to comment on what your experience was, I wasn't there. But I do know that the Greys have technology that allows them to be invisible. You can see right through them. You know, that's not something that's really far off for us, because in my remote-viewing work I have been pushing the idea that we are composite beings, that the soul really exists and the body is just a machine. And so obviously when we die, the body drops off, but we're still there. You can't see a "dead" person any longer, but we're still there. I guess you saw the *Ghost* movie with Whoopie Goldberg? So it's sort of like that, and so apparently the ETs have the technology to mimic this. It's only a matter of time before we'll be able to get our own devices that do the same thing. Right now we have only a very primitive ability to interact between the two dimensions that I call "subspace" and physical reality. But I hope that both the physical side of things and the metaphysical side continue to be a focus of research, so that it's only a matter of time before you get technology that will let us actually interact back and forth between the two dimensions more easily.

PH: What you're doing is extremely exciting.

CB: We have situations where we have remote viewed certain people, and the remote-viewing evidence indicates that they were hybrids of some type. Indeed we did find out medically afterwards that this may be true.

PH: Is that in either one of your books?

CB: No. I had to take that all that out for publishing reasons. I don't publish anything in my books that has any connection to an identifiable real live person. My publisher thinks it is too risky.

PH: So you can't take the chance.

CB: And they don't.

PH: What would you like people to know?

CB: That the remote-viewing evidence is absolutely incontrovertible if you have an open enough mind to look at it, and that it would prove beyond any shadow of a doubt that the human soul exists. It's more and more advanced than any other thing that you've ever seen. The only acceptable hypothesis from this is to accept that there is a non-physical component to all of us—a "subspace mind." But the point is that we now have some scientific proof of this. Any reasonable person can see this. That means that we all are just souls, transforming through light years and transcended through time and space, and that we are virtually unbounded. It is our actual personal selves that are unbounded. Our bodies are nothing more that machines. You don't have to believe it, but we don't have to go to a church or a synagogue or a temple or a mosque to be told it, to hope for it, and to pray for it. Now we know through positive scientific reasons that it's proven that our bodies are nothing more that machines, and that our souls are real.

PH: Is this also included in reincarnation?

CB: That's a whole other story.

PH: Well, you said "in between" lifetimes.

CB: To my knowledge, there's no police force out there that says you can't be reincarnated into another life. So if we know that time doesn't exist, then this idea of reincarnation is actually not exactly correct, because all these experiences are going on simultaneously. They're not happening sequentially.

PH: I know, simultaneously.

CB: The most important thing is that the soul is truly there. The second most important thing is our understanding of time. It is an illusion, a perception, and that means two things; that means everything that was bad, that was ever done by anybody will never go away. That means the Holocaust is still going on right now. That means everything that we do to other people, if we hit our child in anger, minutes later, that means it doesn't ever go away. You can't wipe the pain away. The act is always there. If there's ever a molestation that occurs, and someone is actually guilty of that molestation, they can't remove the event in time to phase it out...it always exists.

PH: It's always there.

CB: The most important thing with regard to time is that once people realize that, I think that people will change for the better. There's a whole new horizon out there that. Nothing ever goes away.

PH: Conversely any good you do is there forever.

CB: The other side of it is that any good you do is there forever. It is so important that you brought up the good side. I was focusing more on the negative, hoping people who do bad won't do it anymore. But the good is always there as well. So those are the two morals of the story— the soul exists and time never fades away.

PH: I'm happy that you're making it scientific, because I'm fighting everybody who says that this kind of work is non-scientific or soft science or pure psychology. It's not, you know.

CB: These public demonstrations took place for six months, and we're going to do it again, we're going to re-do it again sometime. It wasn't like we did it for one day; we did for six months. And the world is watching, and you can now look at the whole, and the data are scientific.

PH: I want to thank you so much.

CB: God bless you.

Chapter 26

The Paranormal Factor

Uri Geller

Energies and ESP

February, 2002

In 1985 Dr. J. Allen Hynek told me that the UFO phenomenon was both physical and paranormal. He said that its connection to the paranormal was not only the most interesting, but also the most difficult to prove. As an investigative journalist, I ignored what I could not prove and what did not fit into my own paradigm of the total  picture, so I excluded the paranormal to avoid being ridiculed or considered "New Age" or incredible to my fellow researchers! Neither did I listen to Dr. John Mack of Harvard University, who, at a 1998 San Marino conference, warned me that unless I took into account this aspect, I would never "see the truth nor become a good journalist."

I did not know myself well enough nor did I realize that this aspect was "the glue" that is the true element that *connects the dots*—those dots that were the verifiable incidents, the unquestionable proof, the credible witness testimony), and the physical evidence that I had been gathering over the years. Now enter: Uri Geller (http://www.observer.co.uk/life/

story/o,6903,615636,00.html), the Pope, Michael Jackson, Phyllis Schlem-mer, Sir John Whitmore, Russell Targ, SRI, and Andrija Puharich!

That same summer a colleague of mine started me reading Stuart Hol-royd's book *Briefing on the Future Landing on Planet Earth* (downloaded it free from http://uri-Geller.com). I was wondering if any ET races had tried to contact humanity, and somehow I began to remember the Uri Geller phenom-ena and how he had supposedly been activated by "an ET being of light" at the age of three and had developed his metal-bending skills.

In 1980, I had told J. Allen Hynek how Uri Geller had erased a whole roll of my film when I confronted him with my camera as he was leaving his dressing room during a show he was doing in Denver, Colo. The lab said it had signs of radiation on the negatives. At that time, I read all I could about his being tested at SRI, and I realized that astronaut Edgar Mitchell as well as physicists Russell Targ and Hal Puthoff had taken a serious interest in these psi experiments (*http://www.fas.org/irp/program/collect/stargate.htm*). In any case, I contacted Geller by e-mail, and he responded, asking me to call him immediately in England. We consequently had a long conversation in which he suggested that I help him meet the Pope when I returned to my home in Rome. He needed to do it quickly! I found this curious, but if one goes on his website (http://uri-geller.com), one sees that Geller is often in contact with high-profile celebrities. This was different, however, as he expressed to me that he had an on-going mission to bring humanity together and bring peace to the world.

I then returned to Italy, thinking about my role, and, as synchronicity would have it, I then had an opportunity to meet and question SRI physicist Russell Targ and his co-author, healer Jane Katra, in Assisi, Italy, at the World Religions Peace Conference that Shantimandir ironically had planned for September 11, 2001.

Early in September, 2001, I had begun to feel history was going to repeat itself in the Middle East and that a heavy spiritual intervention was going to be called for, hence the call to Geller and the desire to go to Assisi to the peace conference. Ironically, the week before September 11, I went on Italian researcher Lilli Astore's radio program, *Radiorama Lecce*, and I antic-ipated a negative event that would happen soon. I asked people to pray or meditate for peace.

As fate would have it, the meeting with Russell Targ was in Vicenza, Italy, where he was giving a remote-viewing workshop, and I intended to verify the experiments done on Uri Geller in the '70s and confirm that the CIA valued psychic phenomena enough to fund certain projects at SRI. (See *Destiny Matrix* by Jack Sarfatti, *http://stardrive.org/Jack/book.pdf.*) For me, it was a matter of seeing the true integration of all this research along with the supposed "nuts and bolts" that the UFO reality always fed to me. I took Russell and Jane's class and discovered that this training can be done with us common folk as well as with natural psychics, and that it produces incredible results. It has to do with a concentration of "energies and the opening of a sixth sense," which some call the "third eye." This technique was used in the military for psychic spying and by the Puharich group in the '70s to peacefully alter history by meditation and concentration of energy. I also verified that Uri Geller had done some amazing things at Targ's home (see *Uri* by Andrija Puharich at http://uri-geller.com.)

In Holroyd's *Briefing* book, it is clear that the placing of people—in this case people with spiritual energy or high psychic ability—can cause a shift in "events," so I began to see connections everywhere. I began to ask why an ailing "Holy Father" like Pope John Paul II physically traveled all over the world in spite of his debilitating circumstances. Did he choose specific times when astronomical conditions were favorable? Was he driven by inspiration to go around the world, South America, the Holy Land, Russia and to even Ancient Sumer. Is he one whose physical energy is placed to cause change? Why can't he just pray from Rome? This Pope survived an assassination attempt when a nun disturbed the aim of a gunman, altering of a chain of future events. What does his presence mean to Earth?

On January 23, the ailing Holy Father chose to go to Assisi by train (with hundreds of body guards), to invite the world religions to accompany him in prayer for peace. This is a switch in philosophy of the churches, each of whom professes to be the one true religion on Earth. Muslims, Jews, Hindus and so forth, all in Assisi.... This was an event that should have shaken the world or altered the ethereal plane, if you will. And why Assisi, dimensionally speaking—the home of St. Francis? Few realized the importance of this event. Perhaps the energies that day altered some events.

It is clear that this particular Pope is both a holy man and an active political participant—one of the major players in this chess game of life. Regarding ET contact, it is significant that the Vatican allowed Monsignor Corrado

Balducci to talk publicly of the importance of UFO witness testimony. More recently, Padre George Coyne spoke in favor of possible diverse life in the universe, which could mean that the time is approaching for open contact, and for this reason Uri Geller wanted to meet the Pope.

The joining of energies for altering social conscience could easily be part of the current ET plan to increase our awareness. The timeliness of events and the synchronistic time we notice them is very important to the *human wake-up* call. I notice, for example, that Michael Jackson was Geller's best man and that a Geller drawing appears inside Jackson's album booklet. The world hears Jackson's pop song, "Cry," but I assure you they are not really listening. Check out his pre-9/11 words:

You can change the world (I can't do it by myself)
You're the chosen one. (I'm gonna need some kinda sign)
If we all cry at the same time tonight
Faith is found in the winds
All we have to do is reach for truth!

Who is the chosen one? What is the sign? Does the synchronistic "crying" at the same time point to a concentration of energies again? What is Jackson's role? I assure you Jackson has the proper awareness "to heal the world." He has donated huge amounts of money to aid human suffering, and he must know that mass "positive energy" causes change! Does "crying at the same time" mean the same thing as "praying at the same time"? Did this intervention happen with Puharich, Schlemmer, and Whitmore in the Holy Land and in Assisi and at the famous Arguelles's "Harmonic Convergence" in August 1987, which is said to have caused a change in the Earth's energetic grid?

In this world of confusion and misinformation, perhaps we need to follow our own "gut instincts," our own wise inner voices, our own common sense, *and* learning to trust our not-so-common sixth sense. The world is not yet at peace, and we must be aware of Earth's pulse to know this. As long as the conflict in the Middle East drips with blood, and we have violent conflicts and classic instability, we are all involved. The top players are probably getting into position. The game may probably soon begin, and we will need some pretty heavy spiritual intervention. It is time to think "outside the box"! Our visitors know this, as they know the future scenario and its possible outcomes. Research tells us that there are many possible futures depending on "our moves on the chessboard." David Icke tells us that the "bad news is that the cavalry is not coming. The good news is that we have the ability to meet them half way!" This can only be done by contact with our visitors. In this way we might have some say in our own future. We become active participants instead of victims, and in becoming participants, we may become the designers of what Col. Philip Corso called "A New World if we can take it."

Now enter Pascal Riolo, a 27-year-old psychic from Liege, Belgium, who has an international following and does many stage shows, mostly pen-and-ink sketches that greatly resemble those of Uri Geller. I was talking to Pascal at his home in Brussels when he told me that a friend had given him Michael Jackson's *Invincible* album. Pascal explained that track 8 has much numerical significance. Eight sideways means infinity; it appears in the Geller drawing; and eight is a cosmic number for change. Interestingly enough, Pascal obsessively designed all the pen-and-ink artwork for his new book almost all in one sitting, while listening to this particular Jackson CD.

It should be noted that Pascal Riolo does not understand the words in English, so the inspiration came from the sounds—the music itself. I explained to him that the Geller drawing was significant because Pascal and Geller had both used much the same style, symbols, and words. I especially noted the similarity of the points outside the drawing. The figure is supposed to be a pharaoh, but its facial features look very much like the male figure in Geller's drawing. The symbols are interesting, and the spacecraft in the right-hand corner with the initials is very interesting. They suggest some type of cosmic connection which he and most people were not aware of inside the *Invincible* album cover. If music is energy, where does the inspiration come from, and where does it circulate, and for what reason?

We need to see who is receiving these messages and ask where the psychic connection takes us. For me, I am reminded of the messages of invitation given to contactees in the film *Close Encounters of The Third Kind*.

Chapter 27

The Paranormal Factor

Synchronicities

http://utenti.lycos.it/paolaharris

April 2002

The continuation of this synchronicity with Uri Geller with possible ET messages is not by any means the "end" of this connection nor the end of this story. The appearance of Uri at the Conference at Bellaria in Italy at the very height of the Middle East conflict suggests a possible correlation with the situation in the book *Briefing on the Future Landing on Planet Earth* by Stuart Holroyd and it became a strong parallel situation.

On April 5 I met Uri Geller in Bellaria, and since I had been corresponding with him for a while, we developed a good friendship. I also had him meet Pascal Riolo (see page 207), who made a special trip from Belgium for Uri's appearance in Italy. Pascal had a flash on the plane that he immediately put on paper. It was a geometric design of what turned out to be the hotel with an infinity symbol in front (one Uri says he uses) which, in actuality, was the swimming pool in the form of a lateral 8.

Pascal had put an X on the 4th floor, where Pascal would lodge and on the 6th floor where Uri was. Pascal's room number he later learned was 704 = the number 11, and Uri was in 611.

I was put on the 5th floor in between them, but I was aware that the connection needed a female energy, as evidenced by the active participation of psychic Phyllis Schleemer in 1973. It just so happened that I called Phyllis in Florida and asked her to intervene spiritually at just the time in Italy when Uri Geller would be on stage. It was a prayer for spiritual and mental awakening and an intervention for world peace!

Uri was clear in his presentation, telling people that it was not his powers that they would witness, but that somehow he was the catalyst for miracles and strange happenings. He purposely avoids the ET connection, and he explained this to me personally. He bent spoons, caused the bending of keys, and demonstrated to the audience that his psychic ability was real. He is very devoted to children and world peace. And then the messages appeared!

With all due respect to Uri, the messages that appeared on the beach in front of our hotel were not from any "human" intervention. It is important that

the reader understand that the placing of high profile, high energy at the right time in the right place causes a change in the *conscious-ness-time* scenario. I believe this is about changing "an event" to cause an alternative future and possibly to avoid an *Armageddon scenario*.

Eleven is a power number. The end date of the Mayan Calendar adds up to 11, Apollo 11 landed on the moon and the tragedy of September 11 may be important synchronicities. One needs to only open one's eyes to understand what we are being led to notice. The 4th, 5th, 6th floors, the number 11, the dates 5+6=11, the huge word in Italian, LA PACE (peace) which appeared as a sign on the hotel next to ours, the words EMERGENZA 11 (emergency 9+2=11) on the orange lifeguard boat under the sign, and the light blue and white Israeli colors all over the beach all seemed to be clear signs.

I noticed all this when I had a sudden urge to leave the back door of the hotel and run to the water. It was then that I turned around and noticed. It was all there before me. But there was one more sign, and it read Rome. I live in Rome, close to the Vatican, and Uri Geller asked me to arrange a future appearance in Rome someday. It is clear that somebody is telling us something!

Chapter 28

The Paranormal Factor

State of the World

---

http://utenti.lycos.it/paolaharris

For a year now I have been writing about the psychic connection, the UFO phenomena, Uri Geller, the SRI studies, remote viewing, Stuart Holroyd's book, *Briefings on the Future Landing on Planet Earth,* and the connection with a group of ET intelligences called "The Nine." It all came together when two of the three protagonists from the *Briefings* book—Phyllis Schleemer Carmel and Sir John Whitmore—decided to meet me in Ft. Collins, Colo., because they were concerned about the developing tense world situation that seemed to be almost parallel to what had been described in the *Briefings* book.

I was happy to meet Phyllis and John, who asked me to gather 25 interested people—researchers, healers, investigators, and people with knowledge and background in UFO phenomena—for a extraordinary channeling of The Nine. The meeting took place in the home of a respected journalist who will remain anonymous. Sir John Whitmore assisted Phyllis Schleemer in allowing Tom, The Nine's spokesman, to speak through her. What follows are Tom's exact words.

Ft. Collins, Colorado, August 15, 2002

Tom (T): I am Tom, Spokesman for the Nine. We are the Nine. We come to thee in love and peace. We greet thee with joy for thy willingness to be with us. We wish to convey our gratitude to each of thee for thy wish to be with us.

John Whitmore (JW): Would you start by telling the group about the situation today that the planet finds itself in these troubled times?

T: Until the nation of Israel has the ability to exist without destruction, your planet Earth will be in turmoil, for the nation of Israel is the representation of your entire planet Earth. It is difficult for many to understand that, but it is a micro of the macro, and it is important that there be peace and harmony. If you will review recent times, you will see that there is more devastation upon your Earth, just as there has been more in the nation of Israel. It is important that it be brought into balance, for you will see that Israel is the center of all the land mass of the planet Earth, and out of it generates the energy for all of Planet Earth. We are in sadness for its devastation and also for the devastation of Ishmael (Palestine). You will view the corruption that now exists also in this country of our doctor [the late Andrija Puharich, meaning the U.S.], and the corruption that will bring about its devastation also, *for those in authority have in themselves a corruption of desire for power and control of humankind.*

Humankind must take into that of self the responsibility not to permit governments to place them in bondage, and humankind has the ability to do that. There are those we call *The Others* who, if they gain control of your planet Earth, will control the universe. You are in a serious time more than has ever existed upon your Planet Earth, and this time is also the time when you have the ability to bring about rapid change, for you have communication among all people in swiftness that did not exist before.

What is now of utmost importance are the youth of Planet Earth and the beginning of changing energy within, and the re-education of those youth who are taught to destroy. We wish to thank those in this abode this evening for your energies are kind and good, which permits us to have clarity. Isn't that joyful, our Sir John?

JW: You have said what the problems are. What recommendations can you give us for our contribution and for what needs to happen to solve these problems, in addition to the re-education of the young?

T: We do not understand how to explain what we know. I will try. You understand the physical DNA? You understand that each group of humans from different civilizations can be traced through that DNA. And you also understand that if there is a disruptive gene, that if one is taken, we can change that. That also exists in *thought DNA*. We had explained this is a time of past to our Jacob, and we had at that time asked that it not be released, for it would also be possible that it would have been manipulated. It is a process that can be changed through prayer, through meditation, and through contemplation.

SIR JOHN WHITMORE, PAOLA HARRIS, AND PHYLLIS SCHLEEMER

A Synthesis

This channeling includes four important pieces of information which, whether you believe in channeling or not, shows the current reality:

1. The Israeli-Palestinian crisis is the key to whether humanity can solve problems in a microcosm. That area is a hot spot and an energy land mass, and it needs to be brought into balance for our entire survival.

2. This is the most serious time in human history, as never before. Later in the rest of the channeling when The Nine were asked of the possibility of war in Iraq, the Nine said "We weep for this. We are in great sorrow, for we had seen a time that humankind would elevate itself in this nation of our doctor (U.S.) and now it is reverting to manipulation, control, and arrogance."

3. In the reference to the existence of The Others, we can infer that there is a classical battle between good and evil on all levels and in all dimensions. Manipulation of thought DNA, or mind control, may be a current reality and a possible cause of the corruption and devastation that we currently experience on this Earth plane. Can we change this? These solutions are given by Tom of the Nine:

T: On that of the physical aspect, write letters; spread through space mail; take responsibility; stand and be tall; voice your opinion; voice who you are; speak to others. When the security of barter is removed, energy and good health will no longer be there, and that is not permissible, so we must create an energy of understanding that we will not permit that. Then we can bring about change. Gather and join with those in a meditative state for 36 minutes when it is 9:00 at night in Israel on Sundays [2:00 PM EST]. If you do this, in gathering with those of ours—and thou also will be of ours, inclusive all over your planet Earth—of three together of one day a month of twelve, then you will see changes coming within."

Information

If you wish to receive further information on The Nine and further channelings, contact Sir John Whitmore at Whitmore33@aol.com

Postscript

I don't know who orchestrated this meeting, which came about by a series of coincidences and mysterious connections, but I feel I am just a catalyst for some kind of evolutionary change by compiling information for those people who are the architects for a future peaceful planet. But if we shall know a tree by its fruit, as it is said in the Bible, then I can conclude that this contact with these entities on the August 15, 2002, was entirely spiritual, peaceful and productive in nature. I needed to add that I did read the book *The Stargate Conspiracy* entirely in order to try to connect the history of Egypt and The Nine and the influence which they seemed to have on the New Age group at Esalen and on New Age thought (in particular generated by the Puharich group.) The book was interesting and informative, but it was written from a certain perspective. Some see The Nine's influence as conspiratorial in the negative sense, but my experience is that The Nine stress the use of free will and freedom of choice, and that is the primary weapon we have against world domination. Instead of possessing a collective consciousness like some species, humanity can still change its future by individual choices. The future, as seen in Spielberg's film *Minority Report,* is not cast in stone. Our future can and will be changed by the collective spiritual intervention of people of good will.

Touching Down

Epilogue

The time has come to talk about a new UFOlogy, one that has emerged thanks to the testimonies, experiences, and research of some people—now my personal friends—such as the late Col. Philip Corso, Dr. Michael Wolf, Clifford Stone, Robert Dean, Dr. Richard Boylan, Dr. Richard Hoagland, Derrel Sims, Dr. Steven Greer and Monsignor Corrado Balducci. Added to the people involved in this significant change in UFO-logic research are the names of Robert Ghost Wolf, Robert Morning Sky and the Lakota shaman Golden Eagle (formerly Standing Elk). It's inspiring to see scientists, military witnesses and Native Americans working together, discussing and debating the nature of our universe. This situation is enhanced by the recent statement made in the Italian newspaper *Il Messagero* by past Vatican Emissary and Demonologist Monsignor Balducci stating the importance of "witness testimony" concerning this phenomenon. Now we must understand the real importance of this change. If we hypothesize that this might suggest "contact," then some of us are witnessing indeed a sociological shift.

I have noticed that things have really changed recently, especially when I compare today's events with those in 1980-86, when I was assisting Dr. J. Allen Hynek in his research. At that time, the "close encounters of the first kind" (lights in the night sky) were a recurrent theme, and some people were surprised by this phenomenon. Today we study the "abduction" phenomenon, the "close encounters" of the fourth and even fifth kind, as witnessed by some CSETI groups directed by Dr. Steven Greer. In some cases humans are receiving messages from alien entities, which seem to be in some other dimension that I call "the outer limits." This incredible reality, which was once conceived as science fiction, is quickly becoming "science fact" today. It is no longer a hypothesis! We are possibly receiving information that foretells upcoming changes, and we are designing a new paradigm.

From this point of view, some parts of the abduction phenomenon may need to be reevaluated because of possible genetic enhancement via alien DNA which may be effecting a startling transformation of the human race to a "Cosmic race" so we can adapt to a *new world, with new responsibilities*. That world will develop into an enlightened one only if we handle it, as the "EBE" (Extraterrestrial Biological Entity) told Col. Philip Corso in 1957. All the while, we walk quickly towards the dimensional door of the year 2012—an evolutionary jump that will make us finally understand, in the end, that we are part of a universe where different races and different realities either coexist peacefully or collide.

All these changes occurring in UFOlogy today pose serious problems to researchers, who, like me, work in the world of information-gathering where news, data, and discoveries travel quickly in real time, thanks to optic fibers and fast Internet access. Sometimes, it is very hard to keep up with these events, since in this field, at every moment something new and intriguing seems to occur. On any given day I might hear from Richard Hoagland researching infrared images from Mars, or Russian researcher Boris Shurinov debunking presumed UFO crash footage, or Dr. Richard Boylan painstakingly collecting data for his UFO Facts list, or Lakota Golden Eagle reporting about Native American prophecies. I might even hear from former Stanford University physicist Russell Targ, or Disclosure Project pioneer Dr. Steven Greer, or researcher Phyllis Schleemer, or even spoon-bending psychic Uri Geller.

In Rome, I now receive at least 50 of these emails a day. Is this some part of a slow release of information programmed by some higher power? By now I am on overload. So I recall when Col. Philip Corso, author of *The Day After Roswell,* used to say to me "Paola, I don't know if the world deserves to know the truth.... Wars continue. There's too much incomprehension in the world of today." This incomprehension is omnipresent even in UFOlogy, where some researchers with their own private agendas frequently absorb misinformation thus becoming victims of a sterile documentation that, instead of helping our planetary research effort, hinders it. Our colleagues begin to criticize each other in an effort to find the "smoking gun" first. So I ask what kind of "cosmic race" are we running here?

It is not important to investigate just "sightings in the night sky" anymore. Yes, SETI has its value, but it seems to me that "The times they are a'changin'," as Bob Dylan sang. I'm sure J. Allen Hynek and his contemporary, James E. McDonald, would agree, too, if they were here now. Instead, from my point of view, it would be smarter to personally inform one's self and keep up to date by reading the newest books and articles that truly reveal the new pieces of this cosmic puzzle. I agree with Dr. Wolf and Col. Corso when they suggest that we should try to take the "halo off of traditional science, and consider other methodologies." As Dr. R. Leo Sprinkle states in his interview, "This phenomenon is both physical and psychical." This theory, or revelation, which is frequently a by-product of contact, should not to be confused with paranoia of the end of the millennium, or New Age prophecies. As I was justly admonished at the San Marino Conference recently by Dr. John Mack: I cannot always intellectualize this phenomenon, but I must instead *open* my heart." Likewise, Dr. Wolf says, "We must see with our ears and hear with our eyes."

In conclusion, I suggest that we start an internal search, more or less spiritual, but intensely personal, as I tried to do in this book, on how to accept this "possible new world" that Corso so often mentioned. Let's not make extraterrestrials our *"star gurus."* They do not have all the answers, and most importantly of all, they do not want to think in our place, and take on our responsibilities. Instead, let's all become more highly evolved citizens of the same galaxy. Maybe they are tired of seeing us carelessly playing with advanced "back-engineered" technologies whose tremendous destructive capabilities threaten to destroy all life on Earth.

It's time for our little blue planet to grow up and rightfully use the new technologies to save ourselves from auto-destruction. It's time to wake up, to wake up our souls, and to stop fighting among ourselves. The time is coming when we must become responsible "cosmic adults," become better people, become better role models for our children, give them "hope" for a viable future, give them better values and a faith in God. This is probably also the only way "to accept truth" when it is revealed. In the upcoming millennium, we may expect a vibrational change and more introspection on the part of our human race.

The years since Roswell have been years of great revelations for someone like me, but I commend the courageous pioneers in this field for forging ahead when it was not very popular, and for attempting to bring truth and enlightenment to the planet. I commend also those who have worked so hard, but are not mentioned here, and all those individuals who are intensely aware of the coming changes and are prepared to "shift gears."

We need to cope, but how? Maybe this way: I remember one of my visits to Chicago, at the home of Dr. Hynek. It was early morning, and I couldn't find him anywhere in the house. Then I finally saw him. He was meditating, with his face towards the rising sun. I was surprised to see that this astronomer-scientist practiced yoga and meditation for an hour every morning. There is a connection to the universe, a spiritual component here. I guess the answer is "faith in the universe," or "blowin' in the wind." The best way we can contribute to this new world—if we can take it—is by being well informed, by being open minded to new perspectives, by conducting our own personal internal searches, and by always being receptive to new information. I wish you the best of good fortune in the changing times ahead.

Biography

http://utenti.lycos.it/paolaharris

Paola Leopizzi Harris is an Italo-American photojournalist and investigative reporter in the field of UFO research and paranormal phenomena. She is also a free-lance writer, widely published, especially in Europe. She has studied UFO phenomena since 1979 and is on personal terms with many of the leading researchers in this field.

Paola Harris has written for *Nexus, UFO Magazine, Notizario UFO* and *Dossier Alieni*. From 1980-1986 she assisted Dr. J. Allen Hynek with his UFO investigations. Initially she was mostly interested in the UFOs sightings. Then she evolved into interviewing experiencers and most recently she has been exploring the

Paola Harris

psychic connections to the UFO phenomenon. She has organized and spoken at many conferences around the world and frequently presents illustrated presentations intended to help make sense of the cosmic mystery.

Paola lives in Rome and has a Masters degree in Education. She teaches history and photojournalism at the American Overseas School of Rome. Learn more at her web site.

PAOLA AND MONSIGNOR CORRADO BALDUCCI

MY MOTHER ELAINE LEOPIZZI, CARLOS DIAZ, AND PAOLA

PAOLA AND COL. PHIL CORSO

CARLOS DIAZ (MEXICAN CONTATEE) , SGT. MAJOR
ROBERT O. DEAN AND COL. PHIL CORSO

WILLIAM HAMILTON, MICHAEL HESSEMAN, COL. PHIL CORSO'S DAUGHTER-
IN-LAW LIZ CORSO, DESMOND LESLIE, PAMELA HAMILTON,
COL. PHIL CORSO, AND PAOLA

Appendix

Books To Read

The following books helped me to *Connect the Dots:*

The 12th Planet - Zecharia Sitchin

Alien Rapture - Ed Fouché

Essential Briefings from Deep Space - Stuart Holroyd

The Catchers of Heaven - Dr. Michael Wolf

Close Extraterrestrial Encounters - Dr. Richard Boylan

Cosmic Explorers - Dr. Courtney Brown

Cosmic Top Secret - Bill Hamilton

The Day after Roswell - Colonel Philip Corso

The Deepening Complexity of Crop Circles:
    Scientific Research & Urban Legends
    - Eltjo Haselhoff

The Destiny Matrix - Dr. Jack Sarfatti

Gene Roddenberry: The Last Conversation - Yvonne Fern

Glimpses of Other Realities - Linda Moulton Howe

Milabs - Helmut Lammer

Miracles of the Mind - Dr. Russell Targ and Jane Katra

The Monuments of Mars - Richard Hoagland

The Only Planet Of Choice - Phyllis Schlemmer

Open Minds, Closed Skies - Nick Pope

Opening Minds:
    A Journey of Extraordinary Encounters, Crop Circles and Resonance
    - Dr. Simeon Hein

The Path of the Explorer - Dr. Edgar Mitchell

Passport to the Cosmos - Dr. John Mack

Penetration: The Question of ET and Human Telepathy - Ingo Swan

Soul Samples:
    Personal Exploration in Reincarnation and UFO Experience
    - Dr. Leo Sprinkle

The Stargate Conspiracy - Lyn Pickett & Clive Prince

The Terra Papers - Robert Morningsky

The UFO Experience - Dr. J. Allen Hynek

UFOs Are Real - Clifford Stone

Underground Bases and Tunnels - Dr. Richard Sauter

Unorthodox Encounters - Uri Geller

Uri - Andrija Puharich

Witnessed - Budd Hopkins

Granite Publishing L.L.C.

has these imprints:

Wild Flower Press

Swan • Raven & Co

Agents of Change

Little Granite Books

Please contact us…

phone: 800.366.0264

fax: 828.894.8454

email: Granitepub@5thworld.com

- or -

Visit our Web Site at

www.5thworld.com

Additional information is at:

www.5thworld.com/Dots